SOCIABLE PLACES

Ranging across literature, theater, history, and the visual arts, this collection of essays by leading scholars in the field explores the range of places where British Romantic-period sociability transpired. The book considers how sociability was shaped by place, by the rooms, buildings, landscapes, and seascapes where people gathered to converse, to eat and drink, to work, and to find entertainment. At the same time, it is clear that sociability shaped place, both in the deliberate construction and configuration of venues for people to gather and in the way such gatherings transformed how place was experienced and understood. The essays highlight literary and aesthetic experience but also range through popular entertainment and ordinary forms of labor and leisure.

KEVIN GILMARTIN is Professor of English at the California Institute of Technology and has been a regular visiting professor of English at the Centre for Eighteenth Century Studies, University of York. He works on late eighteenth- and early nineteenth-century British literature, with a particular interest in the politics of print culture and the history of print media. His most recent book is *William Hazlitt: Political Essayist* (2015).

SOCIABLE PLACES

Locating Culture in Romantic-Period Britain

EDITED BY

KEVIN GILMARTIN

California Institute of Technology

CAMBRIDGE
UNIVERSITY PRESS

University Printing House, Cambridge CB2 8BS, United Kingdom

One Liberty Plaza, 20th Floor, New York, NY 10006, USA

477 Williamstown Road, Port Melbourne, VIC 3207, Australia

4843/24, 2nd Floor, Ansari Road, Daryaganj, Delhi – 110002, India

79 Anson Road, #06–04/06, Singapore 079906

Cambridge University Press is part of the University of Cambridge.

It furthers the University's mission by disseminating knowledge in the pursuit of education, learning, and research at the highest international levels of excellence.

www.cambridge.org
Information on this title: www.cambridge.org/9781107064782
DOI: 10.1017/9781107587779

© Cambridge University Press 2017

First published 2017

Printed in the United Kingdom by Clays, St Ives plc

A catalogue record for this publication is available from the British Library.

ISBN 978-1-107-06478-2 Hardback

Contents

Illustrations

Contributors

DAVID FALLON is Senior Lecturer in English at the University of Sunderland. From 2009 to 2012 he was a British Academy Postdoctoral Fellow at the University of Oxford. He has published on eighteenth-century and Romantic literature and culture and is the author of *Blake, Myth, and Enlightenment: The Politics of Apotheosis* (2017).

INA FERRIS is Professor of English Emeritus at the University of Ottawa. Her books include *Book-Men, Book Clubs, and the Romantic Literary Sphere* (2015), *The Romantic National Tale and the Question of Ireland* (2002), *The Achievement of Literary Authority: Gender, History, and the Waverley Novels* (1991), and *Bookish Histories: Books, Literature, and Commercial Modernity, 1700–1900* (coedited with Paul Keen, 2009). Her current research is on authorship and the printing trades.

KEVIN GILMARTIN is Professor of English at the California Institute of Technology and writes on late eighteenth- and early nineteenth-century British literature, with a particular interest in the politics of print culture and the history of print media. His most recent book is *William Hazlitt: Political Essayist* (2015), and he is currently working on representations of rural poverty in the long eighteenth century.

HARRIET GUEST is Professor Emerita at the Centre for Eighteenth Century Studies, University of York, United Kingdom. She continues to research in eighteenth-century British culture and is currently working on seaside resorts and on portraits of women writers from the late century. Her most recent book is *Unbounded Attachment: Sentiment and Politics in the Age of the French Revolution* (2013).

PAUL KEEN is Professor of English at Carleton University. He is the author of *Literature, Commerce, and the Spectacle of Modernity, 1750–1800* (2012) and *The Crisis of Literature in the 1790s: Print Culture and the Public Sphere* (1999). His edited books include *The Age of Authors: An Anthology of Eighteenth-Century Print Culture* (2014), *Bookish Histories: Books, Literature, and Commercial Modernity, 1700–1900* (with Ina Ferris, 2009), *Revolutions in Romantic Literature: An Anthology of Print Culture, 1780–1832* (2004), and *The Popular Radical Press in Britain, 1817–1821* (2003).

JON MEE is Professor of Eighteenth Century Studies at the University of York. He has written many articles and books on print and politics in the Romantic period, most recently *Print, Publicity, and Radicalism in the 1790s: The Laurel of Liberty* (2016). He is currently working on a book about the circulation of knowledge in the period under the title *Networks of Improvement*, supported by the Leverhulme Trust.

DANIEL O'QUINN is a professor in the School of English and Theatre Studies at the University of Guelph. He is the author of *Entertaining Crisis in the Atlantic Imperium, 1770–1790* (2011) and *Staging Governance: Theatrical Imperialism in London, 1770–1800* (2005) and the coeditor with Jane Moody of *The Cambridge Companion to British Theatre, 1730–1830* (2007). A new collection of essays entitled "Georgian Theatre in an Information Age," coedited with Gillian Russell, was published in a special double issue of *Eighteenth-Century Fiction* in August 2015. He is working on a new book entitled *After Peace and beside War: Engaging the Ottoman Empire*.

MARK PHILP is Professor of History and Politics at the University of Warwick and an Emeritus Fellow of Oriel College. He ran a recent Leverhulme-funded project digitizing and editing Godwin's Diary with David O'Shaughnessy and Victoria Myers (http://godwindiary.bodleian.ox.ac.uk) and a project on Napoleon's Hundred Days with Kate Astbury (www.100days.eu/). He cofounded "Re-imagining Democracy c. 1750–1850" with Joanna Innes (http://re-imaginingdemocracy.com/). Recent publications include *Re-imagining Democracy in the Age of Revolutions: America, France, Britain, Ireland 1750–1850* (coedited with Joanna Innes, 2013) and *Reforming Political Ideas in Britain: Politics and Language in the Shadow of the French Revolution* (2013).

NICHOLAS ROGERS is Distinguished Research Professor in the Department of History, York University, Toronto. A former editor of the *Journal of British Studies,* he is the author of five books on the eighteenth century. The last, entitled *Mayhem: Post-War Crime and Violence in Britain, 1749–7153* (2012), won the John Ben Snow Prize in British history, awarded by the North American Conference on British Studies.

CHRISTOPHER ROVEE is Associate Professor of English at Louisiana State University. He is the author of *Imagining the Gallery: The Social Body of British Romanticism* (2006) and has published widely on the materiality and reception of nineteenth-century literature and culture, including several essays on early photography. He is currently completing a book on romanticism and "close reading" in the interwar years.

GILLIAN RUSSELL is an Honorary Fellow in the School of Historical and Philosophical Studies and School of Culture and Communication at the University of Melbourne. She is the author of *The Theatres of War: Performance, Politics and Society, 1793–1815* (1995), *Romantic Sociability: Social Networks and Literary Culture in Britain, 1770–1840* (coedited with Clara Tuite, 2002), and most recently, *Tracing War in British and Romantic Period Culture* (coedited with Neil Ramsey, 2015). She is currently completing a project on the history of printed ephemera, sociability, and collecting in the long eighteenth century.

Acknowledgments

This collection of essays originated as a conference at the Huntington Library in San Marino, California, in January 2012. The editor is grateful to the participants in that event, and particularly to Robert C. Ritchie, W. M. Keck Foundation Director of Research at the Huntington, when the conference was conceived and planned, and Steve Hindle, W. M. Keck Foundation Director of Research at the Huntington, when the conference took place. The current and former directors of research were generous hosts and stimulating participants in the conference. The Division of Humanities and Social Sciences at the California Institute of Technology cosponsored the event, which would not have been possible without the commitment of Jonathan Katz, Humanities and Social Sciences Division Chair, and Susan Davis, Humanities and Social Sciences Division Administrator. Staff at both institutions contributed to this project at several stages, from conference to publication, particularly Juan Gomez and Carolyn Powell at the Huntington and Sini Elvington and Candace Younger at the California Institute of Technology. Linda Bree, Senior Executive Publisher and Head of Humanities at Cambridge University Press, has been committed to this volume since its inception as a conference. The editor and contributors are thankful to her and to the staff at Cambridge University Press, particularly Anna Bond, Chloé Harries, and Isobel Cowper-Coles. Finally, the editor is grateful to the contributors for their efforts and for their patience at every stage in the development and production of this volume.

Introduction
Locating Romantic-Period Sociability
Kevin Gilmartin

A group of modest merchants, lower gentry, and professional men gather in a village tavern to eat, drink, read, and discuss public matters, and also to select the latest publications for their country book club, some of which will make their way back from the club to the households of individual members and circulate further among wives, sons, and daughters. In the aftermath of prohibitions on public meetings imposed by the Two Acts of 1795, members of the London Corresponding Society (LCS) gather over "bread & cheese & porter" in the home of the clerk and aspiring playwright James Powell, unaware that their host is a paid government informer and that their convivial domestic proceedings will find their way back to an alarmed ministry. In the same years, prominent Tory writers and politicians meet for literary and political conversation in the Piccadilly bookshop of the loyalist John Wright, and some men discretely pass through the shop to a first floor room of Wright's adjoining house to compose and produce *The Anti-Jacobin*. A stage and ring are raised in the Hampshire village of Odiham, and hundreds of people pay half a guinea to see Daniel Mendoza fight Richard Humphries, though conflict spills beyond the ring when, against stout defenses, a mob breaks into the paddock and joins the spectacle. Curious Londoners flock to the Temple of Health in Adelphi Terrace, run by the scientific showman James Graham, where among other wonders they are treated to the famous Celestial Bed, with some couples spending £50 to stay the night and benefit from its supposed procreative powers. In the elegant second floor assembly room of the Lisburn market house, the genteel upper strata of the town's merchant and professional classes join the lower gentry for music and dancing, making the center of the town's commercial life the venue for a voluntary associational culture. The radical philosopher William Godwin brings his own unconventional social habits to bear upon existing class and gender norms as he visits women in their homes and is visited by them in his own domestic quarters. In the wake of the Napoleonic wars, and under the spell of Byron's Childe Harold, British tourists make their way to Rome and the Colosseum by moonlight for an ambiguously introspective and collective experience that epitomizes Romantic sensibility even as it marks the early history of mass tourism. The supposed convenience of the sloop-rigged barges that convey Londoners to the bathing resort of Margate is belied by the distressed attitude of seasick passengers, on their way to a Bartholomew Fair by the sea noted for its confusion of social hierarchies. Ordinary seamen find relief from the hazards of war and severe naval discipline in prodigious drinking and the shipboard pleasures of song and dance and, when docked, the company of wives and women of pleasure.

These episodes are all drawn from the chapters that follow, which explore the range of places within which British Romantic-period sociability took place. The aim is to consider how sociability was shaped by place, by the rooms and buildings, landscapes and seascapes, where people gathered to converse, to eat and drink, and to work and find entertainment. At the same time, it is evident throughout the volume that sociability in turn shaped place, both in the deliberate construction and configuration of venues for people to gather socially, and in the way such gatherings transformed how place was experienced and understood. So, for example, the assumption that members of the LCS could only be alehouse politicians left elites puzzling over domestic radical gatherings, and the perception of Margate as London's East End by the sea led to difficulties in representing a seaside resort that threw together social types that would have remained distinct in London. The aims of the volume are predominantly historical and interpretive rather than theoretical or conceptual. There is, however, explicitly in some essays and implicitly throughout, an effort to move beyond the influential tendency of Jürgen Habermas to privilege rational exchange in a political public sphere that occupied the masculine space of the eighteenth-century coffee house.[1] An interest in forms of social interaction that are not restricted by critical intellect and political aspiration was present already in the publication that introduced Romantic studies to sociability, Gillian Russell and Clara Tuite's 2002 collection of essays, *Romantic Sociability: Social Networks and Literary Culture in Britain, 1770–1840*.[2] That volume traversed lecture theaters, taverns, parks, and shops, and one aim of this collection is to extend a social reconsideration of Romantic-period literature and culture by more fully exploring the reciprocal involvement of sociability and place. Such an enquiry draws, of course, from recent developments in Romantic and long eighteenth-century studies that stress the public and social, rather than private and individual, dimensions of literary and aesthetic expression in ways that involve particular locations: theater studies of course, which has notably transformed Romanticism, but also accounts of travel writing, of radical culture, and of the collective dimensions of literary production and reception.

This volume also follows on recent developments in Romantic scholarship in that it is not restricted to literary expression and literary evidence, developing instead a broader cultural history of sociability. That said, several contributors offer sustained readings of literary texts, notably Ina Ferris on satirical representations of country book clubs, Gillian Russell on the assembly room setting of William Godwin's *Caleb Williams*, Christopher Rovee on moonlight tours of the Colosseum in Byron's *Manfred* and *Childe Harold's Pilgrimage*, and Harriet Guest on the Margate episode of Charlotte Smith's *Marchmont*. Beyond this, the ways in which verbal and visual print culture serves to mediate a situated sociability turns out to be a leading concern throughout. Nicholas Rogers' treatment of lower deck sociability in the British navy from the middle of the eighteenth century to the end of the Napoleonic wars, which might seem to be remote from literature and the arts, engages the songs and ballads that were prized as shipboard entertainment. Studies of collective experience and expression are often set against the individual and introspective associations of canonical Romanticism, so that, as Russell and Tuite suggest, "the sociable occupies the position of the other of a solitary or interiorized Romanticism, . . . partly because there has been no critical tradition of representing a Romanticism in which sociability is a value."[3] Recent scholarship has gone a long way toward establishing such a tradition. In part to indicate the ways in which a suppression of the social has involved a suppression of the specificities of place, of situated human communication and interaction, but also to demonstrate that even the most canonically introspective Romantic forms were profoundly situated and closely involved with sociability, I want to begin this volume by reframing some of its concerns with respect to a very familiar literary text, Samuel Taylor Coleridge's "This Lime-Tree Bower My Prison." The poem can be identified with familiar ways of thinking about social interaction and place that suggest both are meant to be transcended through the individual act of Romantic imagination. While my aim will be to acknowledge a sociable and situated form of Romantic expression, I also want to suggest that such an acknowledgment not only follows from a new attention, for example, to the public cultures of theater and radical assembly, but has been there all along, in the literature and in important strands of critical tradition.

Coleridge laid out the occasion for "This Lime-Tree Bower My Prison," with the date June 1797, in a brief headnote to the first published version of the poem.[4] Having long anticipated a visit by some friends, above all Charles Lamb, the poet is prevented by accident and injury (his wife Sara spilled boiling milk on his foot) from joining an evening walk consisting of Lamb with William and Dorothy Wordsworth, and the poem instead finds compensation through individual reflection in the solitude of a garden bower. The stylized setting may already signal literary convention rather than any particular place or available set of human relationships, and Coleridge's bower has been associated with the influence of William Cowper and with a lyric movement from *hortus conclusus* to consolation in a *locus amoenus*.[5] With a melodramatic excess that has often been noticed, the poem initially presents the bower as prison rather than conventional refuge or retreat, and figures the loss of companionship and natural beauty in extreme terms of blindness and death. Christopher R. Miller has observed that in its simplest terms the poem "concerns the inability to be in two places at once," and the extended process of consolation through which this dilemma is overcome begins with a temporal rather than spatial gesture, a potent "meanwhile" that allows the poet to follow his friends in imagination on an evening walk that he has himself devised.[6] While spiritual typologies and philosophical terms shape the sequence, Anne K. Mellor has offered the most influential account of the poem's itinerary by mapping a distinct series of landscape categories through which the poet "guides his friends up the ladder of the hierarchically ordered aesthetic experiences of eighteenth-century academic art theory," from descent into a picturesque dell through emergence upon a "middle-ground" of beauty to a climactic sublimity with intimations of the divine in a vast prospect bathed in sunset.[7] At the transition from the beautiful to the sublime, Charles Lamb is identified as the poem's particular addressee, and the ecstatic apprehension of divinity in the veiled form of an "Almighty Spirit" brings the two men together in the poet's mind: "So my Friend / Struck with deep joy may stand, as I have stood." With the problems of distance and separation to some extent alleviated, the poem draws to a close by returning to the lime-tree bower with feelings of release rather than restriction and "delight" rather than pain.

What matters about natural setting, about the places represented in the poem, seems to involve the categorical or the typological rather than the particular, with landscape refined in Mellor's terms beyond "an object of rational or even aesthetic contemplation" to become "a mode of consciousness."[8] Or as Michael Raiger suggests in making the case for a spiritual rather than psychological "poetics of liberation," where "the way to liberation is through the power of imagination," there is even in the poem's initial thematics of imprisonment a shift from material to spiritual concerns: "the poet has seen the way out of the prison, which we must constantly remind ourselves is a prison not built of a material nature, but of a spiritual nature."[9] Raiger contends that the reader is carried along by this movement, and in this sense the address to another may be similarly transformed by imagination, as the verbal construction of an absent friend's experience in a remote landscape becomes more confident and emphatic over the course of the poem. The process of consolation eventually yields a compensatory realization about the sufficiency of the immediate bower. "No plot so narrow, be but Nature there / No waste so vacant, but may well employ / Each faculty of sense, and keep the heart / Awake to Love and Beauty!"

Yet a shifting sense of address complicates even as it enriches the identification of "This Lime-Tree Bower My Prison" with the group of Coleridge's "conversation poems." What kind of conversation is this? For Barbara Leah Harman, who considers the poem's opening "Well" to be a self-contained utterance that signals "the continuity of self and the continuity of speech in the absence of a community of speakers," the answer is clear: it is no conversation at all. "The poem substitutes for conversation the self-affirming speech of one person who begins a colloquy with himself" and from this narrates "the gradual awakening of the self to its own powers."[10] In an account that works instead from "the theatrical sense of 'scene'" evident in the dramatically illuminated sunset, Miller associates the poem's lyric speaker with theatrical "speakers of soliloquies," and concludes that despite the ostensible address to Lamb the poem "often sounds like Coleridge's own internal dialogue."[11] The tension between self-communion and communication has figured in some of the most compelling recent readings of "This Lime-Tree Bower My Prison." In an account that pointedly asks, "What does it mean to *pretend* to talk to some one?," Adela Pinch takes the poem as an occasion to explore "different modes of having others in mind," and concludes that Coleridge's apostrophe to the absent Charles Lamb is a "non-voicing" or "not-speaking" that posits the object of address "as an entity that can never truly be spoken in the real beyond apostrophe's reach."[12] For Jon Mee, whose rich study of the "conversable worlds" of the long eighteenth century is shaped throughout by the texture of social circumstance and the value of verbal collision with others, the figure of Charles Lamb is curiously "folded into a kind of monologue." From this perspective, what the individual act of imagination risks losing is the potentially challenging and even combative experience of interpersonal exchange. "Coleridge creates a paradise within himself from the imagined community of his friends. In the process, of course, any resistance from others is also short-circuited by an inclusivity that avoids the collision of difference."[13]

Against this skepticism about Romantic lyric sufficiency, it is worth recalling a critical tradition that was more willing to endorse the rhetorical structure of a poem that seems to dissolve the natural setting and human relationship in the transformative power of the individual imagination. James D. Boulger's 1965 article, "Imagination and Speculation in Coleridge's Conversation Poems," is paradigmatic in part because it is framed by Coleridge's famous definition of the "secondary Imagination" in chapter 13 of the *Biographia Literaria* as an idealizing and unifying process that "dissolves, diffuses, dissipates, in order to re-create."[14] Setting out from the observation that critics interested in the relationship between Coleridge's poetry and his organic theory of imagination have struggled with the conversation poems, Boulger acknowledges formal tensions in these poems but still affirms that "the achievement of unity of any sort is a remarkable tribute to the power of Imagination."[15] To see the conversation poems as a mere "collection of topical references and personal reactions to situations of Coleridge's early married life" is to overlook the fact they are more "essentially about the maker and especially the making of poetry":

> The central theme in each poem is the imaginative power itself, with subordinate themes of the speculative reason pressing to destroy it. The surface play of scenery and friendly dialogue is a mask for the poet's inner struggle to organize the ideas about God and Nature which influenced his early life, mainly of "idealistic" (Berkeleian), traditional Christian, and eighteenth-century mechanist (Hartleian) origin.[16]

There could be no more forceful confirmation of the linked denial of place and sociability than Boulger's dismissal of "the surface play of scenery and friendly dialogue" as "a mask for inner struggle." Approached through "inner struggle" rather than "surface play," the poem opens with mechanistic natural associations, reaches a climactic idealism in the sun drenched apprehension of an "Almighty Spirit," and finds resolution in a delighted return to the bower that makes "the poet's feelings ... the unifying force among conflicting elements." This imaginatively unifying power of individual feeling, rather than topical reference or personal experience, still less situated interaction with others, determines poetic achievement. "The poet's feelings are ... responsible for the choice of imagery and description, and for the associations which are grouped around each selection of natural objects."[17]

Boulger is particularly interested in the way patterns of light and dark track imaginative and spiritual confidence, with "the communicating outward movement of the active imagination into nature ... associated instinctively with light," and the darkness that closes again toward the end of the poem registering fear and doubt. Yet uncertainty about the final image of the rook in flight has less to do with the connection between poet and friend at a distance than with the capacity of imagination to unify discrete image patterns. The act of blessing the bird becomes "a symbolic attempt" to join light and darkness "by an act of the will" that temporarily, if precariously, yields "the identity of subject and object, in a unity between the active and passive elements in the cosmos."[18]

It is hard to deny the impressiveness of this cosmic sense of the poem's scale, yet vastness seems to come at the expense of texture and immediate experience. The same can be said of the proposition that the "communicating outward movement" of the poem involves individual consciousness encountering nature or divinity rather than other people, whether these are friends or readers of the poem. The very notion that "This Lime-Tree Bower My Prison" completes itself as an act of imagination, or (for Harman) an act of self-authorization, is complicated by Coleridge's mischievous habit of eroding formal resolution through serialized closing gestures – the final section of the poem offers a curious sequence of aphorisms, precepts, and figures. And there are a host of further challenges to any sense of the poem as a self-contained act of imagination in the complex history of its composition, revision, transmission, publication, and reception. In a revealing study of the versions of Coleridge's major poems, which indicates how editorial and textual work has transformed our understanding of Romantic literature, Jack Stillinger traces the history of no less than twelve distinct versions of "This Lime-Tree Bower My Prison," beginning with three manuscript letters in advance of print publication: the first to Southey in July 1797, consisting of a fifty-five line poem with no headnote, but with an epistolary explanation of circumstance, and an address within the poem to "my Sister & my Friends" as well as "My gentle-hearted CHARLES"; the second in an undated letter to Charles Lloyd that has partially survived, and that by way of address adds "Sara, and my Friends" to Charles; and the third a seven line excerpt in an October 1797 letter to John Thelwall.[19] Against interpretive claims of imaginative sufficiency, this was clearly a poem that Coleridge wanted to share with his friends. Issues associated with epistolary transmission continue to echo through Stillinger's fourth version, the first publication of the poem in Robert Southey's *Annual Anthology* of 1800, a Bristol volume that included work by others who figure in the social circumstances of the poem (Southey, Lamb, Charles Lloyd). The full title of this first printed version was also notable for the way it identified and located a particular figure of address: "This Lime Tree-Bower My Prison, A Poem, Addressed to Charles Lamb, of the East-India House, London."[20]

The accumulation of friends and intimates throughout the early dissemination of the poem is instructional, since it complicates any reading of "gentle-hearted Charles" as an emblematic addressee who facilitates notional conversation, so that that the poem can ascend (or descend) into monologue and self-communion with nature and divinity. On the contrary, the development of Charles as a figure of address can be understood as part of a more social process of communicating with and through several other friends, in ways that richly inflect the poem's meaning and significance. Critical commentary has explored an intriguing range of individuals and groups identified with "This Lime-Tree Bower My Prison," each involving distinct local associations. The poem was first composed around six months after Coleridge moved out of Bristol and, with the assistance of his wealthy friend Thomas Poole, settled in a cottage at Nether Stowey. The strategic opening of a gate in the connecting wall between the residences of the two men allowed access from Coleridge's cottage garden to Poole's extensive orchard and what would become the poem's lime-tree bower. Relocation from Bristol to Stowey involved social tensions and reconciliations, beginning with Poole's worry that the cottage was inadequate and that the inhabitants of Stowey might not welcome a poet with radical associations.[21] The accommodating gate can be taken as an emblem of the way these stresses were worked through, and the way place can shape and be shaped by sociability and literary expression. If this was a phase of shifting intimacies and allegiances in Coleridge's private life, there were underlying changes too in the historical relationship between private life and the wider public world. Kelvin Everest considers "This Lime-Tree Bower My Prison" to be an important poem in part because it reveals "an emerging distance, in English culture, between the poet and his audience," as Coleridge turns away from "society as a whole" and from explicitly public discourse in favor of "domesticity and retirement," and seeks companionship in "the small domestic community, of family and friends" at Nether Stowey.[22] The conversation poem is distinctive as a literary form in that it requires a specified addressee and auditor distinct from the reader.[23] In this sense, Lamb's mediating role may have less to do with the poet's achievement of self-sufficiency than with a rhetorical management of the pressing claims of a wider reading public.

I will return to Lamb, since he is the poem's most persistent and complex figure of address, but Everest's point about the importance to Coleridge of specific friends within a domestic framework can shape a consideration of other individuals involved in "This Lime-Tree Bower My Prison." Despite Boulger's eagerness to dismiss "topical references" to the poet's "early married life," the domestic circumstances of Coleridge's relationship with Sara Fricker are vividly present from the first letter in which the poem is written out for Southey ("Dear Sara accidentally emptied a skillet of boiling milk on my foot, which confined me during the whole of C. Lamb's stay"[24]) through the initial published headnote, and the poem is made possible by this at once mundane and disturbing incident of domestic impairment, and the network of deprivations, frustrations, and yearnings it triggers. The milk may well have come from Poole through the newly opened gate in the connecting wall.[25] Richard Holmes takes the incident to be evidence of turmoil in Coleridge's married life, and Everest suggests that the poem "manifests a fresh intensity in the potential of Coleridge's ideal retirement" that is antithetically shaped by "actual shortcomings in his domestic life."[26] Yet Rachel Crawford has offered the fullest and most compelling interpretive account of Sara in part by challenging a sense of opposition between domestic life with her and lyric transcendence through address to Charles and other friends. Crawford's approach highlights the link between Sara's disabling accident and the poem's other gendered event, the murder by Charles' sister Mary Lamb of their mother, a "strange calamity" that had generated Coleridge's invitation nearly a year before Lamb's visit took place. Against readings that have "dissociated the poem from the disturbing narratives of Sara's and Mary's deeds," and against an oversimplification of "the speaker's experience of nature by applying to it a kind of aesthetic thermometer which grades the landscape into picturesque, beautiful, and sublime portions," Crawford disrupts aesthetic categories by tracing a contaminating picturesque, with female and domestic associations, through even the most sublime landscapes. Acknowledging that the effort to purify the poem is partly Coleridge's own, she argues for a complex logic of sacrifice that at once obscures and "retains traces of Sara's and Mary's narratives."[27]

Though not as volatile as these two figures of "calamity," other friends have been similarly restored to complex and uneasy presence within the poem, and recent criticism has been particularly attentive to the way lyric communication radiates outward through various circuits of correspondence and social exchange. The three epistolary recipients of the poem are instructive. "This Lime-Tree Bower My Prison" was written at a time

when Coleridge was estranged from Robert Southey, and in treating the
first transmission of the poem to Southey as part of "a breathless appeal for
rapprochement," John Gutteridge has shown that Coleridge infused the
closing movement of his poem with two striking allusions to the recent
second edition of Southey's *Poems*: the first to Southey's "Ode Written on
the First of January, 1794" ("To whom all sounds of Mirth are
dissonant . . ."), and the second to one of the *Botany Bay Eclogues* ("and
thence at eve / When mildly fading sunk the summer sun, / Oft have
I loved to mark the rook's slow course, / And hear his hollow croak . . ").[28]
Working back to the first version of the poem, which addresses "My Sister
and my Friends!" rather than "My gentle-hearted Charles!," Gutteridge
proposes that by fusing the two passages from Southey in his own closing
figure of the creaking flight of the rook at sunset, Coleridge provides a
"link between all the friends in the poem."[29] Even allowing for revisions in
the published version, the apparently triangular geometry of the final
figure – where the bird connects two geographically divided friends – is
complicated by the allusion to Southey. Charles Lloyd, the other epistolary
recipient of the poem, had moved into the cottage at Nether Stowey in
September 1796 as a kind of literary and spiritual disciple who paid £80 a
year for accommodation, tutoring, and companionship, but whose mental
deterioration strained Coleridge's ideals of intellectual influence and sympathetic conversation. By March 1797, a few months before the occasion of
"This Lime-Tree Bower My Prison," he had to be sent away for medical
treatment. Felicity James' revealing and finely grained study of male
sociability and friendship in the relations of Coleridge, Lamb, and Wordsworth suggests that "the growing closeness of Lamb and Lloyd" in London
through the early winter of 1797 was negatively shaped by the fact that
both men felt Coleridge drifting away, as the formation of "a new community at Nether Stowey" that was centered on the Wordsworths relegated Lamb and Lloyd to "onlookers."[30] Again, Lamb's strangely pivotal
yet peripheral role in the poem can be understood in terms of actual social
relationships and specific places as well as spiritual and aesthetic
imperatives.

John Thelwall is by most accounts the least well served of the three
"Lime-Tree Bower" correspondents, and James cites Nicholas Roe's
account of the way both Coleridge and Poole "sacrificed Thelwall's residence in the neighborhood" of Nether Stowey "for the company of
Wordsworth and Dorothy" to suggest how the poem's close rendering of
intimacy and identification would have pained the marginalized friend.[31]
As troubling as this may be, the emotional force of the poem is enhanced

by an appreciation of the range of its attendant relationships. Thelwall has provided some of the more striking registers of place with respect to friendship and social interaction. The possibility that Coleridge might be considered a scandalous presence in Stowey was fully realized when the notorious Jacobin lecturer and veteran of the treason trials visited, and Richard Holmes offers an extract from Charlotte Poole's diary as evidence of communal dismay. "We are shocked to hear that Mr Thelwall has spent some time at Stowey this week with Mr Coleridge, and consequently with Tom Poole. Alfoxden house is taken by another fraternity . . . To what are we coming?"[32] In what may be the most powerful reconfiguration of the poem's key terms and relationships, John Bugg takes the coincidence of Thelwall's arrival in the West Country to visit Coleridge on July 17, 1797 with the first transmission of the poem in the letter to Southey as an occasion to reread "This Lime-Tree Bower My Prison" as a prison poem, shaped by the "force of confinement" and by "the contemporary incarcerations of [Coleridge's] friends and fellow writers."[33] Against the convergence of later published versions of the poem on a malleably imagined "gentle-hearted Charles," no one person can accommodate the varieties of imprisoned experience, nor can the prison be construed (as Raiger would have it) in purely spiritual terms. There is Coleridge melodramatically absorbed in the confines of a pleasant bower become *felix carcer*, Lloyd dispatched to a Litchfield asylum; Lamb despite his own urban inclinations "in the great city pent"; and finally and with more public and political resonance, Thelwall confined during the treason trials of 1794 in the Tower of London and Newgate Prison. "For Coleridge in the summer of 1797," Bugg argues, "'confinement' was an overdetermined concept," so that the poem's ecstatic gestures of transcendence and release cannot be disentangled from a "larger public context" that includes the real threat of close confinement. The significance of the poem's thematics of sound and silence similarly shift against the backdrop of Pitt's terror and the Gagging Acts, and the threat of imminent death seems less melodramatic when considered in light of contemporary prison reform and the hazards of squalor and disease.[34] Bugg's close confinement enriches the framework for lyric communication among friends and compatriots, and forces us to recalibrate the terms of the poet's desire for solace and release.

Coleridge gestures of friendship were notoriously ambiguous, and against Gutteridge's positive account of allusion in the closing movement of "This Lime-Tree Bower My Prison" it is worth considering elements of appropriation and mastery as well as reconciliation. The letter to Southey that included the poem congratulated him on the sale of his recent volume of Poems, but also criticized a phrase from his ballad "Mary, the Maid of the Inn" as "*slipsloppish*."[35] More telling in terms of the poem may be the same letter's effusive praise of the Wordsworths, who had recently settled at Alfoxden House near Stowey. James wonders about the decision to frame the epistolary poem with "a passionate declaration of affection for the Wordsworths" at a time when William Wordsworth was replacing Southey as a mentor figure for Coleridge, and when the failed Pantisocracy scheme with Southey was giving way to a new ideal of retirement among other friends in the West Country. "For Southey," she concludes, "the poem's celebration of friendship must have carried a particular, hurtful charge."[36] The letter's emphatic language of situation and management ("I brought him & his Sister back with me & here I have *settled them*") echoes the way the poem rhetorically guides the movement of friends at a distance, and the elaborate detail Coleridge offers about Alfoxden House provides some fascinating counterpoint to the poem in terms of home, landscape, property, proximity, and walking. "A gentleman's seat, with a park & woods, elegantly and completely furnished—with 9 *lodging* rooms, three parlours & a Hall—in a most beautiful & romantic situation by the sea side—4 miles from Stowey . . . The park and the woods are *his* for all purposes *he* wants them—i.e. he may walk, ride, & keep a horse in them— & the large gardens are altogether & entirely his."[37] In this context, the poem as first transmitted to Southey and then revised in direct address to Lamb becomes striking for the way it does *not* represent what Coleridge was in the process of finding with the Wordsworths, the sociability of neighbors and "a period of happiness in a closed, familial community."[38]

If only because strained intimacy still lay ahead, the relationship with the Wordsworths can be considered the most positive among the several friendships that run through the poem and its early transmission. As Stillinger reminds us, with respect to revisions to the poem in the years after July 1797, this was a period in which "Coleridge and the Words-worths were reacting to one another's writing almost daily."[39] The inter-textual relationship between "This Lime-Tree Bower My Prison" and Wordsworth's "Lines Left Upon a Yew-Tree" has received the most critical commentary, but Richard Matlak tracks other evidence of "poetic exchange," including the sunset scene in Wordsworth's 1794 manuscript *Evening Walk* and the process by which the "shadowy spot" of a shepherd in the same poem becomes a "speck" by 1836.[40] Although she left fewer textual traces, Dorothy was an active presence in these literary exchanges, and Gutteridge has developed striking parallels between her prose and Coleridge's ongoing revisions to "This Lime-Tree Bower My Prison" which serve to link composition and revision with the shared experience of rural walking, and to identify elements of the poetic landscape with "the topography of the Quantocks."[41] In particular the "dark green file of long lank weeds," the climactic feature of the initial descent into the "still roaring dell" in the revised 1800 *Annual Anthology* version of the poem, recalls Coleridge's earlier description of adder's tongue (or rather hart's tongue) in his 1797 fragment poem "Melancholy," and a journal entry for February 10, 1798, in which Dorothy describes the same plant on a walk to a waterfall in Holford Glen below Quantock Combe.[42] Citing evidence from correspondence as well as the journal, Gutteridge concludes that Coleridge drew on Dorothy's prose record of variously shared experiences to "fill in the details" of his own landscape in a way that wound up conflating two distinct places, Quantock Combe and the dell at Alfoxden.[43] In this sense Mellor's landscape categories involve actual places, and one of the poem's more enigmatic landscape features ("a most fantastic sight!") turns out to be one of its most particular.

A poem that can seem to lapse into soliloquy is very much, in James' trenchant phrase, "part of a multi-voiced conversation," a conversation that is shot through with rivalry and tension as well as affection, and that can be securely identified with specific places. It is worth returning to the role of Charles Lamb to reconsider any sense of the poem as an act of individual imagination that effectively manages and silences another on the way to self-realization and spiritual transcendence. Lamb was the most vigorous respondent to the poem upon its publication in 1800, and while early versions were not sent to him directly, the very fact of epistolary transmission has the effect of making his relevant correspondence seem less distinct from the poem as such. Certainly, key passages from his letters have become indispensable to later editors and commentators in elucidating the poem's meaning: on August 6, 1800, to Coleridge, there is his famous irritation at the repeated sobriquet, "my gentle-hearted Charles," and a request that the poet not "make me ridiculous any more by terming me gentle-hearted in print"; on August 14, again to Coleridge, a further reprimand that any subsequent edition should replace "*gentle hearted*" with "drunken dog, ragged-head, seld-shaven, odd-ey'd, stuttering, or any other epithet," along with an objection to "the unintelligible abstraction-fit about the manner of the Deity's making Spirits perceive his presence" that may have shaped Coleridge's revisions; and finally on January 30, 1801 a letter to Wordsworth in response to a gift of the 1800 *Lyrical Ballads* insisting that "separate from the pleasure of your company, I dont mu[ch] care if I never see a mountain in my life."[44]

Though not addressed to Coleridge, this last letter is worth quoting at length since it links the pleasure of place with "the pleasure of . . . company," and goes on to render the *locus amoenus* of the London essayist in terms that provide a bracing counterpoint to the poet's redemptive bower:

> . . . I have passed all my days in London, until I have formed as many and intense local attachments as any of you Mountaineers can have done with dead nature. The lighted shops of the Strand and Fleet Street, the innumerable trades, tradesmen and customers, coaches, waggons, play houses, all the bustle and wickedness round about Covent Garden, the very women of the Town, the Watchmen, drunken scenes, rattles;—life awake, if you awake, at all hours of the night, the impossibility of being dull in Fleet Street, the crowds, the very dirt & mud, the Sun shining upon houses and pavements, the print shops, the old Book stalls, parsons cheap'ning books, coffee houses, steams of soups from kitchens, the pantomimes, London itself a pantomime and a masquerade, all these things work themselves into my mind and feed me without a power of satiating me. The wonder of these sights impells me into night-walks about her crowded streets, and I often shed tears in the motley Strand from fullness of joy at so much Life— —. All these emotions must be strange to you. So are your rural emotions to me.— But consider, what must I have been doing all my life, not to have lent great portions of my heart with usury to such scenes?———
>
> My attachments are all local, purely local—. I have no passion (or have had none since I was in love, and then it was the spurious engendering of poetry & books) to groves and valleys.—The rooms where I was born, the furniture which has been before my eyes all my life, a book case which has followed me about, (like a faithful dog, only exceeding him in knowledge) wherever I have moved—old chairs, old tables, streets, squares, where I have sunned myself, my old school,—these are my mistresses—have I not enough, without your mountains? I do not envy you. I should pity you, did I not know, that the Mind will make friends of anything.[45]

Yet any sharp sense of difference should be qualified not only by Coleridge's own urban inclinations, but also by a recognition that there is much about "This Lime-Tree Bower My Prison" that is similarly "local, purely local," even if the "attachments" involve very different places: Poole's orchard, the cottage at Nether Stowey, Alfoxden House, Hodder's Combe, and the Quantock Hills. With respect to shifting male friendship and personal rivalry, Lamb's metropolitan riposte to Wordsworth resonates across time as well as space. The concern for temporality in "This Lime-Tree Bower My Prison," registered in the potent "meanwhile" and a host of subtle shifts in tense, is more than a matter of language. William A. Ulmer has stressed the fact that, while Coleridge first invited Lamb to visit in a letter of consolation sent immediately after his mother's death, "by the time Lamb could act on the invitation Coleridge had new friends and new interests." As a result "the initial invitation and visit occurred in uncomfortably different social contexts." Where Coleridge might recently have been jealous about Lloyd's influence over Lamb, by the time Lamb arrived "the problem was less that Coleridge had been eclipsed in Lamb's interests by Lloyd than that Lamb had been eclipsed in Coleridge's interests by the Wordsworths." In stressing the Salutation and Cat tavern in Newgate Street near Christ's Hospital, where Coleridge lodged in autumn 1794 and where Lamb joined him for intoxicated evenings of speculation and literary conversation, Ulmer indicates how shifting friend-ships and habits of sociability can set place against place. "Lamb plainly traveled to Coleridge's 'cot' hoping to rekindle the private intimacy of their Salutation and Cat evenings. What he found upon his arrival was a house full of guests and a Coleridge whose attention was divided among them, and not always equally."[46] Shadowing what the poem directly communi-cates about missed emotion and experience, we can discern a distinctly uncomfortable social quality to the walk that Lamb and the Wordsworths would have taken, as former and present intimates of Coleridge converse in the absence of the man himself.

Felicity James has discussed the "stereotypically manly pleasures of public smoking and drinking" and the "rough, pot-house affection" of the Salutation and Cat, accentuating a contrast with the more mixed ideal of domestic rural retirement in 1797.[47] Ulmer traces a different but no less compelling trajectory from London to Nether Stowey. Drawing on earlier studies of Coleridge and Unitarian faith, he offers a remarkable account of "This Lime-Tree Bower My Prison" as a poem driven by spiritual and transcendental impulses even as it is laced with complex social interactions and particular geographical associations. His reading sets out from a pair of propositions that are at once straightforward and strikingly revisionist: "first, that Charles Lamb rather than Coleridge himself is the principal subject of the text's consolatory enterprise, and second that the consola-tions offered are in important respects less imaginative than theological – more specifically, that they are implicitly but crucially Unitarian."[48] Where the second point directly challenges an emphasis on the individual act of imagination, the first more subtly complicates any sense that the poem works to transcend the immediate social circumstances of its composition by reducing the person Charles Lamb to a manageable figure within a solitary lyric exercise. Ulmer's argument is wide-ranging, but for my purposes a key strand involves friendship in theory and practice. Here the point of departure is "the Unitarianism that Coleridge shared with Lamb, but about which they also disagreed," and the prominence of religion and especially the ideas of Joseph Priestley in the Salutation and Cat conversations. When Southey traveled to London in January 1795 to fetch Coleridge back to Bristol and to Sara Fricker, he sought the wayward man at this tavern only to find that he had instead gone with Lamb to the Unitarian chapel.[49] Ulmer draws on Gurion Taussig's study of Unitarian friendship to clarify the poem's approach to male intimacy, and also suggests an intriguing spiritual framework for walking and rural itinerary, with Coleridge's 1796 walking tour in search of subscribers for *The Watchman* linked with the way English Unitarian clergyman visited one another to foster intellectual and spiritual exchanges among scattered meeting-houses.[50] The series of letters between Lamb and Coleridge in the aftermath of his mother's death, initiated by Lamb's request for "as religious a letter as possible," led to the invitation to Stowey but also in Ulmer's account to a broad "theological debate centering on the issue of experiencing God's being and the possibilities of religious friendship and community."[51] In the end Ulmer finds that Coleridge consoled Lamb by working to convert him to a theory of the One Life that was an outgrowth of his own Unitarianism and that provided the spiritual underpinning and "theological ground of human solidarity" and "redemptive community" throughout the conversation poems.[52]

What is striking about this analysis is that, by linking social and spiritual impulses, Ulmer is able to fully develop the experienced and imagined trajectories of "This Lime-Tree Bower My Prison" without privileging either. So, for example, the poem's "narrated tour" turns out to be "a simultaneous exercise in natural description and spiritual allegory," with the poet speaker "endeavoring . . . to keep his eye steadily on Lamb and his moral situation" even as he seems to look "past Lamb without really seeing him at all."[53] This sense of the relation of apparently disparate impulses and elements has been a feature of some of the most rewarding critical accounts of the poem, as in Raimonda Modiano's observation that "visionary expansion nourishes a more refined and a richer sensory awareness," and in Felicity James' account of a revised poem that was "sharpened and improved by Coleridge's persistent return to . . . interconnected questions concerning the poet and his relationship to the external world, the real and the abstract, the particular and the speculative."[54] The difficulty with Boulger's account is not that it celebrates lyric introspection but that it overlooks the way individual imagination and the desire for transcendence remain engaged with other people and places.

This is unexpectedly confirmed by what may be the most vigorously social, material, and topographical reading, Donna Landry's account of "This Lime-Tree Bower My Prison" as a Romantic "walking poem" in *The Invention of the Countryside*. Landry insists on Coleridge's direct and sensory rendering of identifiable elements of the natural world. The "long, lank weeds" that "still grow plentifully in Holford Combe near Alfoxden" are firmly rooted in "blue clay-stone country" by "a geographical reference to secure their specificity." Yet there is no denial of visionary release. The poem's descent into the dell is "a rare vision of animate creation, of vitality in natural objects" that "offers a glimpse of the one life flowing through all things, a naturalist's supranatural find."⁵⁵ Rivalry in friendship is present here too, notably in contests with Wordsworth that extend from skill in "representing nature" to sheer endurance in perambulating "shared land-scapes."⁵⁶ The most remarkable yield of Landry's reading may be that it grasps the orchestration of spectacular visual effects for a posited itinerary in ways that are consistent with the situated social practice of Romantic walking. Drawing on Tim Fulford's provocative mapping of the poet's bower refuge as a zone of "divided and owned land," set against the "unenclosed Quantock hilltops" where friends roam land that is "shareable in common,"⁵⁷ Landry shows how Romantic walking erodes the distinction between immediate experience and visionary transcendence. A walk that is "not undertaken in the flesh, but imaginatively, from memory and projection" is not restricted to lyric consolation, but is instead part of a more widely practiced "aesthetic of perambulation" that can conceive "of weather and the creation of atmosphere as a theatrical performance." The result is what Landry terms "a form of interactive picturesque": "Sometimes a vicarious walk, the literary composition or, by extension, consumption of a walk, can have the same effect as a walk itself."⁵⁸ In this sense Landry's account does not so much deny Mellor's aesthetic categories as it does remind us that such categories were socially mediated and transmitted, and brought to bear upon experiences like walking the countryside.⁵⁹

The familiar contours of Coleridge's bower effusion can seem worlds apart from bookshop lounging, pugilistic spectacle, assembly room entertainment, seaside recreation, and shipboard revelry. Yet key features of sociability and its locations that emerge from "This Lime-Tree Bower My Prison" figure consistently in the chapters that follow, and not merely in the whiff of radical tavern sociability that hangs about Lamb and Coleridge's Unitarian conversations in the Salutation and Cat. To begin with, sociability involves conflict and difference as well as friendly intimacy, and attention to place can highlight the way social interaction requires exclusions that can be painfully felt and vigorously (even violently) enforced. Further, occasions for sociability, however immediate and spontaneous they may seem, are consistently shaped by shared concepts and norms that are brought to bear upon experience; a sense of place again serves to remind us of the way that gardens, homes, and landscapes were experienced through a host of social, intellectual, and aesthetic frameworks. The productive tension between ideal and practice, and between conception and experience, returns throughout this volume. In this sense, locating sociability may not be a single operation, as even the most closely situated experiences are overlaid by other places and other experiences, which may be called to mind by association and allusion. It did not take Coleridge's remarkable powers of imagination to negotiate the pleasures and difficulties of being in two places at once. This kind of double consciousness necessarily involves a sense of perspective, on others and on other places, and the theatrical visual effects in "This Lime-Tree Bower My Prison" can be linked with the wider development of a sociable culture of spectacle, theatricality, reciprocal observation, and even spying, and with the "audience-oriented privacy" that Habermas finds in eighteenth-century life.[60] The acute awareness of time in Coleridge's poem may be immediately driven by a sense of deprivation and separation from others, but it registers a characteristic feature of located sociability, as the present experience of being with others calls to mind other places and other people at other times. And finally, the remediations evident in tracking the circumstances of the poem through letters, correspondence, and publications remind us that the complexities of verbal and visual representation are not merely a matter of the historical record. Even as the poem is driven by a desire for immediate proximity to Charles Lamb, it is overlaid by any number of other friends and other desires that lead outward through the networks of correspondence and publication that make lyric introspection a socially meaningful act. In this sense, as the chapters that follow often demonstrate, an interest in the meanings of sociability and its attendant places is more than our own retrospective concern.

Part I of the volume, "Print Relations," focuses on sites of sociability directly occasioned by literature and print culture. In "Recovering the Country Book Club," Ina Ferris explores distinctive dimensions of time as well as place in a mode of bookish association that falls outside the more closely studied terrain of the subscription library, with its urban, middle class, and aspirational sensibilities. Country book clubs left fewer historical traces in part because they were more isolated and embedded, "an emanation of local place," gathering the existing male elites of country villages and small market towns in an available place such as a tavern rather than a dedicated library or club premises. A "sense of continuance in place" was aligned with a responsiveness to local and seasonal calendars, and with annual patterns of acquisition from booksellers and dispersal to club members that sustain a fascinating "rhythm of centrifugal and centripetal motions that gathered and dispersed club books at regular intervals." Given their contented alignment with traditional modes of rural sociability, it is unsurprising that these clubs were often viewed with disdain from without, and Charles Shillito's mock-heroic poem, *The Country Book-Club*, at once satirizes rural custom and occasions bitter reflection on countervailing developments in urban literary culture. Yet for all their modest embeddedness in existing rural hierarchies and social relations, Ferris shows that the country book clubs had an impact beyond their actual membership, as books made their way to "small clusters of families in 'lonely houses' around the countryside." Despite their isolation, then, these clubs had "blurred boundaries," as a core membership was "supplemented by an informal periphery (effectively an adjunct membership)" with more domestic and feminine associations. In rescuing the country book club and its social rituals and rural locations from historical neglect, Ferris encourages us "to lower our sights" and "reorient our maps" of literacy and print, considering "reading cultures" as well as the more uniform and aggregate category of the reading public.

In "'Bread & cheese & porter only being allowed': Radical Spaces in London, 1792–1795," Jon Mee returns us to urban locations and to the intensely political sociability of the LCS, drawing particular attention to shifts in radical sociability as a result of controls upon public meetings imposed by the Two Acts of 1795. While the LCS was invested in the potentially limitless imagined category of "the people" as addressed through print publication, Mee insists that radical social relationships "were not experienced as an impersonal information economy," and that the particular venues where events took place or were imagined to have taken place are critical to an understanding of radical sociability. John Thelwall's experience in the convivial gatherings of the Philomathian society and William Godwin's diary entries of "tea" as a shorthand for gathering and conversation provide avenues into a complex social world. Against the simple identifications of the LCS "with the plebeian culture of the alehouse," Mee allows "tea" and provisions of "bread & cheese & porter" to open up a more mixed and varied social terrain that extends from the prototypical arenas of the political public sphere (coffee house and tavern) through private and domestic quarters which were less uniform with respect to class, gender, and social style. Drawing on categories developed by Michel de Certeau and James Epstein, Mee encourages us to consider the way "*space*" as "*practiced place*" can indicate how social and political interactions were imagined, organized, and contested. Spy reports and government records reveal that the diversity of radical gatherings in taverns, alehouses, bookshops, and homes confused polite observers and frustrated efforts to characterize the LCS as a motley assortment of low men meeting in unrespectable places for subversive purposes. The presence of women provided ambiguous evidence of respectability and transgression. Disputes over public and private, and domestic and political, in the 1793 trial of John Frost for sedition as a result of a coffee-house republican utterance demonstrate both the relevance and the contested character of "spatial" conceptions of political locations. While Mee acknowledges radical aspiration and the need to seem respectable, he also insists that LCS activities cannot be reduced to "empty mimicry" of available social and political forms. In their "boozy rituals and symbolic toasts," LCS members were "articulating their own version of the theatrical culture of the eighteenth century" and claiming a place in the political nation.

Although bookshops have never received the attention afforded such canonical sites of eighteenth century and Romantic sociability as the coffee-house and tavern, in "Piccadilly Booksellers and Conservative Sociability," David Fallon sets out by considering establishment and conservative bookshops of the 1790s and 1810s in relation to Habermas' theory of the political public sphere. If the concrete and particular dimensions of bookshop sociability expose the idealized limitations of Habermas' conception, Fallon suggests that the concept remains pertinent in part for the way it reveals how social actors sought to understand their own activity. The conservative Piccadilly bookshops explored here, notably John Wright's and Thomas Hatchard's, pose a compelling case since they challenge progressive assumptions about the literary and political public sphere. If conservative bookshops were strongly linked to the government by ideological and financial as well as personal ties, "bookshop sociability" was nevertheless directed for participants "by a self-conception as independent critical thinkers" keen to challenge Whig and radical claims. Wright's shop was a particularly lively and convivial site of "lounging" and conversation, and while to some extent ideologically uniform, there were complexities about actual and conceptual place, with the bookshop functioning "as a threshold between private conversation, a conservative coterie, and broader public opinion." The "Battle of the Bards," an altercation between the satirical poet John Wolcott ("Peter Pindar") and men at Wright's shop, provides an intriguing glimpse of the movement back and forth between print and shop, and between imagination and experience, as satirical publication and review trigger an event that is then recorded and further contested in print. The particular contours and habits of sociability at Wright's are further elucidated by comparison with its successor, the more evangelical shop of Hatchard, with its more genteel "club-like social space" and retiring back room devoted to meetings and formal gatherings. Taken together, the two bookshops reveal linked social and discursive formations that aim to form public opinion by advancing "a highly partial imagining of the public," but that are also subject to disruption by the heterogeneous and diffuse formation of a political readership.

Part II of the book considers "Sociable Spectacle," though print culture remains very much at issue. Daniel O'Quinn's study of the ambiguities of anti-Semitism in "Proxy Israelites: Staging Ethnic Violence in the Ring and the Pit" takes us back and forth between experience and representation, and between blatant stereotype and elusive allegory. In suggestively linking theater and prize-fighting the chapter traverses a range of places and more particular sites within those places – theater, stage, pit, private box, street, paddock, ring – and O'Quinn (like Mee) develops a language of space to chart the various ways that experience and representation get organized and coded across distinct yet related zones of social interaction. And since theater here involves the OP Riots of 1809, sociability shifts from the familiar terms of conversation and convivial gathering to discord and outright violence. If coming to blows would seem to be the most viscerally physical form of human interaction, O'Quinn attends closely to represented spectacle and performance. One striking result is that actor and spectator sometimes wind up on the same side of a complex representational scheme. "The mediation of performance replicates the separation between the space of representation and the space inhabited by performers and audience alike." Within this fluid framework, the anti-Semitism that ran through Daniel Mendoza's spectacular prize-fighting career proves volatile and unpredictable, often reinforcing British national identity and imperial fantasy, but at times sharply set against them. Johann Heinrich's satirical print, *The Triumph*, published a week after Mendoza's second fight with his archrival Richard Humphries, affords a particularly rich sense of the complexities of anti-Semitism even as it demonstrates the way that "the figural space" of satirical print representation extends and "supplements the sociable space of the fight." While boxing can undo anti-Semitic stereotype, notably at the third Mendoza Humphries fight where "acts of staged mercy" allow Mendoza to become "the anti Shylock," theater winds up reinforcing existing codes, notably when John Philip Kemble recruits Mendoza and other prize-fighters to secure order in the pit during the OP Riots, but then seeks to extricate himself from association with Mendoza by staging "two of the most anti-Semitic plays in the repertoire" at Covent Garden in October 1809, Shakespeare's *The Merchant of Venice* and Sheridan's *The Duenna*. If the gambit was not entirely successful, O'Quinn suggests that this is because, unlike Pierce Egan's retrospective journalism, it "takes place in real time and . . . is embedded in the social space of Covent-Garden theatre," and is therefore subject to the ongoing vagaries of contested social experience.

In "Fashionable Subjects: Exhibition Culture and the Limits of Sociability," Paul Keen explores a heady mix of commerce, fashion, science, and display in the distinctive London shows and spectacles of the 1780s. These potentially troubled Enlightenment confidence about the improving and refining effects of increased sociability in commercial society. Keen therefore develops a mixed conceptual framework to evaluate claims for and against public attractions, supplementing varieties of sociability with Lawrence Klein's account of an eighteenth-century culture of politeness and Habermas' ideal of rational critical debate in a political public sphere. Tensions among these ideals, and across the range of styles and sites for sociable exchange, were "exacerbated by the spectatorial nature of eighteenth-century culture," as the public desire for entertainment came to be associated with the corrupting effects of novelty, dissipation, and distraction. The Prussian lecturer Gustavus Katterfelto invoked the values of moral, spiritual, and intellectual improvement to promote his experimental wonders, but critics worried that "relentless sociability" in debased commercial spaces could only foster ignorance and confusion. James Graham's lectures on the benefits of electricity were also wrapped in the promotional language of gentility and refinement, and raised similar concerns, intensified in this case by the illicit suggestions of sexual commerce associated with the restorative powers of his Celestial Bed. The Learned Pig and the balloonist Vincent Lunardi round out a tour of the ambiguous world of London shows in the 1780s, and without resolving the question of their role in a culture of progress, industry, and instruction, Keen invokes the figure of the balloon to suggest that codes of sociability remain contested.

Part III of the book, "Interior Places," takes up some of the specific protocols and demands of sociability indoors, beginning with Gillian Russell's chapter, "'The place is not free to you': The Georgian Assembly

Room and the End of Sociability." To provide context for the assembly room as a venue for confrontation and historical crisis in William Godwin's novel *Caleb Williams*, Russell provides a history of these distinctive features of Georgian provincial life, stressing (against perceptions of decay) that they persisted well into the nineteenth century and spread throughout Britain and the Empire. The typical assembly room was a complex structure, organized around a central space for dancing but including a range of activities and "zones of parasociability." For this reason, Russell suggests that the assembly and assembly rooms were "potentially metasociable," occasioning an enactment of "what it meant for people to join together in an assembly for whatever purpose" and affording reflections on and observations of those purposes. They were also strikingly heterogeneous places, open to men and women, allowing intergenerational contact, and bringing together the gentry and the prosperous middle class. Though governed by ideals of politeness and civility, they could also be venues for dissension, in ways that help account for Godwin's use of a market-town assembly as the setting for conflict between the locally dominant figure of Tyrrel and the newly arrived Falkland. Russell carefully excavates the ways in which "the protocols of the assembly room are used as a means of staging a confrontation between old regime power, embodied by Tyrrel, and the force of public opinion manifested by the assembly," though she stresses the instability of Falkland's claim to speak with the "general voice." In the end, the novel exposes the assembly room's modes of literary culture and social intercourse as weak imitations of courtly values that can neither resolve social tension nor prevent tyrannical violence.

Godwin figures centrally again in "Unconventional Calling: Godwin, Women and Visiting in the 1790s," as Mark Philp draws on his digital edition of Godwin's diaries to explore the norms and possibilities of a neglected dimension of radical sociability in the 1790s: visiting friends and acquaintances, typically in one another's homes. Though philosophically committed to freeing himself from mere social convention, Godwin was neither informal nor knowingly reckless, particularly after the furor over his frank account of Mary Wollstonecraft in *Memoirs of the Author of A Vindication of the Rights of Woman* (1798). His patterns of visiting and being visited by women provide a fascinating lens on the expectations that governed relationships between the sexes, and on the extent to which a radical and unconventional individual might challenge those expectations. If Godwin hoped to contest assumptions about status in the way he visited and was visited by gentlemen, the diary suggests he did not succeed: he called on such men, or was summoned by them, but they did not call on him. The rivalries and shifting intimacies that run through his visiting habits suggest that this was "treacherous social terrain," with Godwin by turns challenging and conforming to established norms. Occasions on which he visited women alone in their home, or was visited by them alone in his, are particularly interesting, and Philp plots the risks to reputation and status that would have concerned women in the period, as well as suggesting some of the distinctions Godwin may have had in mind in making decisions about his own visiting habits. While the familiar figures of Wollstonecraft, Elizabeth Inchbald, and Mary Jane Clairmont account for many such interactions, Philp closely explores the implications of Godwin's visiting with a less well-known woman, Sara Elwes. Legal proceedings between her and her husband over charges of sexual infidelity lead to other places of potentially scandalous encounter (carriages, inns, gardens, legal chambers), while also suggesting what would have been at stake in unconventional domestic visiting. If some of the distinctions Godwin made in his visiting habits remain elusive, this only serves to confirm the complexity of the norms that governed sociability between the sexes in domestic settings.

While movement is at issue throughout the volume, Part IV, "Traveling Sociability," specifically considers occasions for mobile interaction. In "Sociability among the Ruins: The Colosseum by Moonlight, *circa* 1820," Christopher Rovee explores the rise and development of a postwar British touristic fashion for visiting the Colosseum in Rome at night beneath the moon. If Madame de Staël inaugurated the vogue with *Corinne* (1807), Lord Byron massively popularized and refined the terms of a distinctive Romantic experience. The "inward turn" of reverie and oppositional retreat laid out in *Manfred* and *Childe Harold's Pilgrimage* was promulgated as a touristic practice in guidebooks that invoked Byron and encouraged readers to share a version of his experience. This provides Rovee with a central and telling paradox: the experience of the Colosseum by moonlight was at once an experience of autonomous subjectivity driven by a need to disconnect from time and place, and a collective social practice acquired from others and further transmitted in correspondence and publication. In this sense, the solitary and meditative "performance of counter-sociability" was itself a sociable practice. "Indeed rejection of the social might have been the most social thing about visiting the Colosseum by moonlight." Rovee traces these contradictions well into the nineteenth century, and across a range of concerns about past and present, location and dislocation, sound and silence, solitude and company. The post-Grand Tour era of Romantic travel feeds directly into modern tourism, so that there are enduring qualities about the paradoxes associated with postwar Byronic fashion.

In "Sociability by the Sea Side: Margate before 1815," Harriet Guest sets out from eighteenth-century perceptions of the seaside resort of Margate as the carnivalesque East End of London transposed to a coastal fishing village, and then tracks a more particular range of inversions, confusions, and reimpositions of social order in the representation of sociability and leisure at Margate. In satire and in more serious observation, heterogeneity was the recurrent theme, as the mixing of classes in a new and less geographically demarcated setting blurred social differences and dissolved familiar principles of order and regulation. At the same time, representations of Margate clearly trade on a sense of recognition. "What distinguishes Margate is the combination of the strange and familiar; the recognizable London faces and figures transposed into unknown shapes." The trip via the Thames on a Margate Hoy (a sloop-rigged river vessel) was the first stage in a series of confusions that continued through sea and land, on piers and at the beach, and in public rooms, libraries, and other sites of sociable resort. If the absence of any internal principle of social order is a familiar feature of festive representation, what distinguished Margate was again the proximity (geographically and conceptually) to London, and the disturbing but also liberating sense that social types who would know their place in the metropolis were promiscuously thrown together in the seaside resort. The breakdown of boundaries and hierarchies can seem risky, but Guest indicates a number of ways in which representation involves acts of recognition that reinforce social order. In a revealing coda, the Margate episode of Charlotte Smith's 1796 novel *Marchmont* turns out to be an exception, as the tendency to reaffirm eroded distinctions does not prevent a more reformist impulse that envisions the possibility of social change through Margate's reputation for unconventional sociability.

In "Lower Deck Narratives and Sociability in the British Navy, 1750–1815," Nicholas Rogers explores the life and work of the ordinary navy man, "Jack Tar," on ship and on shore. Against perceptions that sailors typified a culture of mobile wage labor, Rogers demonstrates that the consolidation of coastal communities sustained lives in which men moved back and forth between coastal and oceanic trades. At the same time, the life of the sea was acquired rather than inherited, as voluntary and involuntary recruitment drew men from many backgrounds and geographical areas. By the Napoleonic era, the navy was ethnically and occupationally diverse. Shore leave was infrequent, so apart from sometimes riotous periods of demobilization, labor and leisure took place within the confines of the ship. Discipline was strict, with the lash a matter of routine, and hierarchy clearly established both as a matter of social status and the demarcation of space on board, particularly as the naval leadership came to be more narrowly drawn from the landed and professional classes. Occupying cramped and shared quarters, ordinary working seamen had their own hierarchies and forms of rough justice. This was an emphatically masculine realm of foul language and prodigious drink, where hard labor and episodes of danger were set off by leisure and laughter, with song and dance particularly prized. Rogers identifies the drinking habits of navy men with other plebeian groups, even as he distinguishes the particular way in which "men-of-the-line became floating brothels" when anchored offshore. The mutinies of the 1790s reveal a growing confidence among lower-deck seamen, and against accounts that stress outside influences, Rogers discerns "the self-generating collective action of the seamen themselves." Such collective action flowed "from the sociability of the lower deck" and its distinctive ways of understanding authority, discipline, and hierarchy. Naval work privileged youth, and Rogers closes with the struggle of many sailors to find anything like a settled domestic existence after years at sea, suggesting that "the seamen of the Napoleonic era were a lost generation" whose often dismal ends belied the romance of naval heroism.

Notes

1 Jürgen Habermas, *The Structural Transformation of the Public Sphere: An Inquiry into a Category of Bourgeois Society*, trans. Thomas Burger and Frederick Lawrence (Cambridge, MA: MIT Press, 1989).

2 See especially Gillian Russell and Clara Tuite, "Introducing Romantic Sociability," in *Romantic Sociability: Social Networks and Literary Culture in Britain, 1770–1840*, ed. Gillian Russell and Clara Tuite (Cambridge: Cambridge University Press, 2002), pp. 11–13.

3 "Introducing Romantic Sociability," in *Romantic Sociablity*, ed. Russell and Tuite, p. 4.

4 A version of the note appeared in the first published text of the poem, in Robert Southey's *Annual Anthology* of 1800, although the episode recorded in the poem actually took place in July. Except where other versions are indicated and cited, the discussion that follows quotes from the text provided in Samuel Taylor Coleridge, *The Complete Poems*, ed. William Keach (Harmondsworth: Penguin, 1997), pp. 138–40.

5 For this movement, as shaped by Coleridge's fear of vast and empty spaces ("*horror vacui*"), see Max F. Shulz, *Paradise Preserved: Recreations in Eden in Eighteenth- and Nineteenth-Century England* (Cambridge: Cambridge University Press, 1985), pp. 65–68. For Cowper see Tim Fulford, *Landscape, Liberty and Authority: Poetry, Criticism and Politics from Thomson to Wordsworth* (Cambridge: Cambridge University Press, 1996), pp. 228–29.

6 Christopher R. Miller, "Coleridge and the Scene of Lyric Description," *The Journal of English and German Philology* 101 (2002), 520.
7 Anne K. Mellor, "Coleridge's 'This Lime-Tree Bower My Prison' and the Categories of English Landscape," *Studies in Romanticism* 18 (1979), 255, 260–61.
8 Ibid., pp. 265–66.
9 Michael Raiger, "The Poetics of Liberation in Imaginative Power: Coleridge's 'This Lime Tree Bower My Prison,'" *European Romantic Review* 3 (1992), 74.
10 Barbara Leah Harman, "Herbert, Coleridge and the Vexed Work of Narration," *MLN* 93 (1978), 892.
11 Miller, "Coleridge and the Scene of Lyric Description," pp. 526, 529.
12 Adela Pinch, *Thinking about Other People in Nineteenth-Century British Writing* (Cambridge: Cambridge University Press, 2010), pp. 88, 93, 96.
13 Jon Mee, *Conversable Worlds: Literature, Contention, and Community 1762 to 1830* (Oxford: Oxford University Press, 2013), pp. 189, 195.
14 Samuel Taylor Coleridge, *Biographia Literaria*, ed. James Engell and W. Jackson Bate, 2 vols., vol. 7 of *The Collected Works of Samuel Taylor Coleridge* (Princeton: Princeton University Press, 1983), vol. 1, p. 304.
15 James D. Boulger, "Imagination and Speculation in Coleridge's Conversation Poems," *The Journal of English and German Philology* 64 (1965), 691–92.
16 Ibid., p. 693.
17 Ibid., pp. 699, 702–03.
18 Ibid., p. 705.
19 Jack Stillinger, *Coleridge and Textual Instability: The Multiple Versions of the Major Poems* (Oxford: Oxford University Press, 1994), pp. 44–46, and *Collected Letters of Samuel Taylor Coleridge*, ed. Earl Leslie Griggs, 6 vols. (Oxford: Clarendon Press, 1956), vol. 1, pp. 334–36, 349–50.
20 Stillinger, *Coleridge and Textual Instability*, pp. 46–47, and *Annual Anthology* 2 (1800), 140.
21 Richard Holmes, *Coleridge: Early Visions, 1772–1804* (New York: Pantheon Books, 1989), pp. 132, 138.
22 Kelvin Everest, *Coleridge's Secret Ministry: The Context of the Conversation Poems 1795–1798* (Hassocks, Sussex: Harvester Press, 1979), pp. 257–58.
23 See David Bromwich, *Disowned by Memory: Wordsworth's Poetry of the 1790s* (Chicago: University of Chicago Press, 1998), p. 70, for the conversation poems as "meditations on a landscape that need to address a second person apart from the reader, a particular listener to the poet's hopes and fears."
24 *Collected Letters*, ed. Griggs, vol. 1, p. 334.
25 Holmes, *Coleridge: Early Visions*, p. 138.
26 Ibid., p. 153, Everest, *Coleridge's Secret Ministry*, pp. 242–43.
27 Rachel Crawford, "Accident and Strange Calamity in 'This Lime-Tree Bower My Prison,'" *Romanticism* 2 (1996), 193, 199–200.
28 John Gutteridge, "Scenery and Ecstasy: Three of Coleridge's Blank Verse Poems," in *New Approaches to Coleridge: Biographical and Critical Essays*, ed. Donald Sultana (London: Vision Press, 1981), pp. 165–66, and Robert Southey, *Poems*, Second Edition (Bristol, 1797), pp. 61, 93.

29 Gutteridge, "Scenery and Ecstasy," p. 166, and *Collected Letters*, ed. Griggs, vol. I, p. 336.

30 Felicity James, *Charles Lamb, Coleridge and Wordsworth: Reading Friendship in the 1790s* (Basingstoke: Palgrave, 2008), 96–100, 111–12. By the end of 1797, James sees a full transition, with Coleridge finding "the friendship of Southey, Lloyd, and – to some extent – Lamb, frustrating and cloying," and "moving towards a new friendship with Wordsworth" (115).

31 Ibid., pp. 110, 232, n. 21.

32 Holmes, *Coleridge: Early Visions*, p. 155.

33 John Bugg, "Close Confinement: John Thelwall and the Romantic Prison," *European Romantic Review* 20 (2009), 50.

34 Ibid., pp. 50–51.

35 *Collected Letters*, ed. Griggs, vol. I, pp. 333–34.

36 James, *Charles Lamb, Coleridge and Wordsworth*, p. 110. With respect to Thelwall, James points out that the letter containing an extract from the poem also expresses regret that Coleridge cannot help him find a cottage at Nether Stowey, in sharp contrast with an earlier ideal of their shared retirement.

37 *Collected Letters*, ed. Griggs, vol. I, pp. 333–34.

38 Everest, *Coleridge's Secret Ministry*, p. 245.

39 Stillinger, *Coleridge and Textual Instability*, p. 49.

40 Richard E. Matlak, *The Poetry of Relationship: The Wordsworths and Coleridge, 1797–1800* (New York: St Martin's Press, 1997), pp. 74–75, 78.

41 Gutteridge, "Scenery and Ecstasy," p. 168.

42 Ibid., and Dorothy Wordsworth, *The Grasmere and Alfoxden Journals*, ed. Pamela Woof (Oxford: Oxford University Press, 2008), 145, 284. For a close discussion of Coleridge's "long, lank weeds," see Donna Landry, *The Invention of the Countryside: Hunting, Walking and Ecology in English Literature, 1671–1831* (Basingstoke: Palgrave Macmillan, 2001), pp. 224–25.

43 Gutteridge, "Scenery and Ecstasy," p. 168. See Holmes, *Coleridge: Early Visions*, p. 154, for a related observation that the revised poem "draws more powerfully than ever on the Quantocks imagery."

44 *The Letters of Charles and Mary Lamb*, ed. Edwin W. Marrs, 3 vols. (Ithaca: Cornell University Press, 1975), vol. I, pp. 217, 224, 267. See Stillinger, *Coleridge and Textual Instability*, 49, for Coleridge's revision understood in light of the remark about an "unintelligible abstraction-fit," and for a thoughtful treatment of the pertinence of Lamb's critical response to the poem, see Felicity James, "Agreement, Dissonance, Dissent: The Many Conversations of 'This Lime-Tree Bower,'" *The Coleridge Bulletin* 26 (2005), 47–49.

45 *Letters of Charles and Mary Lamb*, ed. Marrs, vol. I, p. 267.

46 William A. Ulmer, "The Rhetorical Occasion of 'This Lime-Tree Bower My Prison,'" *Romanticism* 13 (2007), 23. For the Salutation and Cat tavern, see Holmes, *Coleridge: Early Visions*, pp. 76–77, 83, 85, 87.

47 James, *Charles Lamb, Coleridge and Wordsworth*, p. 23. It is worth noting that James does discern a persistent if elided "tension between fraternal and familial affections."

48 Ulmer, "Rhetorical Occasion," p. 15.

49 Ibid., pp. 15–16. See also Holmes, *Coleridge: Early Visions*, p. 87.

50 Ulmer, "Rhetorical Occasion," p. 16.

51 Ibid., pp. 16, 18.

52 Ibid., pp. 18–19, 21, 24.

53 Ibid., pp. 20, 22–23.

54 Raimonda Modiano, *Coleridge and the Concept of Nature* (Tallahassee: Florida State University Press, 1985), p. 52, and James, *Charles Lamb, Coleridge and Wordsworth*, pp. 106–07.

55 Landry, *Invention of the Countryside*, p. 224.

56 Ibid., p. 221.

57 Fulford, *Landscape, Liberty and Authority*, p. 229.

58 Landry, *Invention of the Countryside*, pp. 223, 226–27.

59 In this respect Modiano, *Coleridge and the Concept of Nature*, p. 208, n. 3, cites John Barrell's observation that by the late eighteenth century, painterly principles of composition were so pervasive "that it became impossible for anyone with an aesthetic interest in landscape to look at the countryside without applying them, whether he knew he was doing so or not." See John Barrell, *The Idea of Landscape and the Sense of Place: 1730–1840* (Cambridge: Cambridge University Press, 1972), p. 6.

60 See Habermas, *Structural Transformation of the Public Sphere*, pp. 51–52, and "Introducing Romantic Sociability," in *Romantic Sociablity*, ed. Russell and Tuite, pp. 9–11.

PART I

Print Relations

CHAPTER I

Recovering the Country Book Club

Ina Ferris

The "reading boom" of the late eighteenth/early nineteenth century was accompanied by a marked proliferation of bookish associations, as private subscription libraries, literary clubs, and reading societies of various kinds fanned out across Great Britain.[1] This expansion of print-based associations has been generally understood as a sign of the increasing penetration into the provinces of an urban "middling"-class culture of politeness and sociability.[2] For David Allan, for example, the springing up of subscription libraries (the "most characteristic form of polite associationalism") in remote areas like the Cornish coast in the early 1800s represents the degree to which "a specifically urban and strongly middle-class form of culture" was taking hold all over the country.[3] Town histories of the period confirm the point, regularly presenting subscription libraries as signs of civic maturation, showcasing their often imposing premises as exemplary of a new modern urbanscape. Complicating if not overturning this story, however, is the less-noticed circulating book club (also known as a "dividing club"), which achieved even greater penetration in the period than did the subscription library but which had (and continues to have) a much lower public profile. Thus, an often-cited account by "A Traveller" in the *Monthly Magazine* in 1821 reports between 500 and 600 book clubs in operation at that date as opposed to around 260 subscription libraries, and this may well be a conservative estimate.[4] But their specificity as a bookish organization has been elided. While accounts of reading and literary associations in the period typically list book clubs, they also typically subsume them into a developmental narrative of the emergence of the modern public wherein the clubs feature as simply precursors to the more advanced form of the subscription library. Many book clubs did indeed turn into subscription libraries, but many did not, and not only because they were often too small or isolated to do so.

Like subscription and circulating libraries, book clubs provided members with access to more new publications than they could afford (or were willing to buy) as individuals. Club members paid an annual fee to finance the purchase of volumes, holding regular meetings to choose books (usually monthly); the members then nominated books, which were circulated according to a set rota. Like other book-lending organizations, clubs hence multiplied and broadened the range of publications an individual member could read, although they did not necessarily extend the parameters of the reading public as a whole. As William St Clair observes, they tended to widen reading among those already within the reading classes but did not do much "to deepen it downwards."[5] This is not to overlook the significant extent to which newer entrants – artisans, laborers, factory workers – formed reading societies, usually building up modest collections. The west of Scotland was particularly rich in such societies, a correspondent to the *Monthly Magazine, and British Register* noting in 1797, for example, the existence of fifty-one laboring-class reading societies in the area.[6] Nor can the lines between different kinds of reading societies be too sharply drawn. At the same time, however, book clubs in general were characterized by a restricted membership, predominantly male, drawn from the elite and more affluent sectors of a community. The key point is that even though they were a feature of late eighteenth-century cities and large towns, notably new industrial towns such as Birmingham and Manchester where they often had dissenting and reformist affiliations,[7] book clubs more properly represent, as John Brewer has argued, "a phenomenon of small towns and larger villages."[8] As he explains, they brought together "the local elite of professional men, merchants, affluent farmers and minor gentry, in the convivial environment of the local inn or tavern, where together they chose the club's acquisitions, debated the issues of the day and last, but by no means least, ate and drank."[9] An emanation of local place as much as a stage in the development of modern mentalities, the country book club functions less as a rudimentary than as a parallel bookish formation, one that stands in more tangled relation than does the subscription library to the drive to "become modern." To register its specificity is to reposition this ubiquitous but shadowy print phenomenon and, in so doing, to shift attention from the formation of a reading public (a question much agitated over in the period and since) to the making of reading cultures.

Under the Radar

On a cold night in October 1990, Keith A. Manley, editor of *Library History* and assiduous searcher after eighteenth-century book clubs, stepped off a train in the remote Cumbrian town of Dalton-in-Furness. He was there to attend the monthly meeting of the Dalton Book Club, founded in the spring of 1764 at the White Horse Inn but of whose continuing existence Manley had been unaware until he ran across a reference to the club in a recent town history.[10] Almost 230 years after its founding, the Dalton continued to hold monthly meetings following well-established custom, from the order in which members sat around the room (starting with the most senior member to the left of the chairman) to the choosing of books by lot and the ordering of two rounds of beer when the meeting turned to the sociable part of the evening. During this entire period, the club had also kept extensive and meticulous records listing the members, detailing their book borrowing, and registering the items purchased by the club – records still extant except for some twenty odd years between 1898 and 1921. This rich archive too had remained unknown to Manley despite his extensive research and traveling in search of data, for like most country book clubs the Dalton defined itself in and through its locality, understanding itself as a limited circulation in more than simply the number of members. Thus, Manley specifies that the "brief history" of the Dalton he would later print in *Library History* was originally written by a longstanding member (Ernest H. Boddy) specifically "for the benefit of the members of the Club."[11] As an explicit "counterpoint" to this continuing history, Manley juxtaposes in the same issue the report of an extinct nineteenth-century book club in the Cornwall township of Wadebridge by R.J. Swanton, professor of medieval English literature. This club had flourished in the 1840s, but its existence had been unsuspected by modern scholars until the recent fortuitous discovery of circulation sheets inserted in the front wrappers of an unbound set of installments of *Martin Chuzzlewitt* acquired by Eton School Library.[12] The sheets assign each item a number, indicate the number of days it may be kept (three days in the case of the monthly parts), and list the names of the members beside columns for date received and date forwarded, to be filled in when each member passed the item on to the next name on the list. Correlation of these sheets with local contemporary records and the census allowed Swanton to largely reconstitute the membership (primarily gentry and clergy), while the columns themselves provide a rare record of the actual transfer of texts from reader to reader. "Within some parts of the list," Manley writes, "the forwarding distance was a matter of merely some yards, or daily professional contact, in other cases up to half-a-dozen miles."[13]

This diptych in *Library History* – one book club long forgotten but
returned to a certain visibility, the other long continuing but invisible –
underlines the elusiveness of the book club phenomenon. Despite their
pervasiveness, book clubs have left few direct traces; nor (in contrast to
circulating libraries) were they much noticed in contemporary commentary. Moreover, the traces they have left are typically found in peripheral
forms and locations: a book plate here, a circulation list there; a set of rules
printed by a local printer; a passing reference in a town history.
A circulation label may surface for a club without a name; another may
be known only as a name. The White Lion Inn Book Society, for instance,
known to have existed in Nottingham before 1816 remained but a name
until 1896, when the librarian of the Nottingham Subscription Library ran
across two of its book labels listing the rules and the members to whom the
books were to be circulated.[14] Paul Kaufman, whose pioneering study of
book clubs appeared in the 1960s, repeatedly stresses the "extreme paucity
of evidence," and laments that original sources proved "meagre, widely
scattered, fugitive."[15] Despite some substantial new findings since his time,
current library historians continue to echo Kaufman's lament. But in an
important sense, this unsatisfactory scholarly situation – the scanty, patchy
data that make for shaky empirical ground – points to the specificity of the
book club, which constituted itself as an organization precisely under the
sign of dispersal. Unlike other book-lending organizations, that is, book
clubs did not accumulate books but sold them off each year, generally at an
auction where the member who had nominated a book was often obliged
to buy it at a certain discount if no higher bid emerged. There were
numerous variations: some clubs sold the books back to the bookseller at
a discount, for instance, while others began to keep a portion of the books,
often in a makeshift room in town. But all eschewed dedicated premises.

To invoke the terms of Kaufman's seminal distinction, these are book
societies with a set to "current functioning" rather than "indefinite continuance."[16] Indeed, the Dalton club removed itself from notions of
perpetuity or permanence in striking fashion from the start by establishing
the club for only one year at a time, and its members continue to decide
annually whether to renew its existence for another twelve months (temporary existence having ironically but symptomatically turned into a
tradition). Without reading rooms or permanent collections, the clubs
are not "libraries" in our common understanding of the term, and they
lack the library's gravitas, signifying what David Allan sees as "a preference
for the fleeting pleasures brought by being able to read a constant succession of new books over the deeper satisfaction of building and owning an

enduring collection."[17] In contrast stands the solid subscription library, a point underlined in Richard Polwhele's 1806 county history of Cornwall. Polwhele reports the establishment of book clubs in "almost every good neighbourhood" in the county but also notes, regretfully, their regular dispersal of books.[18] After a brief section on the clubs, he rapidly moves on to a lengthy promotion of the ambitious Cornwall Library and Literary Society, founded in Truro in 1792, the exact dimension of whose spacious premises he records and the size of whose collection (around 3,000 volumes accumulated in less than fifteen years) he notes with pride. Running below the description in the text is a massive footnote spilling over seven pages and taking up most of the space, where Polwhele prints documents related to the library's founding, including newspaper reports and handbills; its rules and regulations; books nominated for purchase; a letter in strong support, and so forth. Note overwhelms text, much as the solidity of the Cornwall Library and Literary Society displaces the scattered book clubs.

The keynote of book club reading was currency. "The intentions of the *book club* are well known," declared William Hutton in 1780, "to catch the productions of the press as they rise," intentions of which Hutton himself, having risen out of abject poverty largely on the strength of becoming a paper manufacturer, thoroughly approved.[19] So the Edgbaston and Five Ways Book Society declared in 1816 that "[t]he circulation of modern Works of general interest" was its "special object"; while the Market Drayton Book Society, founded in 1814 (and still in operation), passed a rule in 1817 that books must not have been published for more than four years.[20] Seeking to participate in the broad literary culture of the day, "general" book clubs in rural areas like these focused (as did their urban counterparts) on polite letters, a category that by the turn of the century was increasingly being expanded to include novels. In 1800, for instance, the book club at Sedgefield in County Durham ordered a mix of memoirs, agricultural texts, theological works, voyages, and anthologies in the "elegant extract" mode, but it also bought novels, among them Henry Mackenzie's *The Man of Feeling* and Regina Maria Roche's *Children of the Abbey*.[21] The Market Drayton society was even more up to date on popular literature, its list for 1814 including the hottest new publications: the anonymous *Waverley*, Maria Edgeworth's *Patronage*, Sydney Owenson's *O'Donnel*, as well as Byron's *The Giaour*, *Lara*, and *The Bride of Abydos*, among others. The list for that year also records the usual miscellany of nonfictional genres but even here evidences a decided and up-to-date literary bent. Mixed in with travels, biography, history, and a substantial

number of military memoirs of the French wars, we find Elizabeth Montagu's letters, John Dunlop's pioneering history of fiction, and four titles of
literary-philosophical writing by Madame de Staël.[22]

Even as rural and urban clubs shared reading tastes, however, their
dissimilar social composition placed them in different relation both to
literary culture and to the new. Membership of country clubs was typically
made up of those for whom questions of social status and the building of
cultural capital did not weigh as heavily as for the more recent entrants into
the culture of literacy who appear more often in the roster of urban clubs.
The founding members of the Market Drayton club are typical in consisting mainly of lawyers, local gentry, and the usual clergy.[23] Hence, rural
book clubs differed from the urban ones in two significant and related
dimensions: first, they did not operate under the sign of social aspiration or
within the temporality of advancement in the same way; second, despite
their modern organizational apparatus (e.g., written regulations, minutes,
fines, and so forth), they did not function as alternatives to traditional or
customary forms and practices. Urban clubs for the most part corresponded to the category of "social libraries" defined by James Raven as
"social passports and conduits for polite society."[24] Raven's tropes ("passports," "conduits") invoke a mobile urban milieu remote from the country
villages or small market towns, where rural book clubs took hold among
those who had a social place and stayed in place, their interest in new
publications and polite letters not ruling out a commitment to a temporality of repetition and continuity. The Market Drayton Society, for
example, instituted legacy seats a few years after its founding, ensuring a
future largely cast in the traditional time of generational continuity. Both
the longevity of many clubs and the regularity with which the same
families provided members for several generations, as in Dalton and
Market Drayton, make literal this sense of continuance in place.[25]

Such enfolding underlines the second point I noted – that rural clubs
rarely served as alternatives to customary and traditional order. Unlike
provincial subscription libraries, they did not carve out or build a new kind
of place in a town or village, generally aspiring (as one commentator notes)
to "no more than a corner of the local tavern."[26] Not to separate oneself
from, or add to, what is already in the built place constitutes at once a
symbolic and material gesture, registering a commitment to an embedding
within the already existent. In importing modern metropolitan texts and
issues, the country clubs intermeshed old and new forms of sociability,
creating new habits, but at the same time they merged with traditional
rural activities and practices. Thus, Dorothy Wordsworth, writing of the

annual venison feast and ball held by the Kendal Book Club, casually remarks that one of their visitors "goes to Penrith from the Kendal dinner and Ball, but will return before the Races whither John W. is to accompany him."[27] Responsive to the seasonal and local calendar, the clubs usually had different meeting schedules for summer and winter; in market towns, they also often met, as did the Dalton Book Club, on market day (a Saturday in this case). Club meetings themselves were usually convened in the local inn, supplemented by food and/or drink. Indeed the Dalton club resurrected the old meaning of "club" as the division of the bill among those at a dinner table, collecting a "Club of Twopence" from each member at each meeting to put toward the cost of its libations.[28] Moreover, if the annual sale of books that distinguishes book clubs – the decision to operate under the sign of dispersal – was a pragmatic economic move to raise funds and keep membership fees low, it also had the effect of foregrounding the club as a circle of persons rather than a collection of books, one that in rural versions took its place in a customary round of familiar exchange, gossip, conviviality, and festive occasion.

For a literary culture shaped in metropolitan and urban centers, however, rural book clubs tended to appear an incongruity, mongrel formations yoking together the incompatible tropes of "country" and "book." Their very existence perceived as an irony, the clubs prompted literary representation in the low ironic mode: satires, mock memoirs, and caricatures (subscription libraries, by contrast, attracted exercises in the higher encomiastic modes of ode and heroic verse albeit with forgettable results[29]). Pivoting on the familiar trope of country life and manners as a "naive" premodern form of existence, representations of the rural book club drew on the doubled inflection of this trope: on the one hand, a rustic inflection foregrounding a confined brutish existence rooted in the body; on the other, a pastoral inflection highlighting a sociable natural community also intimately tied to bodies – in either case, well outside the mental space of reading. Charles Shillito's *The Country Book-Club. A Poem*, published anonymously in 1788, goes the brutish route, taking as its theme the incompatibility of a traditional masculine sociability, rooted in the convivial body, and a new enlightened sociability focused on disciplined conversation over books. Thomas Rowlandson's caricature etched on the title page sets the stage. The drawing shows six men sitting around a table in an inn while a comely maid serves a tankard of ale. Smoking, drinking, and talking, they pay no attention to the books on the table except for one figure, slightly removed from the group, who (looking anxious) holds a closed volume: he will turn out to be an impoverished curate who has intruded only to check for reviews of a sermon he recently published. On the walls behind the group hang several placards, most prominent among them the "Rules of this Club 1788" and "Liberty of the Press," casting a sardonic eye on the emphatically corporeal scene of conviviality going on beneath them. Reinforcing the sense of incompatible mixture, another placard ("Glanvill on Witches") alludes to Joseph Glanvill, at once fierce defender of modern science and firm believer in witches and sorcerers.

The mock-heroic poem that follows is a predictable enough lampoon, focusing on the meeting of a "cottage Book-club" at the Malborough inn on a village green.[30] Gathering for a meeting at six o'clock by the village clock, the "motley members" (barber-surgeon, vicar, squire, draper, and bookseller) rapidly abandon any pretence at order or interest in books, ignoring the periodical reviews brought in by the landlord to gossip about local scandal and to transmit scurrilous rumours. All the while the punch bowl makes its speedy round, leaving "no vacant time, to think or *read*."[31] Eventually, the gathering degenerates into a carnivalesque scene of "boundless riot" with the members hurling not only words but books at one another (*Country Book-Club*, p. 38). At the same time, the poem is infused with a certain bitterness about urban literary culture (no doubt reflecting Shillito's own disappointed literary hopes), which surfaces in the pastoral idiom of rural retirement. "Ah! happy man," the poet-narrator addresses the bookseller, "thus gently floating down / The placid stream of life, with fair renown: / No rival envies, and no foe reviles / Thy fame, confin'd within three narrow miles."[32] If the "narrow" compass undercuts the bookseller's "renown" (and underlines the poet's own wider prospect), it also attests to a yearning for such local belonging. As a travesty of a true book club, the country book club in the poem images a regressive social order even as the club's disintegration into discord functions in the second degree to mirror the fractured literary culture of the metropolis.

Ambivalence about metropolitan literary culture, subdued in Shillito's poem, assumes prominence in representations governed by the pastoral mode. Retaining the impossible gap between modern urban culture and country manners but flipping around the valorized terms, representations in this mode cast book societies as contaminators of harmonious community, reflecting the way that rural England became increasingly charged in the early decades of the nineteenth century as an idealized locus of the values abandoned by a rapidly industrializing nation.[33] The highly successful collection of sketches published by Mary Russell Mitford as *Our Village* in 1824 sums up this mode, and its nostalgic evocation of a comforting "little world" remote from fast-paced modern life resonates with the sketch of the village of S___ in a familiar essay titled "Country Reading Societies" published a few years later in the *New Monthly Magazine*. In this piece, the urban narrator, adopting the pose of ostentatious fogeyism popularized by Charles Lamb, claims that, whatever the merits of book clubs in the metropolis or in cathedral and large commercial towns, they are "most baneful institutions amidst the simple and uneducated inhabitants of remote country villages, whither, I grieve to say, they are rapidly spreading."[34] As proof he offers a "before" and "after" picture of the village of S____ . A prosperous village of picturesque peasants and "sociable" gentry far from any main road, it was once "the very image of calm and repose":[35] time moved slowly, marked by casual chatter and home-made specialties of food and drink freely offered to the narrator, as he sauntered about the village during rejuvenating visits to an old friend. All this changed, however, following the establishment of a book society by a widow returned from the metropolis, who imposed an alien discipline on the inhabitants (deadlines for returning books, fines for lateness), altering the way they lived in their bodies and in time, turning them into grim souls, unhealthy and competitive, who furiously read books they did not understand in a "constant race after time." "I can no longer enjoy one of my chief pleasures at S___," the narrator complains, "that easy, sociable, unintellectual chat, springing up one knows not how, and leading one knows not whither."[36]

This scenario of sentimental urban imagining (exaggerated as it is) strikes a representative note in mourning the loss of a "natural" sociability marked by spontaneity, randomness, and familiarity tied to unplanned movement through a particular place. For the urban narrator, country book societies disrupted such rhythms, destroying social cohesion and connection. For book club members inhabiting small villages and remote towns, however, they served precisely as connectors, a thickening rather than an attenuation of local ties, as they pulled dispersed bodies and books within a defined geographical area into closer proximity.

Proximities

In more remote areas of the countryside, where isolation was a primary physical fact, book clubs operated as vital channels of connection. Recalling a book club in rural Norfolk in his youth in the early years of the nineteenth century, the writer of a reminiscence in the *Gentleman's Magazine* emphasizes the "deep influence" of book clubs on small clusters of families in "lonely houses" around the countryside. In such houses, he reports, the arrival of a new club book was "an event looked for with eager interest," the books generally "read aloud, *en famille*" before being passed on to the next name on the list.[37] As John Day observes in his study of Northumberland book societies, book clubs were "an essential social and literary asset" in isolated regions, and his point is borne out by Eneas Mackenzie's account of the number of book societies in small Northumberland parishes in his 1825 county history. Bellingham Parish, for example, with 404 inhabitants had set up a "library or book club" in 1809; by the time of Mackenzie's survey, it had around 40 subscribers, roughly 10% of the population.[38] Nor was it only for the practical reason of facilitating book exchange that most clubs restricted membership to those living within a certain radius. What mattered was the regular rotation of books and meetings; indeed regulated motion (rather than conversation or even reading) may be said to lie at the core of the book club, both books and members circulating in a predictable pattern. "For a month the books . . . carried home by the member were his own undisturbed property," recalls the writer of the 1852 reminiscence, "but they all found their way back, from circumference to centre, on the appointed Wednesday night before the full moon."[39] In this alternating rhythm of centrifugal and centripetal motions that gathered and dispersed club books at regular intervals, the writer clearly found reassurance and comfort, recalling Deidre Lynch's argument that the integration of reading into "the time-frame of the routine" was crucial in securing literature as an institution of middle-class life. Lynch's particular focus is the "steadying" cultural and affective force of individual routines of re-reading (later generalized as the canon), but her argument pertains as well to the punctuated routines of bookish groups like the book club, which were equally instrumental in forging what she calls "alliances . . . between literary reception and the temporal order of the everyday," bringing books into proximity not just in the outdoor life of village or town but in its domestic spaces where, as the reminiscence underlines, they entered the rhythms of family life as well.[40]

"Carried home" for a period (like the books borrowed from circulating and subscription libraries), club books also often ended up there, finding their way back into home libraries in piecemeal fashion as they were sold off at the end of each year: a combination of sharing and owning. Such exchanges draw attention to the blurred boundaries of the clubs whose core was supplemented by an informal periphery (effectively an adjunct membership) consisting of family members (e.g., wives, daughters, sisters, young sons), its composition fluctuating over time. Despite the strongly homosocial constitution of most book clubs, they did not (like most other male clubs) detach themselves from the feminized domestic realm; nor do their nineteenth-century literary representations in contrast, say, to the emphatic masculinism of Ambrose's tavern in *Blackwood's Magazine*.[41] Indeed the sense of an informal domestic periphery was so well entrenched by mid-century that it forms the setting for a rather odd little tale, "Fuss in a Book Club," which appeared in *Fraser's Magazine* in 1848. A light satirical story, it targets the proverbial narrow-mindedness of small country towns, much bruited in Victorian writing; what distinguishes it is the adoption of the genre of the it-narrative. The full title reads: "Fuss in a Book Club. As Related by a Copy of Miss Martineau's 'Eastern Life'."[42] This copy of Martineau's controversial book, dispatched to a fictional Knighton Book Club, narrates the "fuss" that ended in its expulsion as an anti-Christian text, its place filled by the more acceptable *Lives of the Queens of England* by Agnes Strickland. The narratorial perspective renders the story a "secret history" of the book club, taking us behind the scenes of official circulation lists and specified rotas to point up uneven and unpredictable actual reading practices. Sent on its rounds with a list of names and dates affixed to its flyleaf, the book begins its circuit in a rectory, having been ordered by the eldest of several daughters, who had been allowed by her father to choose the book "this time." While her more light-minded sisters dismiss it as a dull tome without pictures, the eldest daughter begins to read rapidly albeit with little comprehension until a young curate intrudes, who immediately condemns Martineau's work with an intimidating flourish of theological learning. Thereupon, the book lies unread in the house until the day it is to be forwarded to the next name, that of the local surgeon, in whose home it is read not by the surgeon but by his wife, a sympathetic and spirited reader who engages in a sharp debate with the dogmatic curate. And so it goes. As the book moves from household to household – a country magistrate, another vicar, a retired general – it finds itself picked up and put down by different members in the house and read (or not read) in a variety of ways. Eventually, the curate's pursuit being relentless, it is exiled to Göttingen where, apparently, they tolerate this sort of thing.

Importantly, the choice of narratorial angle foregrounds the book as a physical presence: it is emphatically a book-body, from the weird image of book-birth in the opening sentence ("Can I ever forget the bright summer evening which saw me released from the last, consummating, book-binder's squeeze?") to the concluding scene of German banishment, where it writes the tale with "a schnapps besprinkled cover, and a cigar marking my most spicy page."[43] Taking up space, requiring transportation, inhabiting rooms and corners, club books were inescapably tangible and proximate objects. As Andrew Piper reminds us, books in the first half of the nineteenth century were "repeatedly endowed . . . with the notion of being 'at hand'," and his observation assumes literal resonance in the case of book clubs as associations literally dedicated to getting books into the hands of their members and facilitating their exchange.[44] In the discourse of the clubs, hands are rarely simply metaphoric. The Market Drayton Book Society, for example, did not hold monthly meetings, so when we find that Rule 4 in its Prospectus specifies that books are to begin circulating with the member who ordered them, then sent on to the next name, and so on "until they have passed through the hands of the whole," the statement has a quite literal charge.[45] Clubs routinely imposed fines for mishandling books, the wording of their regulations and record of fines bringing reading bodies and book-objects into tight relation. "If any book shall manifestly appear to be ill-used or in any way abused the person in whose hands it is found shall pay the prime cost and take the book into his own hands." The words are those of the Dalton club, whose minutes record fines for "writing on the fly-leaf" and "dropping a sort of soot in the edge of the leaves."[46] Such set to the material book, while pragmatic enough, also underlines the closeness of circulation in these groups, where books were transmitted and exchanged among members in face-to-face meetings whether in formal assembly or informal individual encounter.

Details of such meetings are virtually nonexistent, but the historian of the Dalton club helpfully provides a description of current proceedings at their monthly meetings "for the benefit of future generations," observing that these "[p]robably have not changed very much."[47] What he depicts is a highly choreographed affair that brings together various modalities of temporality and sociability. On the one hand, the meeting represents the coming together of equal individuals: the same rules apply to all; all pick lots to choose the books; all pay the same "club"; and so forth. The format of the meeting, divided into specified temporal segments (books are brought out at a certain time, members return them during a designated interval, etc.) is a function of homogeneous modern time, which allows for administrative efficiency and organization so as to ensure the ongoing circulation of the books. On the other hand, this efficient routine is also a social ritual: a repetitive set of stylized gestures and motions through which the group constitutes and confirms a collective identity. This is the shaped time of particular forms of continuance we generally denote as "tradition" or "custom," in contrast to the impersonal time of administrative routine. Underlying both is the third hand: the unscripted familiar time of friendship and neighborliness released when the group moves on to conversation, "during which time, it frequently happens that there is some topical business, sometimes serious, sometimes light-hearted to discuss."[48] Fluid and flexible, this temporal modality constitutes the base time of rural book clubs, layered into its more formal temporal modes, and bridging club time and local time, as well as permitting the slippage between formal structures and actual practice noted by most commentators. Witness Peter Brown's dry comment: "As often happened in this society, the resolution was ignored."[49] Whether or not they were quite as structured as those of the Dalton club, the rituals of meeting held together what was scattered and dispersed, providing at once the sense of a common place (temporary as a "corner of the local tavern" might be) and a regular operation that connected books, persons, and the locality. "If this suggests a ritual," Manley commented after he observed the meeting of the Dalton club, "then of course it is; but it is an informal ritual willingly carried out by old friends."[50] Country clubs thus did not so much harness themselves to metropolitan modernity as "carry home" its books, and in the process they disappeared from public space or, more accurately, from the space of the public.

In a literary culture shaped in metropolitan and urban centers, country book clubs appeared either an incongruity (the subject of satire) or simply did not appear at all. For the resolutely urban William Hazlitt, for instance, whose provocative "On Londoners and Country People" was published in the *New Monthly Magazine* in 1823, rural people led an isolated and "lethargic animal existence" from which they were aroused only by "petty, local interests."[51] Inverting the standard country–city trope, he defines the country as the fundamentally unsociable place, its inhabitants living too much apart; instead he posits the city as the crucible of genuine sociability. This is the case, he argues, not just because its public gathering places support "social feelings" but, paradoxically, also because city dwellers "have a sort of abstract existence."[52] In cities, Hazlitt explains, a "community of ideas and knowledge (rather than local proximity) is the bond of society and good-fellowship."[53] Such a "community" is what constitutes a public: "In London there is a *Public*; and each man is part of it," he asserts.[54] Hazlitt here engages in the contrarianism and polemics he so relished, but his recoil from country life speaks more broadly to the way the category of the "public" (including the "reading public") did not readily map onto the inhabited countryside of small villages and towns. In such places, Hazlitt himself found simply a blank: "No shops, no taverns, no theatres, no opera, no concerts, no pictures, no public buildings, no crowded streets" – and the list mounts until, finally – "no society, no

books, or knowledge of books."[55] This list appears in a review of Wordsworth ("On Mr Wordsworth's Excursion") written for Leigh Hunt's
Examiner, and its rhetorical propulsion is no doubt fueled by Hazlitt's
aggravation at the poet's idealization of rural life. But the blocked view is
symptomatic: in "retired and obscure villages," Hazlitt simply cannot see
anything he recognizes as a truly social formation or a "reading public."
Whatever his hesitation about this public, it remains central to the narrative of the evolution of print as a progressive force to which Hazlitt was
deeply committed. In this narrative, the reading public, as a subset of "the
public," is the function of a complex print system. A fundamentally
homogeneous category, it can be aggregated or disaggregated – cut up,
stratified, even pluralized (we commonly speak of "reading publics") – but
the units are commensurate, inhabiting the same space–time.

The notion of a "reading public" remains indispensable. But we also
need to think about the making of "reading cultures," to lower our sights,
reorient our literary maps, and shift attention to articulations and junctures
where large-scale systems bump into, converge with, or are reshaped by
ongoing (if largely silent) histories on the ground. In recent decades,
Romantic studies have become increasingly interested in processes of
adaptation – renewals, remediations, rewritings – concentrating in particular on interchanges between print and other representational media. To
approach the question of adaptation from the bookish perspective of print
reception is to relocate the question, and the country book club provides
an especially suggestive site. Reversing the arrow of adaptation (incorpor-
ating new into old), it throws into relief another dimension of the inter-
laced temporalities that constitute the historicity of everyday life and
within which (to recall Tom Conley's distinction) cultures take shape as
"processes shared by *people*" in the midst of "codes that define a *public*."[56]

Notes

1 On the provincial expansion at the end of the eighteenth century, see Peter
   Clark, *British Clubs and Societies 1580–1800: The Origins of an Associational
   World* (Oxford: Clarendon Press, 2000). For the explosion of reading, see in
   particular Heather Jackson, *Romantic Readers: The Evidence of the Marginalia*
   (New Haven, CT: Yale University Press, 2005) and William St Clair, *The
   Reading Nation in the Romantic Period* (Cambridge: Cambridge University
   Press, 2004).
2 See Peter Borsay's influential *The English Urban Renaissance: Culture and
   Society in the Provincial Town, c. 1680–1750* (Oxford: Oxford University Press,
   1989).

3 David Allan, *A Nation of Readers: The Lending Library in Georgian England* (London: The British Library, 2008), pp. 74, 72.

4 "Facts Relative to the State of Reading Societies and Literary Institutions in the United Kingdom," *Monthly Magazine* 51 (June 1821), 397. This report is the basis for St. Clair's tables on collective reading institutions, *Reading Nation*, pp. 264–66. However, Clark, *British Clubs*, p. 109, estimates there were around 800 rather than 600 book clubs in 1821.

5 St. Clair, *Reading Nation*, p. 247.

6 "Letter to the Editor of the Monthly Magazine," *Monthly Magazine, and British Register* 4 (October 1797), 275–77. Some forty years later, William Howitt extolled the civilizing power of rural book societies on the laboring classes of Scotland, observing that they "send new books to and fro to one another, with an alacrity and punctuality that are most delightful," *The Rural Life of England*, 2 vols. (London: Longman, Orme et al, 1838), vol. I, p. 264.

7 The (still existent) Birmingham Book Club is exemplary. Founded around the middle of the eighteenth century, it met at John Freeth's Coffee-House, a well-known gathering place of liberals and radicals. During the ferment of the French Revolution it became widely identified with the Jacobin Club; see John Horden, *John Freeth: 1731–1808: Political Ballad-Writer and Innkeeper* (Oxford: Leopard's Head Press, 1993), pp. 26–27.

8 John Brewer, *The Pleasures of Imagination: English Culture in the Eighteenth Century* (London: HarperCollins, 1997), p. 182.

9 Ibid., p. 182.

10 Prefatory note to Ernest H. Boddy, "The Dalton Book Club: A Brief History," *Library History* 9.3/4 (1992), 97.

11 Ibid., p. 97.

12 M. J. Swanton, "A Dividing Book Club of the 1840s: Wadebridge, Cornwall," *Library History* 9.3/4 (1992), 106–21.

13 Ibid., p. 112.

14 Peter Hoare, "Nottingham Subscription Library: Its Organisation, Its Collection and Its Management Over 175 Years," in *Bromley House 1752–1991: Four Essays Celebrating the 175th Anniversary of the Foundation of The Nottingham Subscription Library, More Generally Known as Bromley House Library* (Nottingham: Nottingham Subscription Library, 1991), p. 8. The White Lion Book Society was long posited as a possible origin of this library, but Hoare also notes a rival candidate, namely an "unnamed" book society known only from a circulation label inside an assize sermon preached in 1806, also found in the Bromley House archives.

15 "English Book Clubs and Their Social Import" in *Libraries and Their Users: Collected Papers in Library History* (London: The Library Association, 1969), pp. 36–64. This chapter is a shortened version of his article "English Book Clubs and Their Role in Social History," originally published in *Libri* in 1964. Kaufman identified 110 clubs, but he was able to locate original sources for only 6 of these, along with specific information for just 6 more. Kaufman's work prompted a flurry of searches, which yielded new sources and new

identifications. For the most thorough account of the book clubs, see Allan, *Nation of Readers*, pp. 24–61.

16 Kauffman, *Libraries and Their Users*, p. 38.

17 Allan, *Nation of Readers*, p. 46.

18 *The Language, Literature, and Literary Characters of Cornwall: With Illustrations from Devonshire* (London: Cadell & Davies, 1806), p. 98.

19 *An History of Birmingham To the End of the Year 1780* (Birmingham: Pearson & Rollason, 1781), p. 138.

20 *Regulations Adopted at a General Meeting of the Members of the Edgbaston and Five Ways Book Society*, March 27, 1816 (printed by T. Knott, jun.); Peter Brown, *The History of the Market Drayton Book Society 1814–2008* (Market Drayton: TF9 Publishing, 2009), p. 34. Unusually, the Market Drayton club had female members from the outset. Perhaps as a consequence of being a mixed society, it was also not remarkably social. After holding annual break-fasts for a few years, for instance, it discontinued all social events for 140 years.

21 *Rules and Regulations of the Book Societies at Sedgefield, With the Names of the Members, and a List of Books* (Stockton: Printed by Christopher & Jennet, 1800). The extensive list of books (well over 100) suggests that the society did not sell all its books, even though Rule 7 stipulates that books are to be sold to "the best bidder."

22 Brown, *Market Drayton*, pp. 79–84.

23 Ibid., pp. 14–15.

24 "Libraries For Sociability: The Advance of the Subscription Library," in *Cambridge History of Libraries in Britain and Ireland, Vol. 2 1640–1850*, ed. Giles Mandelbrote and K.A. Manley (Cambridge: Cambridge University Press, 2006), p. 248.

25 The Market Drayton society, for example, can trace families with links to the society for up to six generations (Brown, *Market Drayton*, p.3), and Boddy reports that the Dalton club has had continuing links with local families (*Dalton Book Club*, p. 104).

26 Frank Beckwith, "The Eighteenth-Century Proprietary Library in England," *The Journal of Documentation* 3 (September 1957), 83.

27 *The Letters of William and Dorothy Wordsworth. The Middle Years. Part II. 1812–1820*, 2nd ed. Ernest de Selincourt, rev. Mary Moorman and Alan G. Hill (Oxford: Clarendon 1970), p. 556.

28 Boddy, *Dalton Book Club*, p. 101.

29 See, for example, John Corry, "The Newry Literary Society. An Ode" in his *Odes and Elegies, Descriptive & Sentimental* (Newry: R. Moffet, 1797) and John Button, Jun. *The Lewes Library Society; A Poem* (London: W. Button and Son, and J. Johnson, 1804).

30 [Charles Shillito], *The Country Book-Club. A Poem* (London, 1788), p. 15.

31 [Shillito], *Country Book-Club*, p. 31. Not only country book clubs were targeted in these terms. The town club in George Crabbe's *The Borough: A Poem. In Twenty-Four Letters* (London: Hatchard, 1810) prompts a similar question: "How can Mortals think,/Or thoughts exchange, if they thus eat and drink?"

(Letter X, p. 134). Similarly the high-flying bibliomaniacs of the Roxburghe Club were castigated for their "gourmandizing and guzzling," *Athenaeum* 4 (January 1834), 2. The difference is that in the critique of the urban clubs, books did not signify incongruity. Rather, their book practices pointed up the follies and evils of city life (e.g., fashion, decadence, excess).

32 [Shillito], *Country Book-Club*, p. 22.

33 See Elizabeth K. Helsinger, *Rural Scenes and National Representation: Britain, 1815–1850* (Princeton: Princeton University Press, 1997) and Linda M. Austin, *Nostalgia in Transition, 1780–1917* (Charlottesville, VA: Virginia University Press, 2007).

34 [Eliza Walker], "Country Reading Societies," *New Monthly Magazine and Literary Journal* 22 (January 1828), 217. Despite the essay's female authorship, the narrator is gendered male.

35 [Walker], "Country Reading Societies," p. 218.

36 Ibid., p. 221.

37 "Country Book-Clubs Fifty Years Ago," *Gentleman's Magazine* ns 37, pt 1 (May–June 1852), 571.

38 *Coffee Houses and Book Clubs in Eighteenth and Nineteenth-Century Northumberland* (Newcastle upon Tyne: University of Newcastle upon Tyne, 1995), p. 16; Eneas Mackenzie, *An Historical, Topographical, and Descriptive View of the County of Northumberland*, 2nd ed., 2 vols. (Newcastle upon Tyne: Mackenzie and Dent, 1825), vol. II, p. 248.

39 "Country Book-Clubs Fifty Years Ago," p. 571.

40 "Canons' Clockwork: Novels for Everyday Use," in *Bookish Histories: Books, Literature, and Commercial Modernity, 1700–1900*, ed. Ina Ferris and Paul Keen (Basingstoke: Palgrave Macmillan, 2009), pp. 88, 91.

41 Richard Cronin argues that a "new masculinism" entered the literary sphere after Waterloo, reflecting an anxiety of status owing both to the increased participation of women and to the commercialization of authorship, *Paper Pellets: British Literary Culture after Waterloo* (Oxford: Oxford University Press, 2010).

42 "Fuss in a Book-Club. As Related by a Copy of Miss Martineau's 'Eastern Life,' Etc. Etc.," *Fraser's Magazine* 38 (December 1848), 628. The reference is to Harriet Martineau's *Eastern Life: Present and Past* (1848). On the Victorian genre of it-narratives featuring book narrators, see Leah Price, *How To Do Things With Books in Victorian Britain* (Princeton: Princeton University Press, 2012), pp. 107–35.

43 "Fuss in A Book-Club," pp. 628, 634.

44 Andrew Piper, *Dreaming in Books: The Making of the Bibliographic Imagination in the Romantic Age* (Chicago: University of Chicago Press, 2009), p. 237

45 Brown, *Market Drayton*, p. 16.

46 Boddy, *Dalton Book Club*, pp. 99–100.

47 Ibid., p. 105.

48 Ibid., p. 105.

49 Brown, *Market Drayton*, p. 54.

50 Preface to Boddy, *Dalton Book Club*, p. 97.

51 William Hazlitt, *Metropolitan Writings*, ed. Gregory Dart (Manchester: Carcanet Press, 2005), p. 92.

52 Ibid., pp. 93, 94.

53 Ibid., p. 94.

54 Ibid.,

55 Ibid., p. 79.

56 "Afterword: A Creative Swarm" in Michel de Certeau, *Culture in the Plural*, ed. Luce Giard, trans. Tom Conley (Minneapolis: University of Minnesota Press, 1997), p. 151. The italics appear in the original.

CHAPTER 2

"Bread & cheese & porter only being allowed"
Radical Spaces in London, 1792–1795

Jon Mee[1]

From its foundation early in 1792 to its proscription in 1799, the London Corresponding Society (LCS) was the fulcrum of the popular reform movement in Britain. Its position was built around a public role of information gathering and circulation, creating a network of other societies with similar aims, and staging large outdoor meetings, partly to manifest its claims to represent the people at large. In London itself, LCS members met in divisions to pass resolutions, read and discuss, sing and argue, in alehouses, auction rooms, private homes, and shops, as well as gathering more informally in "Sunday evening parties at the residences of those who could accommodate a number of persons," as Francis Place put it, to do much the same things unofficially at much the same gamut of venues.[2] These activities were seriously curbed by the passing of the Two Acts at the end of 1795, which, among other things, made it impossible for meetings of more than fifty people to gather without the explicit permission of a magistrate and increased the punishment for what were deemed seditious activities. Leaving aside the implications for the law of treason, so eloquently discussed by John Barrell, the Seditious Meetings Bill had grave repercussions for the kinds of events the LCS could undertake and the kinds of spaces they could operate in.[3] Effectively, the radical movement was driven underground, although the LCS continued to try and give the movement a public face until its proscription. In this regard, the Two Acts confirmed hostile representations of the Society as incapable of sustaining public discourse, severely constraining its access to the topography of improving London, re-licensing a pre-existing stereotype of the ale-house politician unable to master appropriate forms of political behavior found in James Gillray's print *London Corresponding Society Alarm'd. – vide Guilty Consciences* (1798) (Figure 1).

The LCS's investment in the production and circulation of print in its addresses, periodicals, and other publications made it possible for radicals to imagine themselves addressing a potentially limitless category of "the

Figure 1   James Gillray, *London Corresponding Society Alarm'd. – vide Guilty Consciences* (1798).

people" and for their readers to imagine themselves as citizens within this category, but these relationships were not experienced as an impersonal information economy. The public sphere created by the LCS was not simply "phantom" but focused on relations in its divisions, committees, and a penumbra of other activities around its formal structures.[4] Location is an important issue for thinking about radical culture in this regard. The venues where things happened or were imagined happening changed their meanings, an issue that had legal status when it came to questions of innocence or guilt in trials for sedition, as we will see, but not one that was or is easy to make judgments about. Kevin Gilmartin provides the useful reminder that "the ability to discern the horizons of a public sphere and debate its contours is not our own belated privilege."[5] Such spaces were discerned and contested in the 1790s, not simply in competitions over occupancy, when, for instance, debating societies were driven from taverns and other public houses, but also in terms of what kind of space they could be understood to be. The LCS's idea of itself as an improving public body, for instance, meant that it also shaped various spaces in the image of the associational worlds of the eighteenth century more generally, actively participating, as its members saw it, in the wider republic of letters. In 1797, for instance, the informer (never uncovered), clerk, and aspiring playwright James Powell wrote to Richard Ford his paymaster in the office of the Treasury Solicitor asking for the remuneration he had been promised as a reward for reporting on LCS meetings.[6] Powell's plaintive letter gives an insight into some of the aspirations of at least some of those associated with the LCS.

At the end of 1794, the leading members of the LCS had been brought to trial for treason for planning to call a national convention, a plan – in so far as it existed – that the government construed as a direct challenge to the authority of Parliament. After his acquittal, John Thelwall, by this stage effectively the main public face of the LCS, resigned from the society for a few months, but set up a regular gathering, Powell says, "every Monday evening at his house to which the principal men of the party were invited." "His house" at this stage was in Beaufort Buildings, discussed in more detail later in this chapter, premises he had taken over only a few short weeks before his arrest, where he had lectured, hosted LCS meetings, and lived with his family. Prior to his membership of the LCS, Thelwall was already a veteran of the London's debating clubs that met in various places across the city. From at least 1790, he was also a member of the Philomathian Society.[7] Limited to twenty-one members, this club met weekly – on Tuesday evenings – to discuss various topics, some of which are listed in the diary of William Godwin, a member from 1793. Evidently it was a convivial group, with dining sometimes involved, although it isn't known where or what kind of space it met in. Possibly Thelwall was aiming at something along these lines when he started the conversazione Powell describes very late in 1794 or early in 1795, but with a membership drawn particularly from the leading figures in the LCS.

Powell boasted to his spymaster that his own "conversatione" was "more numerously attended than Thelwalls." Among those who attended Powell's gathering was the radical poet–publisher Richard "Citizen" Lee, who became "a constant attendant on that evening but on every other when I was not at home."[8] When Lee fled to the United States at the beginning of 1796, he went with Powell's wife. Perhaps more surprisingly, at around this time, just after the treason acquittals, Godwin seems to have been meeting with LCS members as a group, including Powell, Thelwall, and probably Citizen Lee. The entry in Godwin's diary for January 17, 1795, refers to "tea Powel's, w. Ht, Thelwal, Iliff, Bailey, Walker, Manning, Hubbard, Lee, Johns, Fawcet & Dyer." Much the same cast assembled on the last day of the month: "tea Powel's, w. Thelwal, Bailey, Hubbard, Vincent, Hunter, G Richter, Walker, Bone, Manning & Lee."[9] By meeting with these LCS members, Godwin may have been practicing what he preached about "the collision of mind with mind" in his *Enquiry Concerning Political Justice* (1793).[10] He was probably already meeting some LCS members at the Philomathians from 1793, including Thelwall, if he remained a member, John Binns, sometime after December 1794, when he arrived from Ireland, and probably John Fenwick too.[11] Members of the LCS who attended the meetings at Powell's may have been thrilled at the chance to meet the philosopher, which is not to say that they necessarily agreed with his ideas. At the very least, meeting with Godwin provided an opportunity for them to demonstrate that they were quite as capable of sustaining moral improvement as he. On the face of it, Powell's provision of "bread & cheese & porter" might seem what would be expected of members for an organization often identified with the plebian culture of the alehouse. "Tea," the term used in Godwin's diary, might suggest, on the other hand, something more "polite," perhaps "domestic" even, as if Powell had brought out the best china to welcome the famous philosopher to his modest "conversatione." But such juxtaposition would be too crude. For a start, Powell probably already knew Godwin.[12] He was from a relatively respectable background; at least his father had been a clerk in the Customs House, "a man of property," by Francis Place's account.[13] Powell junior certainly had literary ambitions. He had already published a play and his theatrical career continued into the nineteenth century.[14] The same general point about literary ambitions holds true for Iliff, Lee, Thelwall, and others in the group.[15] Secondly, the meeting with Powell took place not in an alehouse, but in the potentially "private" and "domestic" space of his home. Powell's wife was evidently a regular presence there. Whether she was a participant or someone whose domestic labor facilitated the event and added to its politeness is not known, although many years later Francis Place – who dismissed Powell as "honest, but silly,"'still not knowing him to have been a spy – claimed she was "a woman of the town."[16] Regardless of Place's judgment, there is no reason to believe that Powells conversatione did not aspire to improvement of the sort Godwin wrote about in *Political Justice*, whatever the philosopher himself might have made of the actual gathering, or those who attended it.

"Tea" is Godwin's description of the meeting at Powell's, but perhaps it wasn't the exercise in politeness that word may imply to modern readers. Godwin's diary seems to use the word for any modest repast served in the home (in the early evening, after dinner and before he sups). In Godwin's diary the term is mainly used to refer to meetings that seem to have included the consideration of weighty philosophical questions and topical political issues, often with women present, and need not imply politeness in a way that militated against the vigorous discussion of political issues. On February 1, 1794, for instance, the diary has "tea at Johnsons, w. Courtenays & Blairs, talk of Brissot, Mirabeau & jurisprudence." Presumably, this was in Joseph Johnson's rooms above his bookshop, with the Whig politician John Courtney, and perhaps his wife. Possibly the Philomathian meetings also took place in domestic spaces, although it may have needed a coffee house or tavern room for its twenty-one members. All these occasions seem to have allowed for the collision of mind with mind, to some degree at least, within the home, even if not within strictly "domestic" circumstances. For my purposes, the main point is that the LCS and its members involved themselves in the diffusion of knowledge across a diversified urban terrain, which included their homes in various ways. The conversations held by Powell, Thelwall, and others were intrinsic to their commitment to reform. They were part of the lateral horizon of the LCS meetings proper, whereby ideas were hammered out and the links of sociability cemented in a convivial environment, perhaps convivial enough to blind LCS members from recognizing Powell was a spy. The creation of and participation in such spaces was part of an attempt to sustain a democratic culture, "where political ideas and decisions," as Seth Cotlar puts it, "would emerge out of conversations among ordinary citizens and not just filter down from their leaders."[17]

James Epstein has argued for a better understanding of the relationship "between the logic of spatial practices and language, or better the production of meanings." Radical culture in the 1790s provides one of Epstein's key examples of the processes of "naming, mapping, tracking, settling, imagining and counter-imagining" as it played out in "taverns, courtrooms and the street." Following Michel de Certeau's understanding of "*space*" as "*practiced place*," Epstein's discussion relates spatial production to "democratic political practice, possibilities of representation, and visions of possibility."[18] The reports that the spy Captain George Munro sent into the Home Office in November 1792 struggled to fit his understanding of popular culture with what he saw at the LCS's meetings. He melodramatically described a gathering at the Cock and Crown on Villiers Street as a group of the "lowest tradesmen, all continually smoaking and drinking porter," but then conceded they were "extremely civil."[19] Such concessions were rare in spy reports. When he started reporting in February 1794, John Groves insisted that it "requires some mastery over that innate pride, which every well-educated man must naturally possess, even to sit down in their company."[20] Perhaps more anxious about his own status, Groves, who was a solicitor, may have felt the need to confirm to his masters that he was of a different order from the men on whom he was reporting. How such men managed to organize themselves into their own version of the public sphere continued to puzzle polite commentators. Where they met was part of the puzzle, especially where practices resisted the idea of LCS members as simply alehouse politicians.

Government papers from the 1790s give a sense of its struggle to comprehend the urban topography of radicalism. At the end of 1792, for instance, the Treasury Solicitor tried to compile lists of the public houses and other spaces where the LCS met, drawing on evidence from spies like Munro, to distinguish between them in terms of attendance and social standing. The Marquis of Granby, near Oxford Market in Marylebone, is described as better attended than those that met at the Cock and Crown or the Red Lion, Kings Street, near Golden Square. In November 1792, Robert Thomson, the LCS's most prolific songwriter at the time and a fellow Scotsman, not suspecting Munro was a spy, let him into the meeting at the Marquis of Granby. The LCS minutes from August inform us that members of other divisions had been encouraged to go to the Marquis of Granby to rouse its flagging members.[21] The Treasury Solicitor's list describes the Red Lion as "more decent" than the Marquis of Granby, but still "extremely low": "Nothing but thieves and pickpockets below stairs." The Cock and Crown was annotated with Munro's comment about "the very lowest tradesmen."[22]

In the build up to the arrests for treason of May 1794, John Reeves undertook a similar exercise, providing the Treasury Solicitor with a "Report on Sedition." He also carefully distinguished from each other what he understood as the key bookshops for the circulation of seditious materials. James Ridgway, imprisoned in 1793 for selling Paine's *Rights of Man*, but with longstanding links to the Whig Opposition, did not "condescend to sell seditious pamphlets of less than sixpence" (not strictly true in terms of pricing, as we will see below, but accurate as a comment on the relative status of Ridgway's clientele). Daniel Isaac Eaton was doing a brisker trade at a cheaper price: "more frequented than any other Booksellers shop in London, and he does more business, with this single difference, that his articles are low priced, and his gains are less." On the lowest rung, as far as Reeves was concerned, was Thomas Spence, forced into a shop after he was arrested at the end of 1792 for selling seditious material from a street barrow: "this man lives in the dirtiest poverty, but his shop is decorated with lines in prose and verse, expressing a determination to carry on this traffic, in spite of Laws and Magistrates."[23] None of these venues appear in James Raven's recent "bookscape" of printing and publishing in London before 1800, even though James Ridgway's shop was fondly remembered decades later as a place where the literati opposed to Pitt gathered to scribble newspaper satires.[24]

From its very inception, the LCS had been active in a diverse urban landscape. John Barrell has provided us with a nuanced map of LCS organization across a range of London boroughs and a sense of how those locations signified in terms of its activities.[25] My concern is less with geography, as it were, and more with the different ways space was understood in relation to the practices of popular radicalism in these places. Michael T. Davis has shown the importance of "the politics of civility" for understanding the LCS. Thomas Hardy's account of the first meeting – in the Bell in Exeter Street off the Strand – described the participants as "plain, homely citizens."[26] The Bell may very well have been neat and homely, especially compared to some of the alehouses where LCS divisions met. Taverns, in contrast, as Ian Newman reminds us, were often elegant establishments, venues for public dinners and other respectable gatherings.[27] Davis notes how much of the LCS's official documentation is concerned with the orderliness of the kind Francis Place was keen to stress in his *Autobiography*. He primarily understands these self-representations as the product of the LCS's need "to represent itself as inclusive, autonomous, as a rule-regulated organization based upon the principle of equality and rational deliberation in order to invert the political messages of loyalists."[28] Iain McCalman suggests this idea of civility extended even to prison sociability, which included visits from Godwin and various other literary figures from respectable backgrounds sympathetic to reform.[29]

The LCS frequently did explicitly represent its own behavior at various meetings as intended to "defeat the various calumnies with which they have been loaded by the advocates of Tyranny & Oppression."[30] But, this self-representation need not be understood merely as a functional need to demonstrate its respectability. There is a danger of constructing the LCS as most authentically itself when involved in "unrespectable" alehouse activities, and somehow deferring to "external" notions of respectability when it met for "bread, porter, and cheese" or even when it met Godwin for "tea." Quite apart from the practicalities involved in running business meetings, the LCS carried on the popular aspect of enlightenment that saw "reform" as an opportunity for participation across the diversity of social worlds available in the city from debating societies to other forms of "literary" sociability.

Of course, these different urban spaces were already subject to complex pressures of policing, representation, and interpretation, official and unofficial, before the 1790s. Taverns and coffee houses were never simply open and convivial spaces where ideas flowed freely. Spies and informers inhabited them throughout the century, and their testimonies had played an important part in prosecutions for seditious libel for decades. Various types of informal and formal censorship had also long been surrounding and intruding upon these spaces. In 1781, David Turner, president of the Westminster Forum, presented its debates as a site for the integration of what he called "public conversation," but acknowledged that sometimes they failed to transcend their "ale-house" (Turner's term) origins. The roughness of the debates, Turner believed, discouraged those with a classical education from attending.[31] Nevertheless, Turner mentions the presence of women in his *History of the Westminster Forum.* On one occasion, in response to a remark on the growth of population, "the brilliant set of ladies in the gallery, spread their fans before their faces."[32] The presence of women was always crucial to how meaning was constructed in social space. They could grant an aura of respectability, although for some commentators their presence could itself function as a sign of transgression. Powell's wife may have passed from one to the other pole of this representation during the life of his conversatione, her disappearance with Lee into exile in America may have confirmed her status as a "woman of the town" from Place's point of view, but to others she may equally have given or been understood to give the gathering the air of a polite gathering.

The spatial understanding of such places could have very real consequences for radical groups as John Barrell and James Epstein have shown in the case of John Frost.[33] Frost was an attorney who had been closely involved with the Society for Constitutional Information (SCI) from its beginnings in the early 1780s and played an important role in its revival under Horne Tooke's leadership in 1791. When Paine fled for Paris in September 1792, Frost accompanied him, writing regularly to update Horne Tooke on their progress. Returning to London in October, he sat on the SCI committee chosen to confer with the LCS over addressing the French Convention. Reporting on Frost's speech to an LCS meeting a few weeks later, the spy Munro described him as "almost the only decent Man I have seen in any of their Divisions." The SCI chose Frost with Joel Barlow to deliver their address to the Convention. On November 6, between his two trips to Paris, Frost had attended the dinner of an agricultural society in London, a sign of his general commitment to improvement beyond political reform, at the Percy coffee house. Matthew Yateman, an apothecary, stopped him on his way out and asked him about France. The two men already knew each other, but their conversation grew heated after Frost told Yateman, "I am for Equality and no King." When Yateman asked if he meant "no King in this country," Frost is said to have bawled out *"no King in this country."* At this point, others became involved in their conversation. A complaint against Frost was made immediately, but the government took no action until it was sure he was back in France and could be portrayed as absconding. Frost wrote from Paris vehemently denying that he had fled from justice. Almost certainly the government wished to avoid a trial, not least because of Frost's possession of correspondence with Pitt on reform from the 1780s.[34] When Frost returned to London, stalemate ensued. Richard Brinsley Sheridan raised the silence on the case in Parliament on March 4, to suggest that the government now wished to drop it.

When the trial finally came on two months later, Thomas Erskine's defense strategy turned on two issues. The first was whether Frost spoke "advisedly," that is, whether he could be charged with intentionally aiming to spread disaffection when he was in drink. The second part of the defense is more important when thinking about the production of spatial meaning. It turned on understanding the coffee house as "private" and properly beyond the reach of a law aimed at those who could be proved to have disaffected the public. Erskine insisted that the "common and private intercourses of life" were necessarily protected from prosecution:

> Does any man put such constraints upon himself in the most private moments of his life, that he would be contented to have his loosest and lightest words recorded, and set in array against him in a Court of Justice?[35]

The prosecution agreed that it was hard to imagine a case in which "the public necessity and expediency of a prosecution should be so strong as to break in upon the relations of a private life."[36] What it rejected was the idea that a coffee house could be imagined in these terms. The case involved was no "breach of the sweet confidences of private life." The word "sweet," as John Barrell suggests, implied something like an understanding of "private" as "domestic," and perhaps even female presence.[37] Few instances from the 1790s reveal more clearly how space was central to the production of meaning. The prosecution's mention of "sweet confidences" at Frost's trial, implicitly using an idea of female spheres of influence to quarantine the domestic from the political, also shows how much questions of gender were continuously involved in the production of spatial meanings.

Political meetings in the eighteenth century were routinely masculine affairs, dominated by rituals of speech-making, toasts, and serious alcohol consumption, equally routinely reported in the newspapers, and, in this regard at least, open to public enquiry and censure. So Charles James Fox's speech to the Whig Club in December 1792, at the elegant London Tavern, a few weeks after the incident with Frost at the Percy Coffee House, and a few days prior to Paine's trial, was reported in the newspapers. As was not uncommon, the report garnered at least one satirical poem in response:

> The zealous Whigs, obedient to command,
> Drink till they stare, and call again for more:
> Nor does the Bottle quit their ready hand,
> Till *Whigs* with *Whigs* lie Tumbling on the floor.

Originally printed in *The Sun* newspaper, the poem also came out in a pamphlet, published by James Ridgway, which included a satirical account of Frost's trip to Paris.[38] Imprisoned for publishing Paine's *Rights of Man* a few months later, it was Ridgway who had put Fox's speech and toasts – or a version of it – into circulation as a 2d pamphlet. Fox's allies in the Whig Club swiftly wrote to the newspapers to distance their leader from the declaration of support for reform he seemed to give in the toasts as published by Ridgway. The satirist makes great play with the price of Ridgway's pamphlet and implied Fox was selling himself cheap in drink, but shows no signs of discomfort at or censure of the bibulous behavior itself. Fox is indulging, as it were, in what men-of-the-world did, without it necessarily compromising his claims to be regarded as a public figure. The satire comes from the idea of an alliance of a statesman like Fox with the principles of Paine in a second pamphlet.

Plenty of other satirists exploited the idea of drunken gentlemen losing their sense of social status by consorting with radicals, or at least seeming to consort with them in sentiment if not in practice. Take, for instance, the satires on the meeting of the "Friends of Liberty" at the Crown and Anchor in 1791. The response of the treasury newspapers to these dinners, in Harriet Guest's words, "oscillated rather uneasily between treating the occasion as a serious threat to national stability and security, and dismissively mocking its folly."[39] "The Political Mirror" of *The World* (July 15, 1791) was self-consciously tolerant in placing the meeting within the context of the political sociability of the time:

> In the circumstance of a set of people assembling for a purposes of conviviality – however numerous the meeting – however mixt – or however riotous and brutal in its conduct and effects, there can be no cause for even momentary alarm.

Having confirmed the idea that traditional British liberties were still very much alive, the paper then suggested that these gentlemen would need to be watched, because they were in danger of losing a properly masculine sense of their social and political identities: "The Englishman who can now avow such rapturous admiration of a Government *unformed* and *inefficient* has lost all due respect for his own – and in a mind thus prone to change, and doating on licentiousness, the transition from thought to action is made with an accommodating facility."

The self-congratulatory tolerance shown to the "Friends of Liberty" was not likely to be extended to the LCS, more liable to be thought of as *"unformed* and *inefficient."* Their activities were at best likely to be understood as a low mimicry of events such as those at the London Tavern, learning, as Sir George Paradyne puts it in Robert Bage's *Man as He Is* (1792), "in an alehouse to imitate, at humble distance, the luxury of the tavern."[40] Sometimes these two worlds mixed in the public sphere of reform, as at the anniversary dinner of the SCI in May 1794 at the salubrious Crown and Anchor tavern. John Horne Tooke invited some few Whig MPs thought to be sympathetic to reform, but also gave away free tickets to LCS members.[41] Among those who attended was the MP for Beverley, John Wharton. Interviewed by the Privy Council after the arrests for treason had begun, Wharton was embarrassed and perhaps fearful, insisting that he had attended only because Horne Tooke had persuaded him he would bring respectability to a "convivial" meeting. Pressed about the presence of LCS members and the toasts given from the chair, Wharton claimed to have been shocked to see them at a meeting of this sort, admitting it dangerous "to give such Toasts to such persons." "So much disgusted with the proceedings of the day," was Wharton, "that I expressed my resolution to many of my Friends that night to have nothing more to do with such societies."[42] Others from a similar social background to Wharton didn't see much out of the ordinary run of conduct at political meetings. The SCI member Thomas Symonds, at his interview, said it "did not appear to him that the people at the dinner were so very inferior a class."[43] Horne Tooke himself was a gentleman in social terms and his conduct was as inebriated as Fox and his friends at the Whig Club. When at their free-and-easies LCS members went through their own boozy rituals and symbolic toasts, they were articulating their own version of the theatrical culture of the eighteenth century, not as empty mimicry, but as an assertion of their own place in the political nation.

As it was, some members of the LCS's own members thought drunken behavior, whatever its source, unworthy of any organization aiming at political improvement. If Francis Place declared the Sunday evening parties "useful and agreeable," he was always more ambivalent about the role of drinking and singing in any aspect of cultural life.[44] Theatricality also had little part to play in his idea of politics: he thought Thelwall's lectures guilty of "bombast and loose declamation." For his part, Thelwall's radicalism tended to be strongly freighted toward the idea of an affective domain that distanced itself from the libertinism of men such as Horne Tooke. In this regard, both Place and Thelwall could be understood as participating in larger historical trends for which the behavior of Fox, Horne Tooke, and their ilk was increasingly deemed inappropriate. *Pocock's Everlasting Songster* (1800) presented its collection of songs and toasts as avoiding "those of a political, wicked or vulgar tendency, which have so long been suffered by Chairmen of different Societies to reign predominant." Its advice was generally designed in part at least to make it more possible for women to be part of convivial meetings: "at this place it will not be amiss to say, that a popular toast which has been the too general rule to give first ('To the Exclusion of every Female,' whose company we ought rather to court than discourage) has been a disgrace."[45]

If women seem not to have been voting members of the LCS divisions, they were present at its associated events, their presence possibly adding to an idea of their improving or polite nature. Thelwall's moral perspective might translate obviously into an idea of separate spheres that would exclude his wife Susan from involvement in his political life. His various poems "To Stella" not infrequently present hearth and home as a place presided over by his wife's genius, from which he is torn by the demands of politics, but the reality of their life was more complex. Beaufort Buildings, where they moved early in 1794, served the Thelwalls as home, lecture theatre, bookshop, and LCS committee room.[46] Invasions of the sweetness of domestic life by informers were central to Thelwall's descriptions of his struggles with political authority, as Corinna Wagner has shown in her account of his "exploitation of privacy."[47] From early on in the 1790s, Thelwall routinely presented his private life as the foundation of his political virtue. At the same time, he represented intrusion into his premises in Beaufort Buildings as an unwonted violation, as if they were separate spheres:

> My hours of conviviality have been attended by spies and sycophants, my doors beset with eavesdroppers, my private chambers haunted by the familiar spirits of an Infernal Inquisition, and my confidential friend stretched on the rack of interrogatory, or order to extort from them the conversation which in the unsuspecting hours of social hilarity may have been uttered at my own table.[48]

The irony, of course, as Wagner points out, is that Thelwall invited scrutiny of the space that he constructs as vulnerable to invasions by public authorities. "The very sphere of life [Thelwall] aims to protect from public interference," as she puts it, "is the sphere he places squarely before the enquiring eyes of the public."[49]

In his rejoinder to the attack on his lecturing in Godwin's *Considerations on Lord Grenville's and Mr. Pitt's Bills* (1795), Thelwall invoked the philosopher's bachelorhood and his supposed social reclusiveness as evidence of his unfitness to judge of politics. A "life of domestic solitude" had rendered Godwin unsympathetic to "every feeling of private, and sometimes public justice." The gendered separate spheres sometimes imagined in Thelwall's poetry are brought into a more complex relation in this criticism. Certainly Susan Thelwall's letters to her brother in the country make it clear she attended political debates with her husband:

> I suppose you have heard by the newspapers that politics run very high at present, but as those papers are generally the vehicles of falshood & corruption, you perhaps may receive truer information from a female democrat. The society which was last winter held at Coach Makers Hall & which has this winter been remov'd to the King's Arms Cornhill has been illegally suppressed.

Obviously self-conscious about the novelty of her involvement in politics, she makes it the occasion of sending the letter at all: "I should perhaps not have written (for I believe you are a letter in my debt) if I was not become a great politician." She goes on to describe a particular debate at the King's Arms, in an "exceedingly crowded room," where "a foolish aristocrate" loaded her husband with "invective and abuse." The meeting eventually broke up in confusion and the magistrates used the furor to suppress the society.

In fact, the King's Arms had not been used as a tavern since a fire in 1778. Largely given over to private accommodation, the building did still maintain a large room for debates, auctions, and the like. Mary Thale and Donna Andrew have shown that there was a history of women speaking at debates in the great room.[50] "The Female Congress" had met there in 1780. Later in the 1780s, another debating society took pride in "the display of female eloquence from which this society has already received so many obligations." *The Times* of October 29, 1788 took the view that "the debating ladies would be better employed at their needle and thread, a good semptress being a more amiable character than a female orator." By the end of 1791, this society has been replaced by one mainly comprised of law students keen to distance themselves from the previous management. Admittedly, there's no evidence that Susan Thelwall participated in the debates she went to with her husband, even if we know other women had been doing so a few years before, but a strong sense of engagement with public affairs emerges from her letters. She seems to have been reading the newspaper reports of Fox's speech at the Whig Club, which she under-stands as more sympathetic to reform than had been anticipated by the radical societies: "Fox's speech, which I suppose you have read, & which is bolder & more explicit, than any body expected of him, has put us poor democrates a little in heart again." Overall her letter communicates pride in her husband's cause, but also her own commitment to radical politics.

Other women participated in creating and inflecting radical spaces. John Reeves noted with indignation that Susanna Eaton "sold publickly and with particular parade the Libel which was under prosecution, and her husband at that time in Newgate for having sold."[51] Amelia Alderson recorded a visit to the shop with her cousin Ives Hurry, when a stranger enters:

> I then told [Mrs Eaton] that curiosity led me to her shop, and that I came form that city of sedition Norwich ... at last we became so fraternized, that Mrs. Eaton shut the shop door and gave us chairs. I will not relate the information I heard, but I could have talked with him all night.[52]

The stranger was of the opinion "that democratic women were rare, and that he heartily wished he could introduce me to two charming patriots at

Edinburgh, who were, though women, up to circumstances." Bookshops were important places for radical sociability in this period, as for other forms of association, but obviously represented a more insulated kind of space than the former tavern visited by Susan Thelwall. When their husbands were in prison or on the run, as he may have at the time of Alderson's visit, women like Susannah Eaton ran their businesses and seem to have hosted radical conversatione. Locking the door and placing the chairs in a circle seems to construe the bookshop space into an intimate configuration, but the conversation follows the latest political news. The mysterious "he" who is in the shop when Alderson arrives, turns out to be Charles Sinclair, recently tried in Edinburgh with the Scottish Martyrs.[53]

Descriptions of the open-air LCS meetings of 1795 record they were "crowded with Citizens, both male and female." In the account published by Citizen Lee, the spatial rhetoric is of a gathering "met in the open face of day," scorning attempts to drive it underground in retreat from "the eye of observation." If the language of invasions of privacy appears in the pamphlet's reference to a victimized cast of "the helpless widow and wretched orphan," women are not confined to the familial role, but implicitly taken to part of "the persevering efforts of reason."[54] Interestingly, this account of the meeting published by Lee ends with an advertisement for a cheap edition of Wollstonecraft's *Rights of Woman*, flanked by others for two scurrilous pamphlets.[55] I have found no evidence that Lee ever brought out the cheap edition of Wollstonecraft, perhaps because he was soon arrested for publishing Iliff's *Duties of Citizenship* among other things. Lee's advertisement suggests we should be careful of any assumption that the radical movement operated with an exclusively masculine and moral notion of republicanism, or, more specifically, assumed that the domestic was in practice a sphere strictly separate from the political. Popular radical culture in the 1790s existed across a complex and variegated urban topography, often structured by ideas of improvement incomprehensible to its ruling elites or uncongenial to nineteenth-century ideas of respectability. No such complex sense of the public sphere of the LCS is granted in Gillray's *London Corresponding Society Alarm'd*. There the spatial practices of the LCS are literally underground, subhuman and beneath contempt. The Two Acts of 1795 made this representation easier to maintain, despite the fact, as John Gale Jones's *Sketch of a political tour through Rochester, Chatham, Maidstone, Gravesend* (1796) shows, the LCS continued to imagine the development of a public sphere out of interactions between citizens in a variety of places beyond the alehouse, including a stage coach, a circulating library, and a dance in a public assembly.[56]

Notes

1 The research for this essay was made possible by an Arts and Humanities Research Council (AHRC) fellowship. At every stage, Ian Newman's advice has been invaluable. Any errors, of course, remain entirely my own responsibility.

2 Francis Place, *The Autobiography of Francis Place (1771–1854)*, ed. Mary Thale (Cambridge: Cambridge University Press, 1972), p. 131.

3 See *Imagining the King's Death: Figurative Treason, Fantasies of Regicide 1793–1796*, (Oxford: Oxford University Press, 2000), especially pp. 551–603, on the Treasonable Practices Bill, and for a summary of the provisions of the Seditious Meetings Bill, see Albert Goodwin, *The Friends of Liberty: The English Democratic Movement in the Age of the French Revolution*, (Cambridge, MA: Harvard University Press, 1979), pp. 887–88.

4 See Bruce Robbins, "Introduction: The Public as Phantom" in *The Phantom Public Sphere*, ed. Bruce Robbins (Minneapolis, MN: University of Minnesota Press, 1993), p. xiii.

5 Kevin Gilmartin, "Popular Radicalism and the Public Sphere," *Studies in Romanticism*, 33 (1994), 549–57.

6 PC 1 23/38a, National Archives, Kew. Mary Thale notes that Powell lived near Somers Town, p. 256 n, not far from Godwin. *Selections from the Papers of the London Corresponding Society 1792–1799*, ed. Mary Thale (Cambridge: Cambridge University Press, 1983).

7 The fullest recent account of the Philomaths is David O'Shaughnessy's "*Caleb Williams* and the Philomaths: Recalibrating Political Justice for the Nineteenth Century," *Nineteenth-Century Literature*, 66 (2012), 423–48. Thelwall's participation is confirmed in his *Ode to Science. Recited at the Anniversary Meeting of the Philomathian Society, June 20, 1791* (London, 1791).

8 See Jon Mee, "The Strange Career of Richard 'Citizen' Lee" in *British Literary Radicalism, 1650–1830: From Revolution to Revolution*, ed. Timothy Morton and Nigel Smith (Cambridge: Cambridge University Press, 2002), pp. 151–66.

9 Godwin's diary at the Bodleian Library, Oxford, was consulted online at http://godwindiary.bodleian.ox.ac.uk/index2.html. It shows that Godwin took tea with someone called Powell at Helen Maria Williams's in 1789. He also saw Powell in company with October 14, 1793, "Thelwal, Dyson & Dibbin dine: tea Thelwal's, with Holcroft, Powel & Belmano." This group from 1793 seems to be comprised of those with theatrical associations. Holcroft and Thelwall were Philomathians, as was Dyson.

10 William Godwin, *An Enquiry Concerning Political Justice*, ed. Mark Philp, vol. 3 of *Political and Philosophical Writings of William Godwin* (London: William Pickering, 1993), p. 15.

11 See O'Shaughnessy, "Recalibrating Political Justice," p. 432.

12 See note 8 above.

13 Place, *Autobiography*, p. 179n.

14 See Powell's *The Narcotic and Private Theatricals* (London: H. D. Symonds, 1793). The publisher Symonds was closely associated with the radical movement. On his

theatrical career, see David Worrall, *Theatric Revolution: Drama, Censorship and Romantic Period Subcultures 1773–1832*, (Oxford: Oxford University Press, 2009).

15 Edward Iliff, present at the January meeting, was an actor who in 1796 published a novel, *Angelo*, dedicated to Godwin's sometime sponsor the notorious financier John King. His pamphlet *The Duties of Citizenship* (1795) played a part in the government decision to arrest its publisher, Citizen Lee, by which time Iliff was in correspondence with Godwin about his literary ambitions. Iliff and Godwin had first met socially on September 30, 1794, according to Godwin's diary, possibly at or after a Philomath meeting that discussed "utility of religion" On February 25, 1796, Iliff wrote to ask Godwin "[i]f I send you a novel . . . will you become my patron." He also asked Godwin whether he had heard anything of *Duties of Citizenship*. Iliff to Godwin, MS Abinger c. 16, f. 3, Bodleian Library, Oxford. Godwin agreed to give him literary advice, but said he had not heard anything about the pamphlet. He also said he did not understand the meaning of the string of names at the bottom of the letter: "King, Marshal, Powel." These were likely Godwin's friend James Marshall, John King, and James Powell. Possibly it is a list of others Iliff had written to for help. Godwin also replied to another letter, now lost, in the following month. See *The Letters of William Godwin, Volume I: 1778–1797*, ed. Pamela Clemit (Oxford: Oxford University Press, 2011), pp. 161–3.

16 Place, *Autobiography*, p. 180. Place described Powell as "a man whose relatives were gentlefolks, well informed respectable people, but he was an only son, had been indulged and spoilt," p. 179. Thelwall also failed to realize that Powell, whom he had known form at least 1792, was a spy. See *Selections*, ed. Thale, p. 256n.

17 Seth Cotlar, *Tom Paine's America: The Rise and Fall of Transatlantic Radicalism in the Early Republic*, (Charlottesville, VA: University of Virginia Press, 2011), p. 8.

18 James Epstein, "Spatial Practices/Democratic Vistas" *Social History*, 4 (1999), 294, 296, and 297.

19 Munro report, November 14, 1792 in *Selections*, ed. Thale, p. 27.

20 Groves report, June 12, 1794 in *Selections*, ed. Thale, p. 184.

21 The list is archived in TS11/959, National Archive, Kew. See *Selections*, ed. Thale, p. 17 for the directive to attend the Marquis of Granby. Given Thomson's reputation for rousing the spirits of members, it is highly likely that he was among them. The minutes show that he was elected its delegate, as the list in the Treasury Solicitor's papers confirms.

22 Anyone interested in further details of the LCS meeting places should consult Ian Newman's excellent website "London Corresponding Society Meeting Places: Exploring the 1790s Alehouse" at www.1790salehouse.com.

23 John Reeves, "Report on Sedition &c, 29 April 1794," TS11/965, ff. 22–23, National Archives, Kew.

24 See James Raven, *Bookscape: Geographies of Printing and Publishing in London before 1800* (London: British Library, 2014). Alexander Stephens described meeting David Williams, Major Cartwright, and others at Ridgway's shop

after Debrett's closed a few years after this period: "Such shops in my time have been what certain coffee houses were in the days of the Spectator." See "Ridgways" in "Stephensiana. No. VI," 138. For more on Ridgway, see Manogue, "The Plight of James Ridgway, London Bookseller and Publisher, and the Newgate Radicals, 1792–1797," *Wordsworth Circle* 27 (1996), 158–66. His career and its fluctuations, like other radical booksellers, would repay a full-length study. Stephens also described Merry and Paine writing satirical attacks on Pitt in the offices of *The Argus* in 1792: "Stephensiana. No. XIV," *Monthly Magazine* 54 (1822), 425–28.

25 See *The Spirit of Despotism: Invasions of Privacy in the 1790s* (Oxford: Oxford University Press, 2006), pp. 16–74.

26 See Davis, "'The Mob Club?': The London Corresponding Society and the Politics of Civility in the 1790s," in *Unrespectable Radicals?: Popular Politics in the Age of Reform*, ed. Davis and Paul A. Pickering (Aldershot: Ashgate, 2008), pp. 21–40, and Thomas Hardy, *Memoir of Thomas Hardy, Founder of and Secretary to, the London Corresponding Society, for the Diffusing Useful Political Knowledge among the People of Great Britain and Ireland, and for Promoting Parliamentary Reform* (London, 1832), p. 44.

27 Ian Newman, "Edmund Burke in the Tavern," *European Romantic Review*, 24 (2013), 125–48. See, especially, his useful note, 144, on the distinction, in terms of reputation at least, between the relatively respectable tavern and the far less respectable alehouse, despite the collapse of the early modern hierarchy between inn, tavern, and alehouse.

28 Davis, "The Mob Club?," pp. 26–7.

29 McCalman, "Newgate in Revolution: Radical Enthusiasm and Romantic Counterculture," *Eighteenth Century Life* 22 (1998), 95–110. Godwin's diary contains numerous references to dinners in Newgate, especially in 1794.

30 Minutes of LCS general meeting July 9, 1795 in *Selections*, ed. Thale, p. 261.

31 [David Turner], *A Short History of the Westminster Forum: Containing Some Remarks upon the Laws; Where in the Nature of Such Societies is Examined*, 2 vols. (London, 1781); vol. II, pp. 134, 219.

32 Ibid., vol. II, p. 90.

33 See Epstein, "'Equality and No King': Sociability and Sedition: The Case of John Frost" in *Romantic Sociability: Social Networks and Literary Culture in Britain, 1770–1840*, ed. Gillian Russell and Clara Tuite (Cambridge: Cambridge University Press, 2006), pp. 43–61, and Barrell, *Spirit of Despotism*, pp. 75–9 and 83–6.

34 See *Trials for Treason and Sedition, 1792–1794*, ed. John Barrell and Jon Mee, 8 vols. (London, Pickering & Chatto, 2006–2007), vol. I, pp. 228–30.

35 Ibid., vol. I, pp. 236–7.

36 Ibid., vol. I, pp. 246.

37 Barrell, *Spirit of Despotism*, p. 85.

38 See *The Speech of the Right Hon. Charles James Fox: Containing the Declaration of His Principles, Respecting the Present Crisis of Public Affairs* (London, 1792), pp. 7–8. Fox's allies denied that he had given the reformist sentiments ascribed

to him in the pamphlet. Ridgway's pamphlet reproduces the correspondence and another poem – "An Answer to the Above Letters"- mocking Fox's defenders Andrew St. John and Robert Adair.

39 Harriet Guest, *Unbounded Attachment: Sentiment and Politics in the Age of the French Revolution*, (Oxford: Oxford University Press, 2013), p. 46.

40 See Robert Bage, *Man as He Is*, 4 vols. (London, 1792), Vol. I, p. 82, although Sir George is complaining about luxurious consumption rather than political pretensions.

41 See the account of the dinner in Goodwin, *Friends of Liberty*, pp. 329–31.

42 I quote from the copy of the interviews before the Privy Council at TS 11/963, ff. 256–67, National Archive, Kew.

43 TS 11/963, f. 586.

44 Place, *Autobiography*, p. 11.

45 *Pocock's Everlasting Songster, Containing a Selection of the Most Approved Songs* (Gravesend, 1800), p. ii.

46 For an excellent account of the arrangements at Beaufort Buildings, see Judith Thompson, "From Forum to Repository: A Case Study in Romantic Cultural Geography," *European Romantic Review*, 15 (2004), 177–91.

47 See Corinna Wagner, "Domestic Invasions: John Thelwall and the Exploitation of Privacy" in *John Thelwall: Radical Romantic and Acquitted Felon*, ed. Steve Poole (London, Pickering and Chatto, 2009), pp. 95–106.

48 John Thelwall, *Natural and Constitutional Right of Britons to Annual Parliaments, Universal Suffrage, and the Freedom of Popular Association*, (London, 1795), p. 79.

49 Wagner, "Domestic Invasions," p. 101.

50 See Thale, "Women in London Debating Societies in 1780," *Gender & History*, 7 (1995), 5–24, and Andrew, "Popular Culture and Public Debate: London 1780," *Historical Journal*, 39 (1996), 405–23.

51 Reeves, "Report on Sedition," f. 29.

52 Tuesday, [1794]; Amelia Alderson Opie to Mrs. Susannah Cook Taylor, Berg Collection, New York Public Library. I'm extremely grateful to Roxanne Eberle for her generosity in giving me have access to her transcription of the original, from which there are slight omissions in the version published in C. L. Brightwell's *Memorials of the Life of Amelia Opie, Selected and Arranged from Her Letters, Diaries, and Other Manuscripts*, (Norwich, 1854), pp. 41–45.

53 See Guest, *Unbounded Attachment*, especially p. 126.

54 *Account of the Proceedings of a Meeting of the London Corresponding Society, Held in a Field near Copenhagen House, Monday, Oct. 26, 1795*, (London, 1795), pp. 4, 5, and 8.

55 Ibid., p. 16.

56 John Gale Jones, *Sketch of a Political Tour through Rochester, Chatham, Maidstone, Gravesend. .&c Part the First* (London, 1796), pp. 5, 26–7, 56–7.

CHAPTER 3

Piccadilly Booksellers and Conservative Sociability

David Fallon

In the Romantic period, bookshops proliferated in fashionable West End London, especially on New and Old Bond Street, Piccadilly, and Pall Mall. *The Picture of London for 1802* notes that those on Piccadilly were "much frequented about the middle of the day by fashionable people" and used as "lounging place[s] for political and literary conversation."[1] They were central nodes in the networks of information and culture stretching across the capital. The *New Annual Register* tells how, on February 21, 1814, "a report was confidently put forth in the city, that an officer had arrived from France, bringing an official account of the death of the French emperor." Stocks rose rapidly before traders became wary; the officer and official dispatches could not be found, and shares fell accordingly. "Those who had planned the knavery were reaping the golden harvest on the stock exchange" whilst "their agents or dupes" spread the account, including "one man, dressed too like a gentleman, [who] went into a bookseller's shop at the west end of the town, and declared that he had seen a letter from the Lord chancellor Eldon, which fully confirmed all the news."[2]

The impostors had astutely identified the fashionable bookshop as a discursive hub which would swiftly transmit their story. Piccadilly was a main thoroughfare in and out of London, close to political centres such as Burlington House, Carlton House, and aristocratic clubs including Almack's, White's, and Brooks's, as well as the theatres. The ruse was effective because the "lounging" bookseller's shop was conceived by the swindlers and the public alike as a powerful site in which news circulated and public opinion was generated. To this end, these shops can be identified with the bourgeois public sphere, defined by Jürgen Habermas as "the sphere of private people come together as a public."[3] Habermas associated the development of the public sphere with gatherings in English coffee houses and Parisian salons, in which rational-critical debate gave rise to "public opinion." He idealizes the process as progressive; people in these forums "readied themselves to compel public authority to legitimate itself before public opinion."[4] J.A. Downie has provided a thorough critique of Habermas's historiography of the long eighteenth century, mainly focusing on the inaccurate picture of late seventeenth- and early eighteenth-century England.[5] Downie picks up on Habermas's claim that the bourgeois public sphere is "a category that is typical of an epoch" and "cannot be abstracted" from the unique circumstances of European history, exemplified in late-seventeenth-century England and eighteenth-century France.[6] Contrary to Habermas's claim to root his analysis in historical context, Downie argues that "several of the key aspects of Habermas's public sphere appear to be largely conceptual," deeply compromising the historical value of this model.[7] By contrast, Michael Scrivener draws on Habermas's "Further Reflections on the Public Sphere" (1992) and later philosophical work to outline a dual function:

> Many critics of Habermas fail to distinguish between the historically variable public sphere, which can have multiple centers of activity and various degrees of rationality, and the presuppositions, logic, and structure of communication itself; the latter implies norms of consensus, universal access, and unrestricted discussion – norms the historical public sphere never fully actualizes.[8]

Perhaps the value of Habermas's account of the public sphere actually lies in this uneasy coexistence of an idealized conceptualisation alongside a more problematic and varied concrete historical existence, with its exclusions and asymmetries of power. Craig Calhoun's notion of "subsidiary public spheres," which are "multiple, sometimes overlapping or contending" is helpful in this respect.[9] Subsidiary groups staking a claim to form and represent genuine public opinion against the distortions of their opponents were obliged to articulate their discourse against rival constituencies and toward a wider and more inclusive sense of the public. Such a duality was also evident at the sociable locations; convivial sites of the public sphere had an important conceptual component, with ideal norms motivating and regulating actual practice. As Markman Ellis points out, "the polite coffee-house of Steele's *Spectator*" was "not a real place" but rather a "utopian vision" represented in the service of reforming actual sociable spaces.[10] To constitute genuine spaces of public opinion, sociable gatherings had to position themselves in relation to rival groupings and always risked incursions by alternative forms of sociability which could challenge their ideal norms, reminding participants of their partial construction of the public.

Bookshops were important subsidiary sites of the political and literary public sphere of 1790s and 1800s London. They were central locations at which the more amorphous and conceptual public sphere mediated through print met concrete sociability. Booksellers completed a circuit of discourse: they published texts and disseminated opinion to the wider public and many of their shops also hosted discussion aimed at shaping public opinion, frequently stimulated by their stock of books and journals. The Piccadilly booksellers' shops were particularly significant as they catered for politicized constituencies of readers and "loungers." In 1763, John Almon set up at 178 Piccadilly, and his support for John Wilkes, his publication of parliamentary reports, and his willingness to publish for American republicans made this establishment a thriving centre of oppositional sociability. Almon's was taken over by his former shopman John Debrett in 1781 and Almon's other former shopman, John Stockdale, founded his own bookshop at 181 Piccadilly in the same year. By the 1790s, Debrett and Stockdale's establishments were renowned for rival Whig and Tory publications and gatherings.[11] These successes led other tradesmen, especially John Owen (187 Piccadilly, 1792–1797), John Wright (169 Piccadilly, 1797–1802), and Thomas Hatchard (173 Piccadilly, 1797–1801; 190 Piccadilly 1801–1820; 187 Piccadilly 1820 onwards) to meet the demand for loyal print and sociable gatherings.

For Habermas, the spaces of the public sphere are inherently liberal, with "private people" able "to compel public authority to legitimate itself before public opinion."[12] However, while Debrett's did indeed provide a space for critique of the Tory government, Stockdale's, Wright's, and Hatchard's shops were self-consciously conservative spaces in which critical discussion aimed at shaping "true" public opinion. Despite strong links between discussants and the government, participants in conservative bookshop sociability were directed by a self-conception as independent critical thinkers, attacking liberal Whig aristocratic power and Whig and radical distortions of media and public opinion. However partial their viewpoints, Whig and Tory clienteles can be perceived as appealing to the norms of the public sphere when claiming to critically produce truth and represent disinterested public concern against the power of their opponents.

Clienteles and sociability in the Tory booksellers' shops contributed to and reflected shifts in conservative ideology.[13] This essay will focus on Wright's as perhaps the most politically powerful of the Tory bookshops, in order to demonstrate that Habermas's distinction between an "apolitical" literary public sphere and the political public sphere fails to do justice to their intertwining in the politicized culture of the 1790s. Likewise, as Downie argues concerning the earlier eighteenth century, claims to represent public opinion by writers and commentators associated with these locations can be seen largely as "for rhetorical purposes."[14] Nevertheless, Habermas's account of the public sphere works on a conceptual level in sociable interactions at booksellers' shops. The larger virtual space of the public sphere mediated by print was frequently imagined in relation to these specific locations, part of a process in which Jon Klancher suggests "the public sphere had itself become an image to be consumed by readers who did not frequent it."[15] However, attempts by conservative groups to co-opt, shape, and manage public opinion from these locations were vulnerable to disruption and exposure as partial constructions, situated within a more complex and heterogeneous world of public opinion.

John Wright's "Celebrated Ministerial Shop"

The Gentleman's Magazine for December 1846 featured a letter William Upcott (1779–1845) wrote in January 1845, describing Wright's and Piccadilly. The natural son of the painter Ozias Humphry, Upcott began his literary career apprenticed to Wright's bookshop. He recalled Piccadilly's dazzling parade:

> I daily saw the greatest literary and political characters of the time, who frequented that celebrated ministerial shop ... At this house the Anti-Jacobin newspaper first appeared; at this house Bonaparte's intercepted correspondence from Egypt, captured by Lord Nelson, came out. The morning of publication to booksellers was a memorable day; a line of carriages reached from St James's Park to purchase them, and the shop was crowded with customers from morn till evening. Was I to enumerate the names of those individuals whom I frequently have seen while residing under that roof, or at John Debrett's, the Opposition bookseller, or John Stockdale's, both houses being within a few doors or Wright's, I might mention a long list of Tory and Whig characters, including literary men of the highest order, viz. Burke, Pitt, Fox, Sheridan, Grattan, Canning, Hawkesbury, Lord Clare, chancellor of Ireland, Dr. Joseph Wharton, George Steevens, Malone, W. Gifford (daily), and I witnessed the quarrel between him and Peter Pindar ... Here, too, I saw W. Seward, Dr. John Moore, father of General Moore, Arthur Murphy, George Rose, William Coombe (Dr. Syntax), Abbé Delille, who usually called with Mr. Canning, Mallet du Pau [*sic*], the French political writer, Mons. Lally Tollendal, Archdeacon Coxe, Mons. Calonne, and the most considerable of the French emigrants; Lord Nelson, Lord St. Vincent, Gen. Moore, Earl Spencer, Duke of Roxburghe, the distinguished book collector, Earl Moira, Joseph Ritson, George Chalmers, T.J. Mathias, Dr. Charles Burney, Dr. Parr, Bishop Porteus, Bishop Watson, Mrs. Montagu, and a variety of literary ladies.[16]

Upcott probably saw Whigs heading to Debrett's or Ridgway's (at 196 from 1784–1787 and at 170 from 1806–1817) rather than Wright's, "the greatest political bookseller in favor of Administration of his day."[17] Despite the "literary ladies," the clientele of the bookshops here is overwhelmingly male.[18] In August 1798, Hester Piozzi directed Penelope Pennington to pick up her *Three Warnings to John Bull* (1798) from "Wright in Piccadilly the Aristocrate Bookseller. *That* Shop teems with Antidotes to the Poyson administered by a neighbouring Shop *Debrett's* so the Folks know where to go for Sweet and bitter Water like Doctor Johnson's Fountains."[19] This reflects how the discourse around the politicized bookshops tended to define each in opposition to their rivals. Despite their polarization, Piozzi perceives the booksellers administering to the same patient: a public body of readers. Both print output and lounging space provided different groups with scenes of similarly conceived if differently inflected sociability.

Even if Upcott personally recalled his master as a "close and uncommunicative man," Wright effectively developed the bookshop as a scene of discussion, apparently centred around the Tory satirist and critic William Gifford, author of *The Baviad* (1791) and *The Maeviad* (1795).[20] When Upcott began, Gifford and the Vicar of Croydon, John Ireland, were daily visitors. Gifford was Wright's "principal Patron, & had brought him into notice," and "secured for him many of the most respectable persons to supply with books."[21] The Royal Academy painter Joseph Farington's diaries provide vignettes of sociable practice in this circle, recording visits to the bookshop from November 1797 to its demise in 1802. His most frequent contacts there were Gifford, the painters John Hoppner and Ozias Humphry, William Combe (a political journalist and former Pitt propagandist, at this time writing for both Wright and Debrett), and his "old crony," the Shakespeare editor George Steevens.[22] Farington also met George Canning, Edward Malone, and Lord Hawkesbury in the shop. These figures populate a space of overlapping cultural and political discussion. Topics discussed included MPs' private lives, Parliamentary debates, Irish and European politics, French invasion, the satirist Antony Pasquin's trial, the merits of T.J. Mathias's conservative satire *The Pursuits of Literature*, the Royal Academy, *The Anti-Jacobin*, publishing matters, and Jacobin–Illuminati conspiracy theories.[23] Farington records one visit to Wright's on 17 April 1798, during which he and William Combe easily switched between criticisms on the style and substance of Bishop Porteous's sermons and Combe's approbation of the ministry "working on the peoples apprehensions" of French invasion.[24] The bookshop was evidently a catalyst for the formation and exercise of judgment on both aesthetic and political matters.

These diary entries suggest that many visitors to Wright's aspired to what Habermas terms rational–critical discourse, the hallmark of the public sphere. Discussion in Wright's lounging bookshop seems, however, to have been largely ideologically homogeneous. The space functioned as a threshold between private conversation, a conservative coterie, and broader public opinion. Farington often came to discuss the frequently politicized intrigues at the Royal Academy, particularly with Hoppner; it seems that Wright's was a congenial space for conservative Academicians.[25] The aristocratic shop provided him with a space in which conservative discourse and arguments could take shape. First, the shop was an environment for semi-private talk and a refuge from clashes with Whig and radical opponents at the Academy itself. Second, the discussions and talk at Wright's would have helped Farington and Hoppner to consolidate their own conservative positions, before they finally returned to the fray of more diverse and divisive opinions beyond the shop. The bookshop lounges, Whig as well as Tory, were spaces for a partial and controlled critical generation of public opinion. At Wright's, Gifford's ability to rub shoulders with MPs and other gentlemen despite his origins as a cobbler might suggest his elevation on the basis of rational-critical discursive skills, but these seem to have been valued only insofar as they supported traditional hierarchy.

Nevertheless, these ideologically hermetic gatherings could be confirmed as public spaces when penetrated by unexpected or unwelcome guests. Farington records that on December 11, 1798, while discussing the publication of secret French correspondence from Egypt with Combe and Gifford in Wright's, the usual loungers were startled to see Henry Grattan enter, "a remarkably mean looking Man," sporting a Whiggish "blue coat and Spencer with half boots." "I never saw a Man in a respectable situation look less like a gentleman. Perceiving that the eyes of the people were turned upon him, He soon quitted the Shop."[26] Grattan's transgression of loyal political space draws forth critical assessment based on norms of gentlemanliness which Farington conceived as integral to the sociability of the shop.

Wright's clientele identified their conversation with public opinion and common interest, but as a social space the shop sat uneasily between an aristocratic club and an accessible shop open to alternative opinions and discursive norms. The poet and former MP Sir James Bland Burges, aiming to help the indigent Irish author Thomas Dermody, opened a subscription at Wright's shop to publish his poems. John Grant Raymond asserts that the plan was thwarted by "the imprudence and strange conduct

of the poet." Dermody, a habitual drunkard, was too shambolic: "His dress
and appearance were such as not to allow of his appearing at Mr. Wright's
shop."[27] Dermody seems to have expected frank literary discussion at
Wright's. Raymond narrates an example of his "independence" and freedom "from literary hypocrisy," which took place at Wright's:

> A nobleman . . . called there one day with a list of subscribers whom he had
> obtained for a book which Dermody was about to publish . . . From the
> various and common topics of the day, the conversation turned upon
> literary disquisition; a kind of argument which Dermody was at all times
> ready to engage in . . . His lordship, unluckily, at last took up a new
> publication from the counter; and putting it into his hands, desired him
> to peruse it at a future period, and give him his opinion of its merits.
> Dermody replied, "My lord, I have already read the book; and found too
> little pleasure in the task, to endure the fatigue of again wading through
> such a mass of dullness." His lordship thanked him for his candid opinion,
> and instantly left the shop.—"Fatal mistake!" exclaimed Mr. Wright: "you
> have for ever lost a friend and patron: his lordship is the author!"

Dermody coolly responded: "Were the king the author, it is badly
written . . . had I known that it was his, I should certainly have told him
the same truth."[28] Wright embodies the cultural capital and unspoken
norms of the shop's sociability, which Dermody could not or would not
master.[29] Although those meeting in Wright's appeared to conceive of it as
a forum for matters of public opinion, their notion of a legitimate public
was narrow and any relaxation of status distinctions remained limited.
Sociable discussion, critical judgment, and creativity were all exercised in
support of the establishment rather than to challenge hierarchy, a point
exemplified by perhaps the most famous title to issue from the bookshop.

The Anti-Jacobin; or, Weekly Examiner

Upcott's account of Wright's shop emphasizes the impact of *The Anti-
Jacobin*. Two journals shared this title: Wright's *The Anti-Jacobin; or Weekly
Examiner* (November 1797–July 1798), edited by William Gifford, and the
follow-up *Anti-Jacobin Review and Magazine* (1798–1821), initially edited by
"John Gifford" (John Richards Green). According to William Cookesley, in
late 1797 "a number of men of brilliant talents and high connection" to the
ministry "determined to establish a weekly paper, for the purpose of exposing to deserved ridicule and indignation the political agitators by whom the
country was then inundated."[30] Targets included "the Jacobin Daily Papers
of the Metropolis,"[31] *The Analytical Review* and *Monthly Magazine*, and

Foxite Opposition Whigs. It was led by Pitt's protégé, George Canning, the MP and under-secretary in the Foreign Office, with the assistance of his friend, also in the Foreign Office, John Hookham Frere, plus George Ellis. Canning regularly visited Wright's and Upcott recalled it was in the shop "that the Anti Jacobin Newspaper was first suggested."[32] Other contributors included the Foreign Secretary Lord Grenville, Viscount Morpeth, Edward Nares of the *British Critic*, and even occasionally Pitt himself. Edward Hawkins describes the extraordinary arrangement:

> [John] Owen, who had been the publisher of Burke's pamphlets, failed. The editors of the *Anti-Jacobin* took his house, paying the rent, taxes, &c., and gave it up to Wright, reserving to themselves the first floor, to which a communication was opened through Wright's house. Being thus enabled to pass to their own rooms through Wright's shop, where their frequent visits did not excite any remarks, they contrived to escape particular observation.[33]

Upcott corroborates the story: "The leading articles were composed in that and the adjoining house—where a large room was set apart for the use of its contributors," "the brightest geniuses of the age—whether as politicians, poets or Divines." Upcott wrote the fair copy to keep contributor identities anonymous.[34] This curious arrangement avoided direct identification between the journal and government ministers, mediating it as a more independent critical enterprise, although Canning was soon publically identified as its moving spirit. The room suggestively constituted a private space proximate to but withdrawn from scrutiny in the more public shop.

The *Anti-Jacobin; or, Weekly Examiner* followed the 1797–1798 Parliamentary session. As Kevin Gilmartin notes, this meant "the corrective representations of the counterrevolutionary press were advanced as a respectful supplement to legitimate parliamentary representation."[35] The journal espoused the cause of "TRUTH" and promised that with the information presented "our readers will, after a very short trial, be enabled to form their own opinion." An explicit aim was to police "lies, misrepresentations, and mistakes" of the "Jacobin" press.[36] Hawkins suggests that contributions embodied the sociable environment in which they were composed:

> What was written was left open upon the table, and as others of the party dropped in, hints or suggestions were made; sometimes whole passages were contributed by some of the parties present, and afterwards altered by others, so that it is almost impossible to ascertain the names of the authors.[37]

For Hawkins, the journal emerges out of sociable writing and embodies evolving collective opinion, rather than individual interests. The journal's poetry exemplifies this; the poems are dialogic and discursive in form and

content. To take one example, "Imitation. Sapphics. The Friend of Humanity and the Knife-Grinder," a parody of Robert Southey's "The Widow:
Sapphics," is introduced as verse "of the *Amœban* or *Collocutory* kind."[38]
Although referring to the generic structure of the poem, it also suggests the
journal's own relational enterprise. The introduction scans Southey's original to highlight how "the pathos of the matter is not a little relieved by the
absurdity of the metre": "Cōld wăs thē nīght wīnd: drīftĭng fāst thĕ snōws
fell." Classical Sapphics distort English rhythms, an aesthetic analogue to the
unnatural experimentalism of Jacobin ideology. The content of the poem
likewise frames Whig and radical discourse as fundamentally uncritical,
dogmatically applying rigid theoretical narrative to more nuanced circumstances, voiced in the leading questions of the "Friend":

> "Tell me, Knife-grinder, how you came to grind knives?
> Did some rich man tyrannically use you?
> Was it the squire? Or parson of the parish?
>   Or the attorney? . . .
>
> "(Have you not read the Rights of Man, by Tom Paine?)
> Drops of compassion tremble on my eyelids,
> Ready to fall, as soon as you have told your
>   Pitiful story."[39]

The Knife-Grinder's bathetic revelation that his tattered garments result
from a drunken scuffle at the Chequers and assertion that "for my part,
I never love to meddle / With politics, sir" infuriate the Friend in his
efforts to solicit grievances, expanding the public sphere. The innately
deferential Knife-Grinder is more than happy to stick to the irrational and
private space of the inn.

The satirical energy of the poem invites critical judgment which will
realign public opinion with sound political principles as well as "natural"
aesthetic norms. Although the poems are presented with the originals so as
to stimulate independent discrimination by the reader, reproducing the
rational-critical discussion the journal considers itself to defend against its
false Jacobin equivalent, their presentation also betrays discomfort, and
echoes the ventriloquism of the poor that it mocks in the "Friend." The
poem's introduction is obliged to spell out Jacobin ideology, the deficien-
cies of Southey's original, and the satire itself: "In those orders and
gradations of society, which are the natural result of the original difference
of talents and of industry among mankind, the Jacobin sees nothing but a
graduated scale of violence and cruelty."[40] If the journal flatters its readers
with an opportunity to exercise their judgments, it also frames the "right"

judgment: what Habermas identifies with manufactured "acclamation" rather than genuine and independent rational–critical discussion.[41]

The Anti-Jacobin self-consciously identified itself with Wright's shop as a site from which public opinion could be ascertained, as well as imagined as a discursive location by readers. In 1798, the twelfth *Anti-Jacobin* complained of a dull attack on it in the January 23 *Morning Chronicle.* "The only symptom of life which the enemy has betrayed . . . had been a *Thing* of four lines (we cannot call it an Epigram)."[42] The response is a grandiose address to the public:

> *Notice is hereby given,*
> That the sum of FIVE SHILLINGS is lodged in the hands of our Publisher, to be bestowed as a Prize on any Jacobin who, within a week from the publication of this notice, shall produce, at the shop of Mr. J. WRIGHT, in Piccadilly, any POEM, REBUS, ACROSTIC, CONUNDRUM, ANA-GRAM, or EPIGRAM, or any other *Thing* whatsoever, not exceeding the number of four lines, true and lawful measure, which shall be judged by three competent Umpires, to be selected, one by Mr. WRIGHT – one by Mr. DEBRETT, and the third by the JACOBIN POETASTER himself, to exceed in dullness, folly, flatness, and stupidity, the *Thing* above printed. If within a week's time a worse performance is not produced, the Prize is to go to the author of the above, and he is thereby empowered to apply for it accordingly.[43]

This *jeu d'esprit* imagines the sociable space of the bookshops as sites for the arbitration of cultural value. Debrett's appearance in the plan purports to guarantee a fair decision, but it also acts as an implicit challenge to that shop's clientele. The fifteenth issue describes the soporific labor of judging entries to "entitle the exulting Author to the *Fowl* and *Sausage,* in which Mr. WRIGHT's Housekeeper had judiciously laid out the *Five Shillings.*"[44] The feature finishes with a letter from Wright's "House-keeper, Mrs. DEBORAH WIGMORE" to her mother. Deborah reports discussing the entries with Debrett's shopman, Peter, before reading more alone. "I swept up my hearth and set my tea-things, and began to read—but I had like to have done myself a mischief, for I fell into a kind of dose at the third Letter, and had my stocking burnt through by a hot cinder— This put me upon my guard, and I kept the tea-pot steaming under my nose till I had got through seventeen—but 'twas all in vain—*I could find nothing that equalled the stupidity of the first.*" Recounting her activities after supper to her master, Deborah "begged him to give the Reward to the 'ORIGINAL EPIGRAMMIST,' for that it was next to impossible that a foolisher one should be found." Agreeing, Wright thanks her and gives her "half-a-crown to buy a ribbon, and said he was very glad it was over, for he felt as if a mountain was taken off his shoulders."[45]

The Anti-Jacobin and its publisher infantilize and ventriloquize the common people. Deborah, as a servant and a woman, is doubly taxed by critical discourse, which even endangers her. She willingly relinquishes her judgment. If the episode distinguishes between true and false public spheres, in the process it also concedes a critical voice to Deborah, as well as betraying Wright and the *Anti-Jacobin*'s subsidiary position within a larger, more diffuse public sphere. The combative pseudo-invitation to Jacobin poets to enter the shop riskily advertises its permeability as a concrete site of sociability, where confident conservative opinion as mediated in print might be forcefully contested by its opponents. For William Upcott, Peter Pindar's attempt to do just this was one of the most dramatic events ever to take place in Wright's.

The "Battle of The Bards"

"Peter Pindar" was the *nom de plume* of the satirical poet and conservative-baiter John Wolcot. Rumors abounded that Wolcot had seduced and bribed Royal staff into yielding personal details about the royal family, which appeared in his mock-epic *The Lousiad* (1785–1795). Pindar's coarse, irreverent humor, and eye for absurd images and rhymes, assured popularity. Politically, Wolcot was Whiggish. His poems lambasted Pitt, and although he remained a constitutionalist whose *Odes to Mr. Paine, Author of "Rights of man"* (1791) satirized democratic agitation, one opponent compared "What PINDAR sings, or PAINE and GODWIN preach."[46] William Gifford begrudged him an attack on his character in the *Critical Review*, which both Wolcot and the *Review* denied he had written. This developed into an ongoing print battle.[47]

In its account of Pindar's *Nil Admirari; or, A Smile at a Bishop* (1799), *The Anti-Jacobin Review* lambasted Pindar as an exemplar of "the vicious spirit of modern times," subverting satire in his "abuse of virtuous and elevated characters" and embodying a "disgusting mixture of obscenity and blasphemy."[48] Pindar's success reflected Whig sociability infecting public discourse. His poems "first attract the applause of some fool of fashion, whose ideas are kindly adopted by his associates, then become the topic of conversation in the circle of round-heads, at Ridgeways, or Debretts, and from those *pure* authorities receive the stamp of general currency."[49] Wolcot discovered the journal's editor was "Gifford," concluding this was William Gifford, whom he wrongly believed had also attacked him in *The Pursuits of Literature*. The postscript to his next poem, *Lord Auckland's Triumph* (1800), attacked T.J. Mathias and "little squinting MASTER AESOP GIFFORD," dubbing each "a rhyme-monger and critic" and undermining their gentlemanly public credentials by mocking their origins in trade.[50] Pindar provided a libellous biography of Gifford, alleging he pimped women for his patron, Lord Grosvenor, and abused *The Anti-Jacobin*, led by "MASTER CANNING," whose attack on Pindar's "poor Pamphlet" was venally motivated and did not distinguish public and private personae: "Not only my *poetical*, but my *moral* character, which I thought a fine haunch of venison, has been converted into dog's-meat under their paws."[51] Nevertheless, his own satire mocks Gifford and Mathias's private lives and deformed bodies while claiming public categories of worth for himself:

> TRUTH and CANDOUR are the DEITIES at whose shrine I sacrifice; or
> may I resemble
>> A poor, mean, sneaking, literary shrimp!
>> *Lie* like M[athias], and like G[ifford] *p*[imp].[52]

The Anti-Jacobin Magazine was actually the journal edited by "John Gifford." William Gifford responded with a vicious satire, *An Epistle to Peter Pindar*, published by Wright in 1800, and threatened to reveal Pindar's recent misdeeds via letters in Wright's possession.[53] Gifford's abuse of Pindar, via a bombardment of nouns, spills over from the literary to the physical, and with it from the virtual to the social public sphere:

> Come then, all filth, all venom, as thou art,
> Rage in thy eye, and rancor in thy heart,
> Come with thy boasted arms, spite, malice, lies,
> Smut, scandal, execrations, blasphemies;
> I brave 'em all. Lo, here I fix my stand,
> And dare the utmost of thy tongue and hand,
> Prepared each threat to baffle, or to spurn,
> Each blow with ten-fold vigor to return.[54]

Gifford's notes and postscript hinted that Pindar was a pederast. Wolcot reacted with a threatening advertisement in *The Morning Chronicle*; Gifford responded by getting Wright to advertise for back issues of *The Times* containing incriminating information.[55] Wolcot then sent an anonymous letter threatening injury, which Gifford rapidly included as a facsimile in the *Epistle*'s second edition.

On Monday, August 18, 1800, Wolcot tracked Gifford to Wright's. Gifford was sitting by the window, reading newspapers.[56] *Lloyd's Evening Post* reported:

Peter Pindar, in consequence of a vile and most scandalous charge, too gross
for the eye or ear of the Public, repaired to Mr. Wright's shop, to wreak his
vengeance on the person who thus calumniated him. As soon as he entered,
he saw his adversary, and advancing rapidly, accosted him thus – "Sir, is
your name Giffard?" On being answered – "Yes!" Peter said – "You are the
fellow whom I have been looking for," and immediately applied his stick to
Mr. Giffard's head. Mr. Peltier, the French Journalist, and several other
Gentlemen present ... interposed their friendship by disarming the
renowned Peter. In the struggle, the latter received a severe blow in his
turn from Mr. Giffard. As soon, however, as Peter got himself loose from
them, he renewed the combat *à la Mendoza*, and put in several blows with
good effect, driving his antagonist to the other end of the shop. Peter was
then again surrounded, and hustled out of the shop, "bleeding (as O'Keefe
says) in his glory!"[57]

Wolcot fares well in this account; *The London Packet* and the next day's
Albion and Evening Advertiser favor Gifford, who dexterously grabbed
Wolcot's cane and managed to break "the head of his assailant with his
own stick."[58] Wright was reported to have "thrust Peter out of the shop,
and locked the door on him," leaving him "in the midst of a mob on the
streets, his head bleeding, having lost his hat and stick."[59] Some accounts
added the slapstick indignity of Pindar's hat being thrown out onto the
street after him.[60]

Wright had actually been out of his shop but published a memorandum
drawn from his shopmen, ending with Pindar's complaints to "a mob of
hackney coachmen, watermen, paviours, &c.... and then, with a troop of
boys at his heels, [he] proceeded to a Surgeon's in St. James's-street to have
his wound examined, after which he slunk home 'With his crack'd pate be-
plaistered and bepatch'd, Like an old paper lantern!'"[61] Wright associates
Pindar with the mob, an illegitimate and heterogeneous outdoor public in
contrast to the gentlemen of his shop, although Piccadilly was a fashionable aristocratic street. The quotation comes from the *Bacchides* of Plautus,
in a note to Gifford's translations of Juvenal, and refers to a pederastic
teacher, obliquely reinforcing the original libel. Wolcot published a
counter-statement in *The Oracle*, asserting he "really was doing ample
and *easy* justice to [his] cause," before being restrained "particularly by a
tall Frenchman," whose "name was Peltier."[62] Print became the means to
renarrate the scuffle and claim victory in the eyes of the public.

The episode was further mediated through two mock-epic accounts of
the fracas: Alexander Geddes's *Bardomachia: or, The Battle of the Bards*
(1800) and Thomas Dermody's *The Battle of the Bards: An Heroic Poem*
(1800). Geddes, a liberal associated with the social circle at Joseph

Johnson's bookshop, fashions the shop as a site of pseudo-public discussion, presided over by Wright, "a most loyal worthy wight, / Ever prepar'd for CHURCH and KING to fight, /'Gainst croaking Democrates."[63] In the bookshop "so spacious and so fair," "The Loyal and the Orthodox" "rack their Doric wit / To sound the praises of celestial PITT." Gifford presides over discussion:

> 'Mong those Mæviades, the chief of all,
> Sits like a Prebendary in his stall;
> Presses, not fills, the arm'd Dictator's chair,
> And deals his dictates with a master's air:
> Dispenses Oracles deep,—deep, though dark;
> And deems his self a second Aristarch.[64]

Geddes merges Gifford's sociable and textual identities, whilst terms such as "chief," "Prebendary," and "dictates" poke fun at Gifford's self-regard and the pseudo-discussion at Wright's. Geddes and Dermody conclude that both writers, in their unseemly print satires and ensuing scuffle, betray the moderate rational norms expected of literature and the public sphere, thereby laying claim to a more adequate representation in their own detached works.

Many accounts of the fracas drew attention to Jean-Gabriel Peltier. As Upcott remembered, the shop was frequented by eminent émigrés and Peltier's presence in a space frequented by Canning and fellow ministers is revealing. Peltier had fled Paris for London in September 1792. In England, he investigated fellow émigrés to sniff out imposters and spies and expose the disloyal.[65] His business was journalism, advocating the full restoration of the Bourbons, spreading reports of Jacobin violence, and promoting war on the revolutionary regime. He edited and wrote counterrevolutionary journals in French, especially *Paris pendant l'année* (1795–1802), which numbered Pitt, Eden, and Auckland as subscribers.[66] Indeed, he corresponded with Pitt, boasting to the Prime Minister of his contacts throughout Europe and in French colonies, and carried out translations for the British government. In 1798 he claimed to have friends running correspondence networks for the ministry.[67] By the time of the "Battle of the Bards," Peltier styled himself "agent of all kings" and was paid by the Comte d'Artois to advocate the Bourbon monarchy's cause.[68] His presence at Wright's reflects his efforts around this time to solicit government financial support for his publications, as well as the shop's value as a site in which he could gather information on British policy as it developed, as well as influence policy and public opinion on the Revolution. Wright's shop was not only a site of British conservative sociability, but also an intersection with the European counterrevolution.

The Anti-Jacobin represents the zenith of Wright's reign as king of the Tory booksellers. James Gillray's correspondence includes letters with Wright about a proposed illustrated edition of *The Poetry of the Anti-Jacobin*.[69] Wright had begun producing expensive collector's editions printed by Bulmer and, according to the advertisement in the subscription book, dated June 10, 1800, this one would be "on Superfine paper, in One Volume Royal Quarto, and accompanied with FORTY Engravings," sold to subscribers for "One Guinea and a Half" and the public for "Two Guineas."[70] Many would have signed up by post or proxy, but subscriptions were collected at Wright's and comprise many of his clientele.[71] Headed by the Duke of Clarence, the five hundred plus names include: *The Anti-Jacobin* team of Canning, Frere, Ellis, and Gifford; government MPs, such as George Rose and George Hammond; Lords, including Auckland; the anti-Jacobin writers T.J. Mathias, John Bowles, and "John Gifford"; the novelist, dramatist, and M.P. Matthew "Monk" Lewis; artists including Ozias Humphrey and Robert Westall; Anglican booksellers the Rivingtons and the editorial team of their review *The British Critic*, William Beloe and Edward Nares; as well as Isaac D'Israeli and Jean-Gabriel Peltier. More surprising is "Thomas Paine, Esq'"; definitely not given in person, it might have been a joke, although it appears in a block of American subscribers in the same hand.[72] Paine was in France at this point, and unlikely to be signed as "Esquire." Despite the self-consciously ministerial identity of Wright's shop, its public nature left it vulnerable to intrusions which reminded its clientele of competing versions of public opinion.

The edition proved a debacle. Despite initial subscriptions by the *Anti-Jacobin* team, cross-party moves toward negotiating peace with the French in 1800 may have caught Wright unawares. The republication with Gillray's *ad hominem* caricatures unnerved Canning and Frere, who wished to inspect the engravings. Upon Gillray and Wright's refusal, the authors withdrew their names from the subscription and encouraged others to do so. Gillray extricated himself from the project, helped by a handsome financial reward from Canning. Wright soldiered on with the edition, now shorn of the caricatures and many subscribers; the government's disfavor revealed his dependence on ministerial custom. He seems to have financially overstretched himself, perhaps caused by expenditure on advertising, moves into producing expensive editions, and costly losses of £500 in a libel case successfully brought by the Irishman Patrick Lattin, over allegations he was a rebel in *A Fair Representation of the Present Political State of Ireland* (1799). When Wright was declared bankrupt in April 1802,[73] Tories already had an alternative bookshop location for their sociability.

Hatchard: The Godly Bookseller

Hatchard's, the last of the major conservative booksellers established in 1790s Piccadilly, reflected shifts in conservative sociability and print culture. According to John Hatchard's biographical memorandum, after work for the Westminster bookseller William Ginger and two apprenticeships, in October 1789, he began as a shopman for Thomas Payne, bookseller, at Mews Gate in St Martins, "the first that obtained the name and reputation of being a Literary Coffee House and Bookseller's combined." Hatchard served until June 30, 1797, when he founded his own bookshop, first at 173 Piccadilly, and then in larger premises at 190.[74] Hatchard's timing was fortuitous. From 1797 he built up business, co-publishing with Wright among others, until it was independent. His evangelical leanings, loyalty, and religious stock brought the patronage of Queen Charlotte. Wright's bankruptcy in 1802 and the waning of Stockdale's business into remainders, auctions, and overwhelming debts,[75] left Hatchard well-placed to become the unrivalled Tory bookseller in Piccadilly.

Hatchard's was a club-like social space:

> In the days of its founder the shop was very ill lit, only oil lamps being used. In the centre by the fireplace was a table, upon which were placed the daily papers, *The Morning Herald, The Morning Chronicle*, and the *Times*. There were also some old-fashioned chairs to match the customary occupants. All this was considered a part of the business, and as much care as possible taken not to disturb the slumbers of those who fell into the hands of *Morpheus*.[76]

The bookshop catered to the genteel; at the door was a bench for "the flunkeys who rode on the platforms behind their masters' carriages."[77] The back room was used for meetings, including the inaugural and early gatherings of the Royal Horticultural Society, from 1804 until 1805.[78] Between January and April 1803, it witnessed evening editorial gatherings for the *Pic Nic Magazine*, bringing together the editor, William Combe, with James and Horace Smith, Richard Cumberland, Sir James Bland Burges, John Wilson Croker, and others.[79] Hatchard attracted many of Wright's previous loungers, providing a conservative counterpart to the rival Whig Ridgway's bookshop, from 1806 at number 170. Hatchard published speeches by ministers, including Canning and Addington, and was frequented by Tory MPs,[80] but the tone of his sociable space suggests an important modulation from the timbre of Wright's.

Reverend William Beloe, assistant editor of the *British Critic*, knew Hatchard from Payne's bookshop and became a regular visitor. In *The Sexagenarian* (1818), Beloe recalled Hatchard as "The Godly Bookseller," a "worthy and conscientious man, whose principal dealings were in religious books and tracts, chief correspondence with individuals of that description."[81] A customer recalled that "He was invariably dressed in black. His coat was of the style of a Bishop's frock coat, waistcoat buttoning to the throat, with an entirely plain front, and knee breeches and gaiters."[82] His appearance set the tone for a serious-minded shop.

The clientele was conservative, with Evangelical leanings. Sydney Smith, a founding contributor to the Whig *Edinburgh Review*, appraised *Remarks on the System of Education in Public Schools*, published by Hatchard in 1809. Smith began with a caricature of sociability in Hatchard's shop:

> There is a set of well-dressed, prosperous gentlemen, who assemble daily at Mr Hatchard's shop;—clean, civil personages, well in with people in power,—delighted with every existing institution—and almost with every existing circumstance;—and, every now and then, one of these personages writes a little book;—and the rest praise that little book—expecting to be praised, in their turn, for their own little books:—and, of these little books, thus written by these clean, civil personages, so expecting to be praised, the pamphlet before us appears to be one.[83]

Smith depicts like-minded gatherings, not a legitimate, debating public, but a petty, self-absorbed coterie with a circular economy of ideas. He characterizes the forum as an antiquated talking shop out of sync with the "tendencies of public opinion" with which the *Edinburgh* engaged, associated as it was with a wider print culture and the more diffuse and modern literary environment of Edinburgh.[84] Smith's review responds to a Hatchard pamphlet by "Senex," entitled *A Letter to the Young Gentlemen Who Write in the Edinburgh Review* (1809). This undermined the *Edinburgh*'s claim to represent public opinion. Senex believed it was conducted by "persons of a very queer description," its reviews "deviate so widely from the common track." Most of all, it expressed "political opinions" with "extreme violence" in "the support of a political party," rather than "the general discussion of literary topics" and treated religion with skepticism.[85] Hatchard's authors and the *Edinburgh Review* were evidently fighting over their claims to represent public opinion.

Smith's portrait is disingenuous. While loyal, Hatchard's firm owed much of its original success to John Bowdler's *Reform or Ruin* (1797), which challenged to the bad habits and practices of the establishment, especially the laxity of the established church. The shop was a focus for reform-minded Evangelicals and in 1802 Hatchard was appointed the publisher of *The Christian Observer*, a periodical particularly associated with the Clapham Sect. Humphreys relates how "a room now used for despatching orders was once a private parlour set aside," where "bishops and clergy of the Low Church Party, stimulated by the teaching of Wilberforce and Hannah More, seceded from the Bible and Sun, Rivington's house in St Paul's Churchyard, and came westwards to the house more in sympathy with their tenets."[86] In the second half of the eighteenth century, the Rivingtons were the established booksellers for orthodox Anglicanism. This defection to Hatchard's shop mirrored ideological shifts in Christian conservatism.[87]

Hatchard's prominence indicates the rise of sober-minded and activist Christian conservatism in the early nineteenth century. There was some continuity with Wright's shop. George Canning was a regular and published most of his writings through Hatchard, whilst Beloe and Nares, the editorial team of the *British Critic*, also visited. Addington arranged for Hatchard to publish Thomas Dermody's *Poems on Various Subjects* (1802).[88] But from the available evidence, the émigrés who attended Wright's were not prominent here, with many returning to France during the peace in 1802.[89] Conservative literary culture was separating into more distinct, albeit overlapping groupings, with a greater choice of booksellers and lounging spaces. Many conservatives of an older stamp would visit Hatchard's for specific titles, but not for the lively sociability associated with Wright's. The atmosphere in the shop seemed to be graver, focused more on political campaigning than literary debate. Gifford, for example, would be found at John Murray's in Albermarle Street, although he occasionally mentions having visited Hatchard's and requested copies of the *Christian Observer*.[90] This might have been the result of ill-health or his workload for the *Quarterly Review*, but Murray's proximity to Hatchard's suggests ideological motivations as well as the more refined appeal of the less public, salon-style sociability at Murray's. Hatchard's reputation for evangelicalism was not to all conservative tastes, with the more literary minded, such as Isaac D'Israeli, favoring Murray, and with High Church Anglicans preferring Rivingtons in Paternoster Row. It remained, however, open enough to attract a varied constituency. With its preference for religious zeal, self-improvement, and nationalist values, Hatchard's seems intuitively in tune with a grouping rising to power in the Victorian period. William Wilberforce's journals record numerous visits to the shop between 1804 and 1818, usually to pick up letters, catch up on pamphlets, reports, and news, to send out books to friends and colleagues, and to discuss projects of reform (such as The Lock Asylum).[91] Wordsworth wrote to Wilberforce to solicit his vote for Southey's brother, Henry, to become Physician to the Middlesex Hospital, and the letter was redirected to "Mr Hatchards, Bookseller, Piccadilly."[92] When, in 1807, Wilberforce and other abolitionists formed the African Institution, superseding the Society Instituted for the Abolition of the Slave Trade, its plan and directors' reports could be consulted and purchased at Hatchard's.[93]

The clientele Hatchard cultivated was loyal in every sense. Despite usually publishing with Cadell and Davies, Hannah More was a committed customer. In early 1809, she used Hatchard to send a copy of *Coelebs in Search of a Wife* (1809) to Wilberforce.[94] More became friends with the Macaulay family, who shared her evangelical outlook. In letters to Zachary Macaulay between 1811 and 1813, she praised their precocious young son, Thomas and, aiming to foster his talents, sent him money, specifically to buy books from Hatchard's.[95] At the end of the eighteen teens, when popular radical journals like Thomas Wooler's *Black Dwarf* and William Cobbett's *Political Register* were thriving, the government called upon More to repeat her counterrevolutionary *Cheap Repository Tracts of the 1790s* in a form appropriate for the contemporary period. Hatchard's was one of the main publishers and sellers of these tracts.[96]

In addition to aiding the alliance of church and state with Christian reform, Hatchard's was also associated with the faith-driven promotion of the British Empire. Marilyn Butler has persuasively placed Byron's Orientalism, especially in *The Giaour*, in the context of evangelical campaigns to promote missionary activity in India.[97] As is evident from an account of eight books in Article IX of the *Edinburgh Review* for April 1808, Hatchard was a major publisher of tracts promoting Christian missions, exemplified by J.W. Cunningham's *Christianity in India: An Essay on the Duty, Means, and Consequences of Introducing the Christian Religion among the Native Inhabitants of the British Dominions in the East* (1808). By contrast, his neighbour James Ridgway published two of the reviewed titles, with Thomas Twining's *A Letter to the Chairman of the East India Company, on the Danger of interfering in the Religious Opinions of the Natives of India* (1807) voicing a more sceptical, Enlightenment approach to the Hindus.[98] Once again, the appeal to public opinion on matters of national concern emanated from similarly conceived and vying spaces of print and sociability.

The Tory bookshop-lounges were concrete spaces of discussion in which participants conceived of themselves as forming public opinion, which would become diffused through print. This was, of course, a highly partial imagining of the public, a point equally true of the gatherings in rival Whig bookshops. Although these social groupings tended to regard themselves as the means by which "correct" public opinion could be formed and disseminated, these idealizations were vulnerable to disruption, both in submitting printed discourse to an increasingly heterogeneous and diffuse reading public addressed by other subsidiary groupings, and in risking the intrusion of undesirable members of a wider public, with disruptive behaviors. Nevertheless, conflict such as that at Wright's arguably served to entrench rather than challenge group identity. To apply Habermas's model of the public sphere to these bookshops is to recognize that it operated conceptually, ideologically, and rhetorically rather than in actuality. Stockdale's, Debrett's, and Wright's clienteles included MPs and clergymen and thus were hardly independent from church and government in the way that Habermas envisaged for the public sphere, but the rhetoric of disinterested concern for the public good in their discussions and pamphlets indicates serious claims to represent public opinion, albeit motivated by a partially construed sense of that independence. The deliberations and sociability of both Whigs and Tories in these spaces did not in themselves guarantee progressive contributions to public opinion, nor even politeness, but rather facilitated the constitution of group identities and, through discussion and print, validation in their members' eyes.

Notes

1 John Feltham, *The Picture of London for 1802* (London: Feltham, 1802), p. 27. For West End booksellers, see James Raven, *The Business of Books: Booksellers and the English Book Trade 1450–1850* (New Haven, CT: Yale University Press, 2007), pp. 188–99, 318.

2 *New Annual Register* (February 1814), 20–1. For the story of the fraud and trials, see Richard Dale, *Napoleon is Dead: Lord Cochrane and the Great Stock Exchange Scandal* (Stroud: History Press, 2006).

3 Jürgen Habermas, *The Structural Transformation of the Public Sphere*, trans. by Thomas Burger and Frederick Lawrence (Cambridge: Polity, 1989), p. 27.

4 Habermas, *Structural Transformation*, pp. 25–6.

5 J.A. Downie, "How Useful to Eighteenth-Century English Studies is the Paradigm of the 'Bourgeois Public Sphere'?," *Literature Compass* 1 (2003), 1–19. See also "Public and Private: The Myth of the Public Sphere," in *A Concise Companion to the Restoration and the Eighteenth Century*, ed. Cynthia Wall (Oxford: Blackwell, 2005), pp. 58–79.

6 Habermas, *Structural Transformation*, pp. xvii–xviii and Downie, "The 'Bourgeois Public Sphere.'" p. 3.

7 Downie, "The 'Bourgeois Public Sphere,'" p. 13.

8 Michael Scrivener, "Habermas, Romanticism, and Literary Theory," *Literature Compass* 1 (2004), 3.

9 Craig Calhoun, Introduction to *Habermas and the Public Sphere*, ed. Craig Calhoun (Cambridge, MA: MIT Press, 1992), p. 37.

10 Markman Ellis, *The Coffee-House: A Cultural History* (London: Phoenix, 2004), p. 203.

11 For Debrett's, see David Fallon, "Booksellers in the Godwin Diaries," *Bodleian Library Record* 24 (2011), 25–34.

12 Habermas, *Structural Transformation*, pp. 25–26.

13 Eric Stockdale, '*Tis Treason, My Good Man! Four Revolutionary Presidents and a Piccadilly Bookshop* (Delaware and London: Oak Knoll Press and the British Library, 2005).

14 Downie, "Public and Private," p. 62.

15 Jon P. Klancher, *The Making of English Reading Audiences, 1790–1832* (Madison, WI: University of Wisconsin Press, 1987), p. 23.

16 *The Gentleman's Magazine*, 26, New Series, (December 1846), 603.

17 Upcott to Miss Temple, January 21 1822, Huntington Library, UP 697, p. 7.

18 The bookshop features in the historical serial *The Protégée: A Tale*. An Evelina-like heroine, supported by a Countess, visits her patron's West End bookseller, Mr. Wright, who helps her place an advertisement for employment. See *The Court Magazine and Monthly Critic* (July 1842).

19 *The Piozzi Letters: Correspondence of Hester Lynch Piozzi, 1784–1821*, ed. Edward A. Bloom and Lillian D. Bloom, 6 vols. (Newark: University of Delaware Press, 1989–2002), vol. II, p. 512. Piozzi refers to Johnson's "The Fountains: A Fairy Tale," in Anna Williams, *Miscellanies in Prose and Verse* (London: T. Davies, 1766), pp. 111–41.

20 Huntington Library, UP 697, p. 8.

21 British Library, Add. MS 32558, 71^v.

22 *The Diary of Joseph Farington*, ed. Kenneth Garlick and Angus Macintyre, 16 vols. (New Haven, CT: Yale University Press, 1978–1998), vol. II, May 11, 1796. For Combe's political journalism, see Harlan W. Hamilton, *Doctor Syntax: A Silhouette of William Combe, Esq. 1742–1823* (London: Chatto & Windus, 1969), esp. pp. 147–213.

23 *Diary of Joseph Farington*, ed. Garlick and Macintyre, vol. III, entries for: November 3 and 23, 1797; December 4, 9, and 21, 1797; January 1, 15, 24, and 26, 1798; February 19, 1798; March 16, 20, and 22, 1798; April 17, 1798; May 29, 1798; August 24, 27, 28, and 29, 1798; November 15, 1798; December 11, 1798; and vol. IV, entry for January 24, 1800.

24 *Diary of Joseph Farington*, ed. Garlick and Macintyre, vol. III, April 17, 1798.

25 Wright's even served as an exhibition space, with Richard Westall advertising prints on display in the shop, where subscriptions could be collected. See *Morning Chronicle*, July 4, 1798.

26 *Diary of Joseph Farington*, ed. Garlick and Macintyre, vol. III, December 11, 1798.

27 James Grant Raymond, *The Life of Thomas Dermody*, 2 vols. (London: William Miller, 1806), vol. II, pp. 166–67.

28 Raymond, *Dermody*, vol. II, pp. 149–51.

29 Alternatively, this may be a refusal led by radical convictions. See Michael Griffin's introduction to *Thomas Dermody: Selected Writings* (Dublin: Field Day, 2012), pp. 1–31.

30 "Eponymous" [William Gifford Cookesley], "Memoir of William Gifford" in John Nichols, *Illustrations of the Literary History of the Eighteenth Century*, 8 vols. (London: The Author, 1817–1858), vol. VI, p. 5.

31 *The Anti-Jacobin; or, Weekly Examiner*, 27 (May 14, 1798), p. 210.

32 Upcott to [Miss] Temple, January 21, 1821, Huntington Library UP 697, pp. 7–8.

33 Edward Hawkins, "Authors of the Poetry of the Anti-Jacobin," *Notes & Queries*, 1st ser., 3 (May 3, 1851), p. 349. The space was itself significant; John Owen published loyalist texts, including Mathias's *The Pursuits of Literature* (1794–1797), and Edmund Burke's *A Letter to a Noble Lord* (1796) and *Thoughts on the Prospect of a Regicide Peace* (1796).

34 Huntington Library, UP 697, p. 8.

35 Kevin Gilmartin, *Writing Against Revolution: Literary Conservatism in Britain, 1790–1832* (Cambridge: Cambridge University Press, 2007), p. 120.

36 Prospectus, in *The Anti-Jacobin; or, Weekly Examiner*, 2 vols. (London: J. Wright, 1799), vol. I, pp. 2, 8.

37 Hawkins, "Authors of the Poetry," p. 349.

38 *The Anti-Jacobin; or, Weekly Examiner* (November 27, 1797), 71.

39 Ibid., p. 72.

40 Ibid., p. 70.

41 Habermas, *Structural Transformation*, pp. 176, 178.

42 For the origin of these articles, see Roy Benjamin Clarke, *William Gifford: Tory Satirist, Critic, and Editor* (New York: Colombia University Press, 1930), pp. 92–95.

43 *The Anti-Jacobin; or, Weekly Examiner* 12 (January 29, 1798), 420–1.

44 Ibid., 15 (February 19, 1798), 522–3.

45 Ibid., 16 (February 26, 1798), 552–6.

46 *Peter Not Infallible! or, a Poem Addressed to Peter Pindar, Esq., on reading his Nil Admirari* (London: Chapple *et al*, 1800), p. 31.

47 For the build-up and so-called "Battle of the Bards," see Tom Girtin, *Doctor with Two Aunts: A Biography of Peter Pindar* (London: Hutchinson, 1959), pp. 191–210 and Clarke, *William Gifford*, pp. 103–11.

48 *The Anti-Jacobin Review and Magazine* 17 (November 1799), 325.

49 Ibid., pp. 321–3.

50 Peter Pindar, *Lord Auckland's Triumph; or the Death of Crim. Con. A Pair of Prophetic Odes* (London: West and Hughes, 1800), pp. 45–6.

51 Ibid., p. 48. Pindar alludes to Goldsmith's poem *The Haunch of Venison* (1776).

52 Pindar, *Lord Auckland's Triumph*, p. 52.

53 William Gifford, *An Epistle to Peter Pindar; Third Edition with Considerable Additions to the Postscript* (London: J. Wright, 1800), pp. 36–8.

54 Ibid., p. 25, ll. 57–64.

55 Ibid., "Postscript to the Third Edition," pp. 35–61. Wright advertised in *The Sun*, July 24, 1800, above the advertisement for *An Epistle to Peter Pindar*.

56 *Whitehall Evening Post*, August 21, 1800.

57 *Lloyd's Evening Post*, August 18, 1800.

58 *Albion and Evening Advertiser*, August 19, 1800.

59 *London Packet or New Lloyd's Evening Post*, August 18, 1800.

60 *Albion and Evening Advertiser*, August 19, 1800.

61 *The Morning Post*, August 22, 1800.

62 *Bell's Weekly Messenger*, August 24, 1800.

63 [Alexander Geddes], *Bardomachia: Or, The Battle of the Bards, Translated from the Original Latin* (London: J. Johnson, 1800), p. 10.

64 Ibid., pp. 10–11.

65 See Simon Burrows, *French Exile Journalism and European Politics: 1792–1814* (Woodbridge: Boydell Press, 2000), p. 53.

66 Ibid., p. 77.

67 Ibid., pp. 70–1.

68 Ibid., p. 87.

69 See British Library Add. MS 27337, 55^r.

70 Ibid., 56^v–57^r.

71 See Josceline Bagot, *George Canning and His Friends*, 2 vols. (London: John Murray, 1909), vol. I, pp. 170–71 for John Sneyd's request that Gillray "put down my name at Mr. Wright's as a subscriber."

72 British Library, Add. MS 27337. The subscriptions run from 57^v to 68^r.

73 See *London Chronicle or Universal Evening Post*, February 20, 1800 and *Oracle and Daily Advertiser*, February 21, 1800. Raven, *Business of Books*, pp. 295–96, notes tight margins and a peak of bankruptcies for booksellers between 1800 and 1804.

74 Arthur L. Humphreys, *Piccadilly Bookmen: Memorials of the House of Hatchard* (London: Hatchards, 1893), pp. 11, 6–7.

75 See Stockdale, *'Tis Treason*, pp. 380–89, and Raven, *Business of Books*, p. 297.

76 Humphreys, *Piccadilly Bookmen*, pp. 64–65.

77 Ibid., p. 65.

78 See Harold R. Fletcher, *The Story of the Royal Horticultural Society: 1804–1968* (Oxford: Oxford University Press, 1969), pp. 21–23, 37–42.

79 Hamilton, *Doctor Syntax*, p. 218.

80 Hatchard is depicted humbly fawning to the aristocracy in Derek Hudson, *A Poet in Parliament: The Life of William Mackworth Praed, 1802–1839* (London: John Murray, 1939), pp. 131–2.

81 [William Beloe], *The Sexagenarian; or, The Recollections of a Literary Life*, 2nd edition, 2 vols. (London: F & C Rivington, 1818), vol. II, p. 283.

82 Humphreys, *Piccadilly Bookmen*, pp. 63–4.

83 *The Edinburgh Review, or Critical Journal* 16 (August 1810), 326.

84 See the Advertisement to the first issue: *Edinburgh Review; or, Critical Journal* 1 (October 1802).

85 "Senex," in *A Letter to the Young Gentlemen who Write in the Edinburgh Review* (London: J. Hatchard, 1809), pp. 3, 22, 25. Worcester College, University of Oxford, XY.7.42(5).

86 Humphreys, *Piccadilly Bookmen*, p. 61.

87 Henry Curwen, *A History of Booksellers, The Old and the New* (London: Chatto and Windus, 1873), pp. 302–3.

88 *Thomas Dermody*, ed. Griffin, p. 30.

89 Burrows, *French Exile Journalism*, p. 179.

90 See Gifford's letters to Octavius Gilchrist of January 6, 1803 and December 16, 1807: National Library of Scotland, MS 42242, 4^r and 16^r.

91 Robert Isaac Wilberforce and Samuel Wilberforce, *The Life of William Wilberforce*, 5 vols. (London: John Murray, 1838), vol. III, p.186; vol. IV, pp. 88, 127–28, 221–22, 226–27, 319.

92 May 20, 1815, *The Letters of William and Dorothy Wordsworth*, ed. by Alan G. Hill, 8 vols. (Oxford: Clarendon Press, 1993), vol. VIII, p. 158.

93 *The Edinburgh Review* 14 (July 1809), 322–23.

94 More to Wilberforce, January 4, 1809, in *The Correspondence of William Wilberforce*, ed. Robert Isaac Wilberforce and Samuel Wilberforce, 2 vols. (London: John Murray, 1840), vol. II, pp. 45–46.

95 More to Zachary Macaulay, July 8, 1811; September 21, [1812]; August 1813. Cited in Anne Stott, *Hannah More: The First Victorian* (Oxford: Oxford University Press, 2003), pp. 290–91. *Letters of Hannah More to Zachary Macaulay, Esq*, ed. Arthur Roberts (New York: Robert Carter and Brothers, 1860), p. 48. For further use of Hatchard's, see pp. 116, 122, 174.

96 Stott, *Hannah More*, p. 310.

97 Marilyn Butler, "The Orientalism of Byron's *The Giaour*," in *Byron and the Limits of Fiction*, ed. Bernard Beatty and Vincent Newey (Liverpool: Liverpool University Press, 1988), pp. 78–96.

98 *Edinburgh Review*, 12 (April 1808), p. 151.

PART II

Sociable Spectacle

CHAPTER 4

Proxy Israelites
Staging Ethnic Violence in the Ring and the Pit
Daniel O'Quinn

The title of this volume implicitly links sociability to the experience of space. In its most direct reading "sociable place" points toward zones of conviviality, spaces where people come together for pleasure and companionship. It would seem by its very definition to exclude violence and discord. And yet this would be at variance with two of the most important and commented upon spaces of sociability in the late eighteenth and early nineteenth centuries. The theatre was the preeminent space of public entertainment in the Georgian period – the place where Londoners convened on a nightly basis not only to socialize with one another, but also to observe interpersonal exchange both on and off the stage. I have written elsewhere about the auto-ethnographic nature of these entertainments and Julie Carlson's superb reading of Hazlitt's analysis of theatrical sociability demonstrates the degree to which audiences and critics alike saw theatrical space as a social laboratory.[1] But we tend to forget that the patent theatres had historically been sites of intense rioting and violent disturbance. Even when the whole house was not enveloped by disorder, the papers inform us repeatedly of instances of physical conflict in the lobbies, the pit and the galleries. The employment of bruisers to keep order was commonplace.

Potential violence was in some ways endemic to the theatrical experience in the Georgian period and one could develop a sliding scale of disorder from the momentary interruption required to eject a drunk from the pit to the all out insurrection that enveloped Covent Garden Theatre during the OP riots in 1809. I will be discussing the latter events in the second half of this essay, but I will get there by way of a second form of sociability whose theatricality meant that it was equally the subject of the attention of the press. Prize-fighting was an illegal practice in the late eighteenth century, but it often moved beyond the watchful eye of the magistrates and manifested itself in a number of semi-legitimate, fashionable but not polite venues. Because of the huge stakes involved, fights invariably made their way into the papers, not in the form of advertisements, but as part of the society news. Prize-fights did not occur with the same regularity as plays, but their mediation was in many ways modeled on theatrical reporting. The fights themselves, including the events leading up to and following the event, were represented first in the daily newspapers, in drinking songs, in broadside poetry and then in satirical and non-satirical prints.[2] The papers developed a set of discursive parameters for narrating the fights that saw the blow-by-blow account set off from the rest of the paper by the use of miniscule font. This separation is reminiscent of the way that the theatrical intelligence separated its summary of the plot from the rest of the review. In both cases, the mediation of performance replicates the separation between the space of representation and the space inhabited by performers and audience alike. This is a key issue because the conflict staged in the former imaginary space constitutes a pretext for the forms of sociability specific to the theatre and the prize-fight. In a sense, the small font is a useful heuristic because it demonstrates that the staged events were not the most important thing in these sociable spaces: the large font was reserved for discussions of the performance of both the players and the audience.

This is not to say that real events don't happen on stage and in the ring, but rather to emphasize two things. First, on-stage events frequently take on higher levels of figural meaning in this period: the tendency to engage in topical allegory among Georgian theatregoers is no less prevalent among the Fancy. The Fancy was a blanket term used to characterize the subculture that both surrounded and activated the prize-fighting world. A heterogeneous social entity, the Fancy included some of the most elite men in the kingdom, but one of its defining qualities was a self-imposed antinomianism that allowed men, and some women, of all ranks to socialize together if not on equal footing then at least in the same space. The Fancy developed its own complex argot, and a series of rituals aimed at regulating the complex betting procedures that underwrote its activities. This idiom became so arcane, and yet so crucial, that a number of dictionaries were published to keep everyone on the same page.[3] The highly stylized works of writers such as John Badcock and Pierce Egan, whose *Boxiana* series modified earlier print materials into an extended narrative of boxing's history in England, leaned heavily on allegory and allusion to playfully aestheticize the pugilistic world, and that aestheticization warrants our attention because of the way that it handles differences of rank, ethnicity and race.

These differences are important because the most famous fights of the period were "multi-ethnic spectacles." The term was developed by Michael Ragussis in order to characterize a largely ignored shift in the representational economy of the Georgian theatre.[4] Ragussis's analysis of the vast proliferation of ethnic types on the Georgian stage persuasively demonstrates that one of the things being negotiated in the social space of the patent theatres was the place of Irish, Jewish, Scottish and Anglo–African minorities in the social fabric of Georgian Britain. A similar argument can be made with even more force with relation to the world of prize-fighting. The most famous fights in the period were contests between specifically English fighters and representative challengers who were identified with their ethnicity or race. I have written elsewhere about the racial anxieties precipitated by the bouts between Tom Crib and the "Baltimore Black" Tom Molineaux.[5] In this essay, I focus on perhaps the most famous fighter of his generation: Daniel Mendoza, popularly known as the "Star of Jerusalem" and declared by "One of the Fancy" in *Blackwood's Edinburgh Magazine's* 1819–1820 series "Boxiana; or Sketches of Pugilism" "the great founder of the Jewish School" of pugilism. In the first section of the chapter, I analyze the mediation of Mendoza's rise to fame in the celebrated fights against Richard Humphries immediately before and after the French Revolution in order to argue for a crucial alteration in the way that ethnicity, sociability and space are figured at this historical moment.

This focus on mediation emerges out of my own work on the dynamic relation between the theatre and the press in *Entertaining Crisis in the Atlantic Imperium* and from Diana Taylor's theorization of the "repertoire." The repertoire is composed of "all those acts usually thought of as ephemeral, non-reproducible knowledge"; and while some performances disappear,

> performances also replicate themselves through their own structures and codes. This means that the repertoire, like the archive, is mediated. The process of selection, memorization or internalization, and transmission takes place within (and in turn helps constitute) specific systems of re-presentation. Multiple forms of embodied acts are always present, though in a constant state of againness. They reconstitute themselves, transmitting communal memories, histories, and values from one group/generation to the next. Embodied and performed acts generate, record, and transmit knowledge.[6]

As the expression of received culture, enacted and re-enacted in the performance of the everyday, the repertoire shares much with Bourdieu's notion of the habitus, but Taylor activates the term to draw attention to often ignored zones of political contestation that are proscribed from the archive itself. Because the repertoire is mediated, the traces of these contestations are omnipresent, often just out of focus in a conceptual space immediately adjacent to the highly resolved objects of archival analysis and documentation; it is not that the repertoire is occluded by the archive, but rather that it seems to inhere just below the level of evidentiary legitimacy. For this reason this essay attends very closely not only to the ephemeral worlds of the daily press and visual print satire, but also to the transient performance history of the repertoire of anti-Semitism. As we will see, newspapers and print satires both describe evanescent acts of social performance and allegorize it according to recognizable patterns of aestheticization and spatial displacement.

After looking specifically at how Mendoza and the Fancy are described and figured in the outdoor space of the prize ring, I follow him indoors to the space of the theatre at a very specific moment in its history. One of the most under-discussed aspects of the O.P. Riots was the cultural impact of John Philip Kemble's decision to issue orders to Daniel Mendoza, Dutch Sam and other Jewish pugilists to maintain order in the pit. The anti-Semitism that everywhere surrounded Mendoza's career erupted into the space of Covent Garden Theatre, thereby instantiating one of the most significant and sustained ethnic conflicts in the Romantic period. One of my primary objectives in discussing the Mendoza/Humphries bouts and the O.P. Riots in the same essay is to show that Daniel Mendoza's actions in the ring and in the pit are consistently understood in relation to prior theatrical performances that paradoxically defined both the repertoire of anti-Semitism and of British patriotism. Two of these plays were staged repeatedly while these events were unfolding and their key Jewish characters were lightning rods for ethnic hatred and derision – namely, the role of Shylock in *The Merchant of Venice* and the role of Isaac Mendoza in Sheridan's *The Duenna*. But these bulwarks of anti-Semitism were shadowed by an entirely different patriotic repertoire that regularly aligned Britain and the tribes of Israel – namely Handel's Israelite oratorios whose resuscitation was central to the reconsolidation of national and imperial fantasy in 1780s and beyond. As we will see, the complex interplay of these apparently discordant repertoires is crucial to Daniel Mendoza's transit through the mediascape of Georgian England, and tracking his journey will give some insight into the shifting constitution of the ethnoscape during this period.

Tell it Not in *Gath* – Repeat it Not in The Streets of *Askelon*

On May 7, 1789, the aged Charles Macklin, no longer able to remember his lines, was forced to leave the stage in what would be his final performance in the role of Shylock. Macklin had played Shylock to universal acclaim almost fifty years earlier in 1741 and had fundamentally shifted the performance protocols associated with the part. Prior to Macklin's epochal performance, Shylock was played as a buffoon; in Macklin's hands Shylock's speeches were delivered seriously and despite the actor's claims to realism the role became an exercise in malevolence that horrified his audience. As Frank Felsenstein states, "the consummate savagery of his performance came through most powerfully of all in the trial scene (act IV scene i) . . . In performance, Macklin would stoop down and whet his knife on the stage floor, this mute action causing on one occasion a young man in the pit to faint dead away."[7] Despite vicissitudes in his career, from the mid-eighteenth century onwards *The Merchant of Venice* belonged to Shylock and Macklin.[8] Because Macklin's performance in the role was so iconic and so fully intertwined with the representation of Jewishness in the period, it is worth considering the spectacle of the aging actor losing control over the character, failing to realize the part on this particular evening. It would perhaps be too much to suggest that with Macklin's incapacity came a dissolution of his Shylock's efficacy in the ethnoscape of London, except that another man's celebrity had been fully achieved only the day before, and his emergence as a public figure, like Macklin's rise to fame fifty years earlier, altered the representation of Jews in Georgian London.[9]

On May 6, 1789, Daniel Mendoza, in the second of his fights with Richard Humphries, was declared victorious before a crowd of between 1500 and 2000 onlookers in the town of Stilton. Mendoza fought Humphries in three widely discussed matches between January 1788 and October 1790: Humphries won the first fight at Odiham, but controversy surrounding the intervention of his second prompted a rematch; Mendoza won the second and third fights at Stilton and Doncaster respectively due to his greater "science." Mendoza was not a large man and his success lay in his courage, his endurance, and his ability both to land frequent, quick punches, and to dexterously stop the majority of his opponents' blows. But Mendoza's exceptionalism was more than pugilistic. Well before the advent of innovators in the realm of sports writing like Pierce Egan and John Badcock, Mendoza used the medium of print to reconfigure both the sport and the image of its central protagonist. His publication of *The Art of Boxing* in 1789, shortly after his defeat of Humphries, and of his *Memoirs* not only argued for the central place of a newly codified pugilism in the British national imaginary, but also stated in no uncertain terms that the ideal practitioner of this new "defensive" art was actually an internal exile. As John Whale has persuasively demonstrated, Mendoza's self-representation as an icon of pugilistic art is intimately tied to his Jewishness.[10] Put simply, Mendoza argued that his capacity to exceed ethnic specificity in the ring proved the liberality of English identity.[11]

But Mendoza's arguments and his anecdotes about overcoming Christian prejudice both in the streets and the ring are staged against a dynamic field of anti-Semitic discourse. One of the most intriguing things about the Mendoza/Humphries fights is that this discourse changes across a relatively short time frame and that change can be registered by attending to spatial representation. The *Morning Chronicle's* brief account of the first fight at Odiham is the exception that proves the rule:

> The combatants, accompanied by their seconds and bottleholders, mounted the stage between one and two, and the context lasted for near twenty-five minutes before it was ended by Mendoza's giving out. In the early part of the combat Mendoza had apparently so much of the advantage, that bets were 100 to 70 in favour of Mendoza, but an unlucky blow driven in an unlucky place (under the left ear) changed the wagers completely, and made them 70 to 100 in favour of Humphries. Mendoza rose, but could not stand another blow, and complained of having sprained his leg; the consequence was, the battle was decided in favour or Humphries.[12]

As pugilistic reporting goes this is remarkably terse; in all the other papers a great deal is made of the space in which the fight took place, of the wet weather that severely impeded Humphries, of the controversial interruption of the fight by Humphries's second when it looked like Mendoza was going to win, of Humphries ostensible sportsmanship and of the horrible injuries sustained by both fighters. This anomalous report foregoes all of this material to focus attention on the gambling while at the same time eliminating all traces of the gamblers: the Fancy is quite literally ghosted in this report. This is also the case in all but one of the visual representations of the fight to which I will be turning shortly. Gillray's multiple illustrations of the event do not represent the audience.

This erasure is significant because as soon as the Fancy is spatially integrated into the scene – i.e. when they come into representation – the newspaper reports are permeated by anxiety:

> So high was the public anxiety on the issue of the bruising match which was decided yesterday, that neither the distance from town, nor the state of the

weather, could prevent a very large body of people from assembling at the scene of action in Odiham. Several hundreds of people paid half a guinea a piece to gain admission within the paddock where the stage was raised. The paddock was well defended against the multitude by Tring, Ryan, Dunn, and a number of the other of the strongest men in England, who with clubs looked like so many giants; but what can resist the shock of an English mob? The paddock was broken down, and the torrent rushed in.[13]

That this torrent of Englishmen quite literally engulfs Mendoza, his second, and his bottle holder – the only three Jews in this scene – fundamentally alters perception of the match. The intensity of the desire to see the fight testifies to the symbolic threat posed by Mendoza. Predictably, that threat requires repeated delineation and a carefully articulated opposition at the level of character:

> The Jew's stile of fighting was very different from that of his adversary. He fought low, and with cunning: with much dexterity, but without grace— While the look and attitudes of Humphries, continually presented those beauties which a Painter would have arrested every moment, to make them his own.[14]

The opposition between cunning and grace is matched elsewhere by assertions of Humphries's gallantry and of Mendoza's ostensible infringement of the rules. This latter issue is a point of some contention: both Gillray and the *Whitehall Evening Post* focus attention on the moment when Humphries's second Johnson interrupted the fight at a crucial moment and foiled Mendoza's victory. The fact that this controversy and the anxiety provoked by Mendoza remained unresolved instantiated the second fight.[15]

But I am more interested in how two key representations of the fight transcend the spatial specificity of the paddock near Odiham. Johann Heinrich Ramberg's elaborate satirical print entitled *The Triumph* was published seven days after the fight and its heroic treatment of Humphries would seem to enact the aestheticization articulated above (Figure 2). Seated on a chair and carried by the Prince of Wales, a drunken butcher, an alderman, and a grotesque sailor, Humphries's god-like body dominates what is essentially a triangular composition. Just as Humphries is elevated, Mendoza is cast down on the left among a group of conspicuously Jewish figures including a Rabbi who points to the recently converted George Gordon behind him. The representation of this bearded quartet is decidedly racist, but it is balanced by the no less aggressive representation of the Prince of Wales, George Hanger, and Major Topham on the right. The morals of this fashionable triumvirate were very much in question and

Figure 2   Johann Heinrich Ramberg, *The Triumph* (London, 1788) Engraving. Trustees of the British Museum.

it is no surprise to see them visually aligned both with the prostitute on the far right and the mob in the right background.[16] In light of the Prince's financial embarrassments, Dorothy George's argument that "The Prince and Hanger exult at the discomfiture of the Jews representing money-lenders" makes a great deal of sense, but I think it also moves too quickly to a specific reading of the image.[17] There is nothing explicitly aligning the Jewish figures with usury aside from their beards and the general sense of dissipation among Humphries's supporters isn't fully accounted for. The inscription below the image emphasizes that "there was a great Multitude, yea verily a mixed Multitude, & they rent the Air with shouts & Acclamations." The phrase "mixed Multitude" carries great weight here not only because it figures the blending of rank typical of the Fancy, but also because it resonates with the use of the phrase in Exodus 12:38. In Exodus, the "mixed Multitude" of slaves and mercenaries accompanies the tribes of Israel out of Egypt; in the terms set by this print it suggests that all of the constituencies figured beneath Humphries are blended together in a procession led not by Moses but by womanizers, scandal-mongers, and a failed soldier. The comparison is made to emphasize the very "unchosen" qualities of Humphries's supporters. This gains added significance when we remember that George III had personally endorsed the allegorical alignment of Britain and the Israelites by sponsoring the resuscitation of Handel's Israelite oratorios in the wake of the American War. The patriotic repertoire of the 1780s is replete with performances of fragments of *Israel in Egypt, Judas Maccabeus,* and *Saul* in concert halls, assembly rooms, theatres, and churches. Even if this image does not directly cite *Israel in Egypt,* the allegory remains operative and it indicates in no uncertain terms that the new Exodus figured here is mired in corruption.

Ramberg's satire makes two key substitutions. First, it replaces the paddock in Odiham with the allegorical space of Biblical Egypt. And that allegory replaces the Fancy with representative figures of fashionable dissipation. This has a fascinating effect on Humphries because his heroism and his scowl become multivalent. Although his pose and his glance distinguish him from Mendoza's sorry state, his heroism is radically undercut by his celebrants' appropriation of his celebrity. Ramberg's image both separates Humphries from and connects him to the corruption around him. In this regard, it perfectly captures the ambivalence of most representations of pugilism in the period: the image simultaneously celebrates Humphries as a scion of Christian/English manliness and links his "Triumph" to those most publicly aligned with the demise of Christian Britain. This is only re-enforced by the obvious visual comparison between the downcast figure Mendoza and Christ. The triumvirate of figures on the left is a parody of countless paintings of the Lamentation of Christ, and thus Ramberg's image not only predicts Mendoza's "resurrection," but also aligns Humphries and his supporters in the Fancy with Pilate and Judas.[18] Both Old Testament and New Testament allegories conjoin to radically complicate any notion of "Triumph."

At one level *The Triumph,* like much of the press, stereotypically differentiates Mendoza from Humphries in terms of of bodily representation. But this axis of differentiation, like the fight itself, is merely the pretext for a much more elaborate satire. The figural space of Ramberg's satire supplements the sociable space of the fight in a way that paradoxically highlights and attacks the integration of Jews and Christians in the Fancy. If, as Dorothy George suggests, the Prince and Hanger are celebrating because the money-lenders have been struck down, then the print is also arguing that fashionable society is dangerously unaware that such a victory is the very opposite of a triumph for the celebrants because it does nothing to mitigate their financial reliance on the defeated. To put it bluntly, the scowl on Humphries, face indicates that he and all of the other figures in this image cannot separate themselves from the Jews, in spite of his infamous declaration after the fight that "I have done the Jew and am in good health."[19]

Ramberg's print captures a host of social anxieties revolving around Mendoza's rise to prominence, but tilts the satire away from a mere derogation of Jewish upstarts to offer a wide-ranging social critique. In this regard it is merely elaborating on an earlier gesture published in the *Morning Herald* shortly after the fight:

> Of the little topics which occasionally agitate the public mind, few have excited more attention than the present combat. The known science of each antagonist—their muscular prowess, and their repeated victories, joined to the prevailing passion for this exercise, occasioned in the bosoms of numbers the most eager anxiety.
>
> But what is yet more whimsical—*Christianity* and *Judaism* were actually set in opposition to each other, and those who never thought of *religion* in any other shape, were interested for those who were supposed to champion the cause of their respective *creeds.*[20]

The assertion that the first Humphries/Mendoza fight had become a symbolic battle between Christian and Jew is hardly surprising, but the insinuation that this reading is "whimsical" and that the fighters have only a "supposed" relation to their creeds opens onto yet another allegorical displacement:

> But there were yet more substantial reasons for this anxiety, as *twenty-five thousand pounds* were actually staked on the issue of the combat, by the inhabitant's of *Duke's Place* only.[21]—Then "Tell it not in *Gath*—repeat it not in the streets of *Askelon*"—the victory has fallen to the share of the *Christian!*[22]

The passage in quotation marks is a double allusion, both to 2 Samuel 1:20 and to the "Elegy for Saul and Jonathan" from the third act of Handel's *Saul*. Charles Jennens's libretto takes a rather confusing and repetitive narrative from Samuel and re-fashions it into a highly dramatic tragedy. Saul's jealousy of David's martial success instantiates a return to madness and at his lowest point Saul attempts to kill his own son Jonathan. Having averted that horrible fate, Saul regains sanity, recognizes his hubris, but nonetheless continues to pursue David, this time with the assistance of the Witch of Endor. The witch summons the ghost of the prophet Samuel who foretells Saul's death at the hands of the Amalekites because he disobeyed God in an earlier conflict with Amelekites in which he was enjoined to slaughter the remaining survivors as a sacrifice to God. Saul is killed in a battle on Mount Gilboa, and the bodies of Saul and Jonathan are carried in to the strains of the Dead March. It is at this moment that David interrogates Saul's killer, who turns out to be an Amalekite.

As Ruth Smith has demonstrated, the death of Saul at the hand of the Amalekite takes on very specific resonances, because in scripture the

Amalekites, like the French, are the eternal and permanent enemies of Britain's proxy the Israelites. But in this case, Saul's wounds are largely self-inflicted: the Amalekite only finishes off the job and his function is to fulfill Samuel's prophecy. The upshot here is, as Ruth Smith argues, "even God's anointed cannot escape the consequences of breaking God's Law."²³ Smith has demonstrated that at the time of *Saul*'s composition the allegory was used to chastise Walpole's abuses of government and to figure forth a return to the patriotic ideals of Liberty and just governance associated with the Glorious Revolution. I have argued that the same allegory was reactivated during the Handel Commemoration of 1784 in order to critique the mishandling of the American war and to inaugurate a new era for British imperial fantasy.²⁴

The repetition of this same ideological construction informs the *Morning Herald's* invocation of these specific lines, but it alters the terms of the allegory. In Samuel, David laments the death of Saul as follows:

> The beauty of Israel is slain upon thy high places: how are the mighty fallen!
> Tell *it* not in Gath, publish *it* not in the streets of Askelon; lest the daughters of the Philistines rejoice; lest the daughters of the uncircumcised triumph.

Since Mendoza is firmly aligned with Saul, the speaking voice of the passage in the *Morning Herald* takes on the mantle of David trying to avert the celebrations of the Philistines/Christians. This has the curious effect of not only rehabilitating Mendoza's greatness, but also aligning Humphries with the Amalekite and thus subtly separating him from the "Christians" who would celebrate his victory. In both Samuel and in *Saul*, David has the Amalekite executed on the spot as an "Impious wretch, of race accurst! / And of all that race the worst!." By triangulating the allegorical scenario, the *Morning Herald* condemns Humphries and those who would celebrate his victory because they have lifted their sword against the anointed. In terms of the patriotic allegory appropriated from Handel and redeployed here, the Amalekite and those who gain from his victory – i.e. the "Christian" Fancy – are ejected from the space of patriotic fantasy to become the embodiment of Britain's enemy. This is why the report proactively undermines the Fancy's claim to Christian virtue. Humphries and the Fancy suddenly find themselves in the position traditionally occupied by France. The point is I believe clear. The *Morning Herald* is stating in no uncertain terms that this social entity is an internal threat to Britain no less dangerous than the Amalekites across the English Channel.

The allegorical re-territorialization of the fight in the *Morning Herald* and in Ramberg's *The Triumph* demonstrates the immense disease with the mixed sociability of the Fancy. That this discomfort is registered through a spatial transposition from the ring to the phantasmatic spaces of Mount Gilboa and Egypt that were so crucial to the ongoing patriotic utility of Handel's Israelite oratorios indicates that the anxiety activated by the Mendoza/Humphries fight was deeply connected to concerns that Britain's ruling elite were once again devolving into the corrupt entity that failed the nation so miserably in the American war.

But this critique also allowed for Mendoza's partial rehabilitation. The alignment of Mendoza and Saul is telling because David's interpretation of Saul's demise in both Samuel and in *Saul* emphasizes that he was great in spite of the ferocity that threatened to undermine him. And his greatness was sealed by David's succession. In a sense this is precisely what happens to Mendoza in the mediation of the second and third fights. When he beats Humphries at Stilton in May of 1789, all the associations with cunning, deception and ferocity – i.e. the very characteristics of Saul – dissolve to be replaced with encomiums to his "art" – i.e. to his David-like accomplishments. Even the most anti-Semitic report concludes by placing Mendoza firmly on the human side of the opposition between art and animality:

> Among the events of this week, we must mention that the Jew Mendoza has grievously beaten, bruised, and insulted the Christian Humphries. This is accounted one of the triumphs of art over brutal force and animal courage.[25]

The equivocation registered in the word "accounted" can't be denied, but the reporting of the second fight elsewhere in the press is decidedly neutral in its treatment of ethnicity and creed. The papers simply describe the rounds without any explicit slurs or complex allegorical gambits.

This is not to say that anti-Semitism disappears, but rather that it becomes less rhetorically active. Significantly, the assymmetrical sociability of the event itself remains the same – Mendoza and his Jewish seconds are spatially isolated in a sea of Christian onlookers – and the betting remains in favor of Humphries largely because of his ethnicity. The crowd for this fight was double that of the first bout and "about ten rows of seats in an octagon shape were built for the company, which was from 1000 to 1200 persons; the spectators ascended a ladder to the top row, and the combatants only were admitted at a door underneath."[26] This immediate audience is also augmented by the mediated national audience of the daily press whose addressees are assumed to be uniformly Christian. But the press also imagines a supplemental spatial regime and an auxiliary form of mediation, one that links the space of the fight to the very heart of Jewish London:

> A carrier pigeon was sent off with the intelligence to Duke's Place; and it
> was somewhat remarkable, that not above two or three of the tribe of
> Abraham were observed to bear testimony to the victory of their brother of
> the beard.[27]

This self-conscious representation of a communicative act between the
Jews in Mendoza's company and those in East London posits a form of
mediated ethnic sociability that in many ways presages Mendoza's entry
into the public sphere of print.

It is in the wake of his victory in Stilton that Mendoza publishes *The Art
of Boxing* and explicitly argues that his system of boxing is not only a
healthy exercise, but also "a national mode of combat, and is as peculiar to
the inhabitants of this country as fencing to the French."[28] As Whale
argues, Mendoza's text is riven on the one hand by the opposing claims of
brutality and art or system, and on the other by the opposing tasks of
explaining the "science" and vindicating his own conduct in handling the
public dispute with his arch-rival Humphries. As he states,

> This second mode of personal vindication is characteristically couched in terms
> of propriety of behavior and in the furtherance of an attack on extant forms of
> social "prejudice." From a wider perspective, therefore, Mendoza's Jewishness
> might thus be said to accommodate itself to and contribute to the production
> of a developing version of British identity which would later replicate itself in
> an even more dominant imperial guise because of its contribution to a
> regulated, sanitized and rule-governed version of a dangerous sport.[29]

What we see across the mediation of the Mendoza/Humphries fights is a
shift in the function of prejudice. In the reporting of the first fight,
Mendoza is the subject of predictable anti-Semitic representation, but
his Jewishness also provides a discursive assemblage to derogate the Fancy.
When he defeats Humphries, the direct attacks on his ethnicity abate and
he strangely becomes the scion of a new kind of rational masculinity
associated with "British liberality." He quite literally becomes the Jew
whose Jewishness is overlooked in a self-serving fantasy of toleration.

This is amplified during the third fight at Doncaster because Mendoza
showed remarkable restraint when he had clearly destroyed Humphries.
All of the press and the visual images arising from this fight focus on
Mendoza's remarkable acts of "humanity":

> Several times when, in the act of closing Humphries was about to fall, he
> prevented him by holding him round the neck with one hand; and lifting
> the other in the air for some moments proved to his antagonist and the
> spectators what he had it in his power to do,—when, instead of striking the
> decisive blow, he let him down gently and carefully, without the least hurt,

to the ground. This action was more to be admired, as one stroke given at such a moment, would have ended the battle immediately; and Mendoza was much and deservedly applauded for it by all parties.[30]

In these acts of staged mercy Mendoza becomes the anti-Shylock, and in so doing makes a crucial intervention in the ethnic imaginary of Georgian Britain. The fact that this act of mercy is repeated again and again throughout the latter phases of the fight should give us pause, for it is a pedagogical performance. It is as though Mendoza is fighting not only against Humphries, but also against the cultural legacy of Macklin's performance whose very repetition required multiple acts of mercy on Mendoza's part to become visible.

If this seems like an over-theatricalization of Mendoza's performance, we need only look to Egan's account of the fight roughly twenty-five years later in the popular *Boxiana* series:

> Mendoza, in conquering so noble and distinguished a competitor, added considerable fame to his pugilistic achievements; but the greatest merit attached to the conquest was the manner in which it was obtained. Prejudice so frequently distorts the mind, that, unfortunately, good actions are passed over without even common respect; more especially when they appear in any person who may chance to of a *different* COUNTRY, *persuasion,* or *colour*. MENDOZA, in being a Jew, did not stand in so favourable a point of view, respecting the wishes of the multitude towards his success, as his brave opponent—the feelings are somewhat raised when we read:–
>
> > You may as well go stand upon the beach,
> > And bid the main flood 'bate his usual height;
> > You may as well use questions with the wolf,
> > Why he hath made the ewe bleat for the lamb;
> > You may as well forbid the mountain pines
> > To wag their high tops, and to make no noise,
> > When they are fretted with the gusts of heaven;
> > You may as well do any thing most hard,
> > As seek to soften (than which what's harder)
> > His Jewish heart!
>
> But truth riseth superior to all things, and the humanity of MENDOZA was conspicuous throughout the above fight—often was it witnessed that he threw up his arm when he might have put in a most tremendous blow upon his exhausted adversary, who perceiving that the victory was certain, nobly disdained to hear it observed,
>
> > —'Tis a cruelty
> > To load a falling man.[31]

I've quoted this passage at length because it brings the derogation of the Fancy articulated during the first fight to its logical conclusion. Egan now deploys Antonio's speech from Act IV scene I of *The Merchant of Venice* to characterize the corruption and the anti-Semitism of the Fancy. Ramberg's insinuation of dissipation has progressed to the point where the Fancy hides its hatred behind a veil of Christian propriety. As damning as this is, Egan still casts Mendoza as Shylock, but this is not *The Merchant of Venice* as performed by Macklin, or his notable successors Tom King or George Cooke. It is rather the new version of the play and the part associated after 1814 with Edmund Kean.[32] Kean's more sympathetic interpretation of Shylock, which foregrounded the moral shortcomings of the Christian characters to provide a rationale for Shylock's malevolence, has provided Egan with a script for comprehending Mendoza's historical significance.[33] Significantly, this redeployment of Shylock and the question of mercy, like the invocation of the debate on mercy between Cranmer, Gardiner and Cromwell in the fifth act of *Henry VIII*, accords human frailty and aggressivity to the combatants, the observers and their allegorical doubles.[34] But it also argues that it is these very prejudices that need to be overcome to consolidate a fantasy of national election and masculine efficacy. Egan's subtle appropriation of Kean's performance allows us to see, somewhat belatedly, the complexity of Mendoza's self-stylization, for like Kean, Mendoza had to enact Shylock's threatening alterity in order to indict the anti-Semitism that thoroughly surrounded the immediate and the mediate space of the ring. This is another way of saying that Mendoza had to be both dangerous and human in order to counter the repertoire of ethnic hatred.

Covent Garden Synagogue

That Mendoza continued to be lauded by Egan in the 1820s is remarkable because the fighter's reputation was thoroughly damaged by his part in the OP Riots of 1809. The riots and their cultural significance have been the subject of extensive scholarly enquiry, but I will be focusing on the outpouring of anti-Semitic performance following Kemble's decision to issue orders for Mendoza, Dutch Sam, and other boxers to keep order in the pit. As Marc Baer argues, gesturing to E.P. Thompson's arguments about the moral economy of the crowd, the OP disturbances were directed at Kemble's innovations in pricing and seating. On the opening of the new Covent Garden Theatre in September, audience members protested the imposition of new prices, the sale of private boxes, and the employment of the Italian singer Madame Catalani. Because Drury Lane had recently burned down the rise in prices was objected to because the Licensing Act gave Kemble a monopoly. The private boxes became a flashpoint because the maintenance of private entrances not only led to charges of immoral behavior, but also to objections to the privatization of what was by law a national institution. And Madame Catalani became the object of explicitly ethnocentric slurs. All through September this complex combination of nativist rhetoric, moral outrage, and national fantasy coalesced into increasing acts of disorder in the theatre itself that predictably dominated the press. By the end of the month modes of performance, including the OP dance, had solidified into recognizable forms of cultural resistance. Kemble's arguments that the changes were necessary on financial grounds were vindicated by an external committee and ignored by the rioters.

On October 6, the Jewish boxers made their first appearance in the pit and suddenly a fourth element to the conflict permeated both the theatre and the print media. All through October, audience members in the galleries started hanging placards and distributing handbills with anti-Semitic mottos and epigrams. Expressions such as "Turn out the Jews"; "Oppose Shylock and the whole tribe of Israel"; "Shall Britons be subdued by the wandering tribe of Israel?"; "The Covent Garden Synagogue, Mendoza the Grand Rabbi"; "Genius of Britain support our cause / Free us from Kemble and Jewish laws" were now displayed in the theatre, printed in the press and integrated into visual representations of the conflict. Notably many of these placards explicitly separate England or Britain from the figural construct of the proxy Israelites, nowhere more forcefully than in the following placard: "And lo! It came to pass, that John Bull was sorely vexed, and smote the Israelites."[35] This earlier patriotic allegory, so active in the 1780s and early 1790s, was now obsolete. Kemble's action had activated an anti-Semitic firestorm.

As Baer and others have argued, the OP riots generated complex modes of performance that traversed all the regions of the playhouse. The very performativity of the rioters, referred to as OPs, often matched or overwhelmed the performances on-stage. Furthermore, the events in the pit were regularly mediated as if they were theatrical productions. The blurring of the boundary between theatrical and pugilistic performance seen in the first part of this essay now operates in reverse. For example, shortly after the introduction of the boxers to the pit, the press started issuing faux-advertisements for a new "Tragic-Comedy" entitled *Hockley in the Hole* with "Principal characters by Messrs. Mendoza, Belcher, Gregson, Cribb, Will Perry, Harry Lee, Dutch Sam, Solly, Richmond, and Pittone" (*Theatrical Examiner*, 53). There is much to be said about the way that a theatrical genre is being used to mediate social unrest, but it has rarely been remarked that the list of "performers" here cuts across a broad swath of pugilistic fame. The list incorporates Jews, Italians, displaced African Americans *and* icons of English loyalty such as Cribb, Gregson and Belcher. This is significant because the public reaction to the new "pugilistic sociability" of the pit was directed solely at Mendoza and Dutch Sam: in this strange arena before the stage, all pugilists became Jews, and they became the ethnic other around which a particularly resistant fantasy of John Bull coalesced.

This performative economy was more than figural. Michael Ragussis has recently drawn attention to an incident where one of the OP sympathizers, dressed as a Rabbi, was ritually ejected from the theatre.[36] The turning out of actual Jewish audience members ensued on other occasions. As he argues, both the call for and the enactment of expulsion reprise not only the media storm that surrounded the ill-fated Jewish Naturalization Act of 1753, but also the historical act of Jewish exclusion after the Edict of Expulsion in 1290. However, the mock-Rabbi warrants our attention because the audience was constructing a form of Jewish identity manifestly at odds with the Jewish pugilists in the pit. As the *Covent Garden Journal* reports, the audience member playing the Rabbi "suffered himself to be pushed about the pit, by his companions, without betraying the slightest symptoms of displeasure. While he was the object of attack, many exclaimed 'a Jew! a Jew! turn him out.' The sham Israelite kept up the deception until he was quite exhausted."[37] By emphasizing the passivity and the silence of the mock-Rabbi, the *Covent Garden Journal* is constructing a fantasy of Jewishness in direct opposition to Mendoza's persona. As we have seen, Mendoza's celebrity is directly tied to his ability to defend himself both physically in the ring and verbally in the press.[38] All through the month of October 1809, the press regularly reports on the violence of the Jewish pugilists both inside and outside the theatre and carefully tracks the fate of various affidavits issued by Mendoza defending his conduct. This effectively rehearsed the collocation in the press twenty years before of accounts of Mendoza's fights and of his printed rebuttals to various insinuations during his rivalry with Humphries. These printed statements were eventually collected in *The Art of Boxing* and make up a considerable part of his *Memoirs*. The mock-Rabbi is not just any Jew; he is the anti-Mendoza.

What we are witnessing here is a step-by-step dismantling of Mendoza's secular persona. If the mock-Rabbi can be best understood as a reversion from the manly pugilist who warrants respect for his courage and defensive "science" to an earlier effeminate and notably religious stereotype, then we

Figure 3   George Cruikshank, *Killing no Murder* (London, 1809) Engraving. Trustees of
the British Museum.

can detect other forms of regression in the OP archive. Perhaps the most
revealing is Cruikshank's famous print *Killing no Murder* (Figure 3) The
print shows Dutch Sam, Mendoza, and other bruisers assaulting well-
dressed audience members in the pit while other non-combatants look
on from the orchestra and the lower boxes. Like so many satires from the
period, its meaning is multivalent. The title is taken from a famous
seventeenth-century pamphlet arguing for the assassination of Oliver
Cromwell. That text argued that killing Cromwell was not murder because
it would constitute an act of loyalty to rightful monarchy. If we were to
read the title without irony then the print would appear to be arguing, as
Kemble did, that the actions of the bruisers were justified because the OPs
were challenging the status quo and thus were seditious. But this reading
of the title is complicated by the violence of the image itself and by the un-
decidable politics of the OPs. As Marc Baer argues,

> The ideology of the OPs and their supporters does not exactly conform
> either to radical or conservative positions . . . In comparison to radical
> theory, OPs held not to a progressive but instead a backward-looking model
> of English society; yet the contemporary radical notion of the popular

convention was much in evidence in their dealings with Kemble. They praised the British constitution and monarchy . . . But their attitudes towards law and order, the rights of majorities, and protection of private property were anything but conservative.[39]

The Cruikshank print demonstrates that the amalgamation of loyalist ideology and revolutionary praxis exhibited by the OPs constitutes a disturbing, because unreadable, form of sociability. In many ways, the disease with the social heterogeneity of the OPs is reminiscent of the anxiety regarding the "mixed multitude" of the Fancy. Kemble's strategy was to deploy the bruisers in a way that activated the same kind of critique of "mixed" disorder that accompanied much of the reporting of pugilism.

Notably, the ambivalent representation of the OPs in *Killing no Murder* does not extend to Mendoza or the two armed-figures who flank him. The man in the centre of the image, who may or may not be Dutch Sam, is savagely beating a medal-wearing OP with a club; to his immediate right, Mendoza kneels on the chest of his well-dressed victim and states "Down down to H__l with all OPs & say t'was Dan that sent thee there." To the right of Mendoza is a man identified by Dorothy George as a sewerman brandishing two bones astride an unconscious gentleman. These two lower-class ruffians framing Mendoza serve to exacerbate the horror of both his actions and his words. But there is something much more inflammatory going on here. Mendoza is separated from his murderous associates at the level of costume; he is dressed like a fashionable gentleman, but not just any fashionable gentleman. Like many of the satirical images of Kemble during the riots, the actor manager's "Roman" nose is being transformed into Mendoza's "Jewish" profile.[40] The pugilist and the actor are one in this image. It is also notable that Mendoza is using his fists: like Kemble, this is a man revered for turning performance into a scientific art. At one level to unite Kemble and Mendoza in the same figure literalizes the relationship between management and muscle, but it also asks us to consider their interchangeability. What about these two men is commutable? The answer to this complex question lies on the bench next to Mendoza in this print, the plangent object around which the entire scene of violence revolves. I am referring of course to Mendoza's knife.

The knife was the crucial prop in Macklin's performance of Shylock and here Cruikshank returns us to the very phantasmatic scene that Mendoza had resolutely attempted to obviate in the third fight against Humphries. In the earlier fight, Mendoza's victim, to quote Dorothy George's gloss of this print, is "at the mercy of his assailant"; now there is no question of mercy.[41] With the knife near at hand, this Mendoza has reverted to the condition of the murderous Shylock that dominated the London stage prior to the advent of Kean in 1814. What is so striking here is how this replicates the reversion exhibited in the performance of the mock-Rabbi. Mendoza is being refigured as an earlier avatar of Jewishness. Just as the former performance suppressed Mendoza's masculine efficacy and reconstructed a fantasy of Jewish passivity, this rendering of Mendoza reconstitutes all the malevolence and ferocity of Shylock. This two-pronged re-invention of Mendoza is crucial because it so rigorously moves backwards in time. In the era following the third fight with Humphries, Mendoza is the ideological face of ongoing integration of Jewish and Christian communities during this period. His successes in the ring were marshaled to construct a fantasy of universal British courage and martial skill. But here precisely the opposite procedure is underway. Mendoza is returned to earlier stereotypes and his "positive" qualities are slowly migrated to the emergent entity of John Bull. He now becomes both the source and the foil for this national fantasy.

This movement backwards away from Mendoza's persona of the 1790s toward earlier manifestations of Jewishness culminated in a remarkable act of programming on Kemble's part. Although violent acts continued for the duration of the riots, the Jewish pugilists' role was largely done by the end of October. As one letter writer to the *Morning Chronicle* bemoaned: "the Jews are routed, the Constables are almost, [sic] wearied out, all seems at length to yield to the voice of justice, why are the Managers still obstinate? . . . "[42] Actual violence in the pit was largely replaced by mock-battles, but anti-Semitic vitriol was disseminated in all media well through November and December. As noted above, many of the placards displayed in the theatre not only aligned Kemble with Jewishness, but also specifically referred to Kemble as Shylock.[43] Even as late as November 20, this equation is being made." . . . very few of the pitites [sic] wore the O.P.; an opposition medal had in a great measure usurped its place; it is about the size of a crown piece, the front represents Mr. KEMBLE as the 'Jew that SHAKESPEARE drew;' on the reverse were inscribed the letters O. P. O. B. D. T. P. O."[44] This adaptation of Pope's famous epigram on Macklin's performance of Shylock from 1741 gives us some sense of the degree to which earlier moments in the repertoire proliferated through the ethnoscape at this moment.

But just prior to the Royal Jubilee on October 25, Kemble himself tried to break the figural linkage between himself, Mendoza and Shylock, and he did so in a particularly revealing fashion. He decided to mount *The Merchant of Venice* and Sheridan's *The Duenna* for successive performances on October 18 and 19. In the face of the outpouring of anti-Semitic rhetoric and performance in the house, the staging of the two most anti-Semitic plays in the repertoire could be read as either foolhardy or cynical. However, I believe Kemble was actively extricating himself from association with Mendoza by using the repertoire not only to align himself with Antonio, but also to reconfigure Mendoza first as Shylock and then as Isaac Mendoza. As we will see, this latter move is not at all distant in its objective from the performance of the mock-Rabbi in the pit.

In order to understand this, it is helpful to look at Kemble's relation to the play's performance history. As we have seen, Macklin played Shylock at Covent Garden when Kemble first came to the stage. As Shattuck states, when Kemble went to Drury Lane Theatre in 1783, Shylock belonged to the actor Tom King except for a brief period when King was absent. For the rest of his time at Drury Lane, Kemble played Bassanio. "When Kemble took over management of Covent Garden in 1803, he wisely ceded Shylock to George Frederick Cooke, and he flattered this formidable employee-rival further by supporting him in the role of Antonio"[45] Cooke was brilliant in the part and maintained the legacy of Macklin's performance: "his features are thoughtful, bold and marked, and calculated to give the expression of scorn, envy, hatred, brutal ferocity and overbearing pride with unrivalled force and effect.[46]

On the evening of October 18, 1783, Kemble stood before the raucous house as the threatened Christian character and Cooke took on the mantle of Jewish malevolence: "In *The Merchant of Venice*, which, with *Who Wins? or, the Widow's Choice*, was last night performed, Mr. COOKE gave a masterly delineation of the vindictive Jew and the Play went on in a very flattering manner till towards the close of the third act, when the performances of the evening were first interrupted by hisses; and the half price commending shortly after increased the uproar."[47] The importance of Kemble's distancing of himself from Shylock should not be underestimated because as we have seen it also amounts to an attempt to dissociate himself from Mendoza and other pugilists still in his employ. However, as a performative strategy it was no doubt hindered by the performative economy of the riots themselves, for the now standard practice of drowning out the mainpiece at half-price entry meant that the all important scenes where Shylock enacts his ferocity and Antonio declares that it is impossible to "soften his Jewish heart" were obliterated:

> *The Merchant of Venice* was played last night; but whether COOKE in *Shylock* was the Jew that SHAKESPEARE drew, or any other Jew, it was

impossible to ascertain, the performers who played the characters, hissers, groaners, c. being determined that themselves alone should be heard, particularly in the last two acts.[48]

Kemble's attempted dissociation relied on a simultaneous return to the script of Shakespeare's play and to the state of decorum necessary for its effective production. It would seem that the audience and the press was happy to re-insert Mendoza into the role of Shylock; but Kemble's attempt to migrate to the position of Antonio would take considerable time to unfold.

A similar blockage occurred during the subsequent night's performance of *The Duenna*:

> The bulletin of the *Row* last night was 'Much the same.' The performances were *The Duenna*, the last act of which was converted into Pantomime, and *All the World's a Stage*, of which not a single word was heard. The latter was pretty accurately exemplified in the house, where the greater part of the audience were, as usual, active performers. The house, towards the conclusion of the Opera, and throughout the whole of the Farce, was fully equal to that of any former night. The Gentlemen of the Pit devised a new mode of amusement; during the performance of the Farce, they formed circles, and had several mock battles.[49]

The shift from the *Merchant of Venice* to *The Duenna* is replete with significance here. If staging the former play constitutes an attempt to re-position Mendoza back in the role of Shylock in order for Kemble to emerge as the victim Antonio, mounting *The Duenna* effectively replaces the cultural threat embodied by Shylock in the post-Macklin era with a return to performances of the Jew as the inefficacious buffoon. The character of Isaac Mendoza in Sheridan's opera is a fool who thinks he can outwit the Christian characters around him. In this regard he is very proximate to Shylock as the role was performed in the pre-Macklin era by comedians like Thomas Doggett who played the role in Granville's adaptation *The Jew of Venice*.

If we see the staging of the *Merchant of Venice* and *The Duenna* as a response to the anti-Semitism of the OP riots, then Kemble's action is primarily one of dissociation. He reconstructs the threat ostensibly posed by the Jewish pugilists by returning the most famous of them to the most harmless and defenseless of his stereotypical precursors. Mendoza the merciful and rational pugilist is aligned first with the malevolent and unmerciful Shylock perfected by Macklin and replicated by Cooke and then subsequently downgraded to the condition of his namesake, Isaac

Mendoza – a farcical buffoon more suitable to the pre-Macklin representation of Jews on the London stage. In this light, what we see here is the active dismemberment of all that Mendoza endeavored to symbolize in the wake of the Humphries fights. However, this derogation of Mendoza by the OPs, by the press, and finally by Kemble was ultimately enacted in the name of a mystified loyalty. The figural regression of Mendoza's public persona to an earlier cultural construct left behind an all important residue of "masculine liberality" that was immediately cannibalized by the amorphous entity of John Bull. In contrast to the way that liberal sentiment was retroactively manifested in Pierce Egan's deployment of Shakespearean literariness in his account of the Mendoza/Humphries fights, Kemble here is attempting to use the repertoire to exculpate himself. He is less successful than Egan because Egan can rely on the restricted economy of print; Kemble's rhetorical gambit takes place in real time and perhaps most importantly is embedded in the social space of the Covent Garden Theatre and is thus beyond his absolute dominion.

Notes

1 See Julie Carlson, "Hazlitt and the Sociability of the Theatre" in *Romantic Sociability: Social Networks and Literary Culture in Britain, 1770–1840*, ed. Gillian Russell and Clara Tuite (Cambridge: Cambridge University Press, 2002), pp. 145–65 and my *Staging Governance: Theatrical Imperialism in London, 1770–1800* (Baltimore, MD: Johns Hopkins University Press), pp. 1–42.

2 For a compelling analysis of boxing discourse as itself performative, see David Snowdon, "Drama *Boxiana*: Spectacle and Theatricality in Pierce Egan's Pugilistic Writing" *Romanticism on the Net*, 46 (May 2007).

3 See, for example, John Bee [John Badcock], *Slang. A Dictionary of the Turf, the Ring, the Chase, Pit, of Bon-ton, and Varieties of Life, Forming the Completest and Most Authentic Lexicon Balatronicum . . . of the Sporting World* (London, 1823) and his *Sportsman's Slang; a New Dictionary* (London, 1825). The daily papers also published brief lexicons; see for example *The Pilot*, October 10, 1811.

4 Michael Ragussis, *Theatrical Nation: Jews and Other Outlandish Englishmen in Georgian England* (Philadelphia, PA: University of Pennsylvania Press, 2010), pp. 24 and 43–45.

5 Daniel O'Quinn, "In the Face of Difference: Molineaux, Cribb, and the Violence of the Fancy," in *Race, Romanticism, and the Atlantic*, ed. Paul Youngquist (London: Ashgate, 2013). See also John Whale, "'Imperfect Sympathies': The Early Nineteenth-Century Formation of Responses to Black Fighters in Britain," *Moving Worlds* 12.1 (2012), 5–18.

6 Diana Taylor, *The Archive and the Repertoire: Performing Cultural Memory in the Americas* (Durham, NC: Duke University Press, 2003), pp. 20–21.

7 Frank Felsenstein, *Anti-Semitic Stereotypes: A Paradigm of Otherness in English Popular Culture, 1660–1830* (Baltimore, MD: The Johns Hopkins University Press, 1999), p. 171.

8 See Ragussis, *Theatrical Nation*, pp. 43–86 for a thorough discussion of Macklin's capacity for ethnic masquerade.

9 See Felsenstein, *Anti-Semitic Stereotypes*, pp. 229–31, and Todd M. Endelman, *The Jews of Georgian England*, (Philadelphia, PA: University of Pennsylvania Press, 1979), pp. 219–23.

10 John Whale, "Daniel Mendoza's Contests of Identity: Masculinity, Ethnicity and Nation in Georgian Prize-Fighting," *Romanticism* 14.3 (2008), 259–71.

11 This argument recurs frequently in the highly self-conscious writing on boxing in the period. See for example the cancellation and re-inscription of Molineaux's racial difference in "The Sable School of Pugilism" in "Boxiana No. VIII," *Blackwood's* 8 (October 1820), 64.

12 *Morning Chronicle and London Advertiser*, January 10, 1788.

13 *London Chronicle*, January 8–10, 1788.

14 *The World*, January 10, 1788.

15 This is typical of many interracial fights: perceived infractions or infringements of the rules become flashpoints where the representation of racial, ethnic, or cultural differences is most pointed and least susceptible to rhetorical control. See my "In the Face of Difference" for a discussion of how this played out in the Cribb/Molineaux contests.

16 *Pancratia* frequently reports the presence of the Prince of Wales and Hanger at the fights; see for example 79.

17 M. Dorothy George, *Catalogue of Prints and Drawings in the British Museum: Division I: Political and Personal Satires* (London: British Museum, 1938), vol. VI, p. 552.

18 Ramberg's rendering of Mendoza's figure is almost a direct copy of Van Dyck's 1634 *Lamentation of Christ*.

19 *Pancratia, or a History of Pugilism* (London: W. Hildyard, 1812), p. 77.

20 *Morning Herald*, January 10, 1788.

21 The home of the Great Synagogue, Duke's Place was the epicenter of Jewish London.

22 *Morning Herald*, January 10, 1788.

23 Ruth Smith, *Handel's Oratorio's and Eighteenth-Century Thought*, (Cambridge: Cambridge University Press, 1995), p. 331.

24 Daniel O'Quinn, *Entertaining Crisis in the Atlantic Imperium, 1770–1800* (Baltimore, MD: The Johns Hopkins University Press, 2011), p. 315–24.

25 *Whitehall Evening Post*, May 7–9, 1789.

26 *Morning Post and Daily Advertiser*, May 8, 1789.

27 *General Evening Post*, May 7–9, 1789.

28 Daniel Mendoza, *The Art of Boxing* (London: 1789), p. vii.

29 Whale, "Daniel Mendoza's Contests of Identity," p. 265.

30 *Diary, or Woodfall's Register*, October 2, 1790.

31 Pierce Egan, *Boxiana, or Sketches of Ancient and Modern Pugilism* (London, 1829) vol. I, p. 265–66.

32 See *Morning Chronicle,* January 27, 1814, for a description of how Kean's noted volatility rendered "the conflict of passions arising out of the contrast of [Shylock's] situation."

33 See Judith W. Page, "'Hath Not a Jew Eyes?'": Edmund Kean and the Sympathetic Shylock," *Wordsworth Circle* 34.2 (2003), 216–19.

34 *Henry VIII* was one of the center-pieces for patriotic performance in the period.

35 *Morning Chronicle,* October 11, 1809.

36 Ragussis, *Theatrical Nation,* p. 121.

37 *Covent Garden Journal* (London, 1810), p. 232.

38 The remark on exhaustion clinches the opposition because Mendoza was famous for his endurance.

39 Marc Baer, *Theatre and Disorder in Late Georgian London*, (Oxford: Clarendon Press, 1992), p. 86.

40 Ibid., p. 216.

41 M. Dorothy George, *Catalogue,* vol. VIII, p. 874.

42 *Morning Chronicle,* October 30, 1809.

43 See for example the *Morning Chronicle,* October 12, 1809.

44 *Morning Post,* November 20, 1809.

45 Charles H. Shattuck, "Introduction to Shakespeare's *Merchant of Venice,*" *John Philip Kemble Promptbooks,* 11 vols. (Charlottesville, VA: University of Virginia Press, 1974), vol. VI, p. i.

46 Quoted in A. Hare, *The Eighteenth-Century English Stage,* p. 130. See Desmond Shaw-Taylor, "Eighteenth-Century Performances of Shakespeare Recorded in the Theatrical Portraits of the Garrick Club," in *Shakespeare Survey 51, Shakespeare in the Eighteenth Century,* ed. Stanley Wells (Cambridge: Cambridge University Press, 1998), pp. 107–24.

47 *Morning Post,* October 20, 1809.

48 *Morning Chronicle,* October 20, 1809.

49 *Morning Post,* October 21, 1809.

CHAPTER 5

Fashionable Subjects
Exhibition Culture and the Limits of Sociability
Paul Keen

If, as Harriet Guest has noted, "in recent years some of the most exciting work on late eighteenth- and early nineteenth-century British cultures has focused on issues of sociability," this may in part be a result of the enormous force that the idea of sociability enjoyed in the age itself, both as a description of what Peter Clark has called the "associational" nature of modern life and as an ideal against which those relations might be judged.[1] This popularity may, in turn, have been at least partially the result of the ability of the idea of sociability to offer people a way of mediating a profound sense of change with inherited codes of distinction. Whether one embraced the transformational power of commerce as progress or lamented it as a sure sign of decline, few truths were more widely acknowledged. This sense of almost tectonic change simultaneously foregrounded the question of how Britain's emerging social order could best be understood and organized, and heightened the enduring appeal of traditional value systems. The idea of sociability was crucial to both, or more accurately it was crucial because it allowed people to have it both ways, though this very elasticity inevitably created problems of its own. The fluid and contested nature of this changing discursive topography is dramatically foregrounded in the particular claims that were associated with some of the most popular attractions in the early 1780s, which I will turn to in the second half of this paper: the self-described "scientific" lectures of Gustavus Katterfelto, the unique mixture of sexual promise and social distraction offered by James Graham's Temple of Health and Hymen, the performing wonders of the Learned Pig, and, perhaps most of all, the ballooning craze that caught hold of almost everyone's imagination following the first flight ever in 1783 and the first flight in Britain the following year. As the intense mixed reaction to each of these examples makes clear, the extraordinary popularity of these attractions helped to unsettle the very forms of sociability that they seemed to promise.

I want to begin to think about both the multiple roles that the idea of sociability played within these debates and the problems that were an unavoidable part of these roles by way of a fairly long passage from David Hume's essay "Of Refinement in the Arts," an account of a process of urbanization driven by improvements in the mechanical and liberal arts that marks a high point in eighteenth-century tributes to the promise of sociability:

> The more these refined arts advance, the more sociable men become: nor is it possible, that, when enriched with science, and possessed of a fund of conversation, they should be contented to remain in solitude, or live with their fellow-citizens in that distant manner, which is peculiar to ignorant and barbarous nations. They flock into cities; love to receive and communicate knowledge; to show their wit or their breeding; their taste in conversation or living, in clothes or furniture. Curiosity allures the wise; vanity the foolish; and pleasure both. Particular clubs and societies are every where formed: Both sexes meet in an easy and sociable manner; and the tempers of men, as well as their behaviour, refine apace. So that, beside the improvements which they receive from knowledge and the liberal arts, it is impossible but they must feel an increase in humanity, from the very habit of conversing together, and contributing to each other's pleasure and entertainment. Thus *industry, knowledge,* and *humanity,* are linked together by an indissoluble chain, and are found, from experience as well as reason, to be peculiar to the more polished and, what are commonly denominated, the more luxurious nations.[2]

Modernity, in this account, is a rising tide buoyed up by a network of interwoven forms of moral, cultural, and economic improvement that, collectively, constitute "the spirit of the age."[3] The future isn't just friendly, if this scenario is to be believed, it is nothing short of utopian. Inspired by a growing love of conversation and armed with a repertoire of ideas, these economic free agents up and "flock" to the city – the word suggests both the spontaneity and the overwhelming popularity of this shift away from an older rural order, which, it implies, is also a move from ignorance to enlightenment, from barbarity to refinement, and from a masculinist homosociality to "easy and sociable" relations between the sexes. Contrary to the warnings of critics such as John "Estimate" Brown, for whom the growth of luxury was nothing more than a source of inexorable corruption, the culture of display these new urban dwellers revel in only heightens their sociability, and with it, their humanity. One need only think of Oliver Goldsmith's scathing critique of the corrosive effects of luxury in his 1770 poem, "The Deserted Village," or William Cobbett's account, decades later, of the decline of traditional rural communities to register the full extent of Hume's idealism.

The concept of sociability functions in these sorts of descriptions as a portent of the end of history in the doubled temporality that structures Francis Fukuyama's argument about liberal democracy: it is both the horizon toward which history was always ineluctably unfolding, and a sign of historical arrival. The unprecedented degree of conviviality charted by Hume – an entire city full of people "conversing together, and contributing to each other's pleasure and entertainment" – was reinforced by what critics hailed as the radically social nature of a commercial nation generally. John Trenchard and Thomas Gordon, the anonymous authors of *Cato's Letters*, argued that commerce promoted a spirit of "mutual confidence" as the "only possible way . . . to maintain publick honour and honesty."[4] For advocates of Britain's new commercial order, this mutual dependence, and the vulnerability it entailed, was commerce's greatest moral asset. "In civilized society," Adam Smith insisted, the individual "stands at all times in need of the co-operation and assistance of great multitudes . . . In almost every other race of animals each individual, when it was grown up to maturity, is entirely independent, and in its natural state has occasion for the assistance of no other living creature. But man has almost constant occasion for the help of his brethren."[5] An article entitled "On the Commercial Ideas Prevailing in some Parts of Europe" in the *European Magazine* insisted that "every branch of commerce forms a link in this great chain of universal acquaintance; none, therefore, can be annulled, without loosening the bond of reciprocal union and friendship, and setting men at a greater distance from each other than they stood before . . . The neglect of commerce would be attended with the most destructive consequences."[6] Descriptions of this "great chain of universal acquaintance" reimagined the inherited ideal of a Great Chain of Being in terms that reflected the relentlessly intersubjective reality of a new commercial order.

The influence, as well as the limits, of emerging forms of sociability were most clearly marked, I want to suggest, in their ambivalent relation to two equally powerful associational ideals: Jürgen Habermas's vision of a bourgeois public sphere, on the one hand, and a Shaftesburian ideal of politeness, on the other. These three ideas overlapped in important ways, but this common ground should not obscure the equally important differences and tensions between them. By its very nature, ideas about sociability merged with Habermas's configuration of the bourgeois public sphere as a public made up of private individuals, but this shared emphasis did not necessarily entail a related emphasis on rational debate and political agency. Hume's refusal to distinguish between curiosity and vanity, wit and good breeding, a love of knowledge and a desire to show off one's taste in clothes or furniture, so long as these traits help to inspire a companionable spirit, is difficult to reconcile with what Robert Jones has described as Habermas's "rather stilted" model of the bourgeois public sphere as a scene of purposeful rational debate in which "the private people, come together to form a public, readied themselves to compel public authority to legitimate itself before public opinion."[7] And yet, for all of that, it is important to remember their considerable similarities as transformative visions of an urban society in which people were engaging each other in various forms of sociable exchange in unprecedented ways and with far-reaching consequences.

Building on Dena Goodman's argument that we have underestimated the complexity of Habermas's historical model by overlooking his identification of "the market of cultural products" as one dimension of the public sphere, Gillian Russell's work has argued for the close connections between the public sphere and various forms of sociability, which, Russell argues, constituted "the ideological and material battleground on which [the] struggle" to establish the limits of the public sphere was fought.[8] Revisionary challenges to the gap between the public sphere's universalist rhetoric and its hierarchical social assumptions often redeploy the idea of the public sphere, less as a discursive space than as a rhetorical process – "public sphering" as a unique form of J. L. Austen's speech act theory, as Robert Miles has recently described it – that was predicated on particular forms of what we might describe as strategic sociability.[9] Punning on the ways that the phrase "counter-public sphere" might be taken to suggest the shop counter, and shopping more generally, as an important form of sociability capable of enabling "women of the English middle classes [to] acquire the ability to articulate certain aspects of their existence as 'public' issues," Deidre Lynch has argued suggestively about the ways that "relations between commerce, the public sphere and women's historical agency" were being reinflected by the tendency of "the birth of a consumer society" to "institute a new horizon of intersubjectivity."[10]

Recognizing the full extent of this mix of shared assumptions and alternative inflections is crucial if we want to understand the ideological force of ideas about sociability in the period, but these tensions were complicated further still by the mediating force of the ideal of politeness, a concept that was neither distinct from nor wholly reducible to either Habermas's vision of the bourgeois public sphere or accounts of sociability. As Lawrence Klein suggested in his study of *Shaftesbury and the Culture of Politeness*, Shaftesbury's deployment of the idea of politeness as part of his struggle to dislodge the authority of the church and court may have aligned the idea with the transformative energy of the bourgeois public sphere, on the one hand, and with emerging definitions of sociability, on the other, but its ethos of genteel accommodation remained more restricted than either the rationalist self-image of the public sphere or the commercial hub-bub of new forms of fashionable sociability. "'Politeness' concerned sociability but was not identical with it ... 'Politeness' was a refined sociability, bringing aesthetic concerns into close contiguity with ethical ones."[11] Or to turn this around, not all forms of sociability merited (or even aspired to) the more elevated and aestheticized notions of refinement that critics such as Shaftesbury were aligning with the discourse of politeness. The "nodal points" of this Shaftesburian discourse of politeness may have been the "coffeehouses, clubs, assemblies, gardens and theatres" of this "new urban culture," but its ethos of gentlemanly accommodation also served as a means of subduing "the babble, diversity, and liberty of the new discursive world of the Town."[12]

If this model of politeness sustained its influence by appealing to this relatively inclusive "new urban culture," descriptions of the bourgeois public sphere had a great deal to gain by absorbing the genteel implications of the discourse of politeness. Grafting an ideal of politeness onto the Habermasian notion of a public of private individuals engaged in seemingly endless rational debate privileged an ethos of accommodation – an ability to make others feel at ease – even as it reinforced a politics of distinction. The *Spectator* may have famously aligned itself with an appealingly democratic version of Socrates who "brought Philosophy down from Heaven, to inhabit among men" by bringing "Philosophy out of Closets and Libraries, Schools and Colleges, to dwell in Clubs and Assemblies, at Tea-Tables and in Coffee-Houses," but in the same issue, Addison also distinguished between the sorts of "well regulated Families" who might be inclined to make time to read his periodical over tea, and who were already refined enough to be able to benefit from its lessons, and "the thoughtless Herd of their ignorant and unattentive Brethren" whose craving for distraction disqualified them from the sort of refined community that could be said to be distinguished by polite sociability.[13] If the idea of the public sphere emerged out of an increasingly urban social order meeting in coffee houses and salons, in philosophical societies, and through the pages of their favorite periodicals, the ideal of politeness simultaneously registered the upwardly mobile pretensions and the contradictions of this new Whiggish social order.

Ideas about sociability were indelibly marked by these tensions between the three concepts, each of which may be best thought of, not as a unified discourse but as "the ideological and material battleground on which [the] struggle" between competing hegemonic orders was being waged.[14] If sociability seemed, in accounts such as Hume's, to be more expansive than the gentrified tone of many descriptions of politeness, the two merged in their role as both "a norm and also a goal of discourse": a vision of self-regulating subjects in a world whose hierarchical order was under pressure from the carnivalesque energies of daily life.[15] Recent studies of the strategic power of competing ideas of sociability have displaced Habermas's "highly stylized" account of a coffee house culture in favor of a far more nuanced emphasis on the specific locations and practices that mediated these initiatives: the "particular clubs and societies" alluded to by Hume which functioned as "nodal points" of the new urban culture. However, as many of these studies have also emphasized, this more particular attention to specific cultural locations must itself be doubled by a corresponding acknowledgment of the extent to which these actual sites were mediated by their cultural location within a complex discursive economy marked by the ambivalent relations that I have been delineating among these three influential concepts: politeness, sociability, and the idea of the bourgeois public sphere, none of which could be reduced to either of the others despite their many points of common ground. They might best be thought of, perhaps, as cultural co-ordinates that helped to organize the changing topography of Britain's social, political, and intellectual order. One's relative proximity to each of these concepts, which is to say, the degree to which one's identity could be reconciled with each of them, offered a powerful means of establishing one's location within the changing world of commercial modernity.

To think about the sites of sociability then, is not just to insist on the importance of greater historical particularity but also to recognize the specificity of the practice's location within this larger field of discursive relations. The sheer multiplicity of the many different versions of sociability that have been a feature of recent contributions to these debates – private sociability, old-style sociability, new-style sociability, and fashionable sociability as one element of new style sociability (Peter Clarke's terms), metropolitan sociability and domiciliary sociability (Gillian Russell's terms), "tavern sociability" (Jon Mee's term), polite sociability, commercial sociability, and so on, is itself an index of the internal complexity of this discursive topography that was marked by the powerful connections and differences between these three ideas. Descriptions of the geographical specificity of various sites of sociability must be complicated by an acknowledgment of the shaping influence of their location within this field of relations marked by both the overlap and the tensions between these three associational ideals.

These tensions were exacerbated by the spectatorial nature of eighteenth-century culture, not in the more rarified terms of either Steele and Addison's Mr Spectator or Smith's "impartial spectator" in *Theory of Moral Sentiments*, but in the public's widely noted thirst for entertainment. The association of theatricality with a love of spectacle, and by extension, with an unreflecting desire for novelty, opened it to charges that it represented the most trivial rather than distinguished elements of modern life: evidence of what a letter to the *Gentleman's Magazine* dismissed as the "refined dissipation" of the age. "Where this prevails," it continued, "it engrosses the time, and effectually excludes every thing which is manly and great."[16] "The passion of this age is in vain display," Dr. Fordyce agreed two years later.[17] It was, the *European Magazine* insisted, an "age of luxury and dissipation" in which "the only idol is *Appearance*, at whose shrine almost all the world pay homage."[18]

Concerns about what the *European Magazine* elsewhere dismissed as "this age of giddy dissipation, when ignorance is every day becoming more and more the character of the people of fashion" were reinforced by a second problem inherent in the theatrical nature of many of these forms of fashionable sociability – the tendency of visual spectacles to divert people's attention from one another.[19] Hume's vision of mixed-sex sociability was predicated on the idea that people "must feel an increase in humanity, from the very habit of conversing together, and contributing to each other's pleasure and entertainment," but this implied that their focus was on one another, rather than elsewhere. If conversation, both as an actual practice and as a metaphor for mutually enriching intercourse, was a crucial aspect of most ideas about sociability, how far could this conversational emphasis be reconciled with the theatrical dimension of modern life? Could watching the same activity, which amounted to consuming culture in parallel, really constitute a basis for sociability? And did it matter what they were watching?

I want to pursue these questions by focusing on the public entertainments that dominated London in the early 1780s, and on the mixed reactions they inspired. Too late to figure in most accounts of eighteenth-century literary history, whether in terms of Augustan poetics, the Scottish Enlightenment, the mid-century novel, or the vogue for sensibility, and too early for Romanticism, the 1780s decade has rarely figured as a central focus in its own right. Yet life in London during these years was marked by an extraordinary range of public entertainments, both the now familiar attractions of the "theatre and opera, puppet shows, pleasure gardens, circuses, assemblies, model exhibitions, lectures, shows (such as Cox's Museum), clubs, learned societies, taverns, and debating clubs" that had been noted by the Duchess of Northumberland in 1773, and a succession of more recent acts whose extraordinary appeal seemed to many critics to exemplify the best and worst of fashionable modernity.[20] The most notorious of these was Gustavus Katterfelto, a Prussian lecturer and conjurer who had enjoyed brief but intense popularity in the early 1780s, and whose trademark phrase was "WONDERS WONDERS, WONDERS AND WONDERS." Using a device known as his solar microscope, Katterfelto claimed that "in a drop of clear water, the size of a pin head, there will be seen above 50,000 insects, the same in beer, milk, flower, cheese, &c. and there will be seen many surprising insects in different vegetables, and above 200 other dead objects."[21] Katterfelto's public lectures fused a sense of religious wonder (his ads invited spectators to behold "these wonderful works of Providence") with Enlightenment promise. He reassured the public that "Mr. KATTERFELTO has . . . by a very long study, discovered at last, such a variety of wonderful Experiments in Natural and Experimental Philosophy and Mathematics, as will surprise all the world."[22] Continually updating his advertisements, Katterfelto was soon promising to combine his "Experiments in Natural and Experimental Philosophy and Mathematics" with "his whole regular Course of Philosophical Lectures," which would be "delivered in twelve Different times, a lecture and an experiment every day, and every evening at 7 o' clock."[23] "All hail Philosophy, it's sovereign aid / Each climate owns where Science is display'd, / Where Art transcendent o'er dull Error rules, / Arts duly drawn from philosophic schools" proclaimed another advertisement in the form of a (syntactically garbled) poem entitled "On Seeing Mr. KATTERFELTO's Grand Exhibition on Saturday night last."[24] Readers and spectators were invited to appreciate Katterfelto's blend of intellectual preeminence and personal virtue. "Ye curious Britons, who'd instruction draw, / With care attend to truth's unerring law," another ad began. "Learn this important truth from me, / 'Tis virtue only gives true dignity."[25]

Part of Katterfelto's appeal lay in the historical coincidence of his own arrival in London with the 1782 influenza epidemic. Exploiting popular anxiety, Katterfelto linked his demonstration with fears of infection in ways that infused his rationalist credentials with an ennobling rhetoric of public service, even as his scare-mongering preyed on the insecurities of frightened Londoners. His solar microscope, his ads insisted, would display "those insects . . . that alarm this nation . . . in the highest perfection, as large as an ox . . . He will shew those insects which are so numerous in the air, which are the cause of that raging distemper, called the influenza."[26]

Other ads carried even more explicit promises to "shew those most surprising insects, which have been advertised in the different papers, and which have threatened this kingdom with a plague, if not speedily destroyed." Raising the stakes still further, he went on to remind his readers that "they are of the same kind, by all accounts, which caused a great plague in Italy in the year 1432. They will be magnified as large as an ox, and a hundred persons may have a view at one time."[27] And having exposed the source of the problem, he dutifully offered to cure "any person in London afflicted with the above complaint, by taking one of Dr. BATTO's bottles of medicine and sold by Mr. KATTERFELTO, and at no other place in London. A bottle for 5 s. will certainly cure a person in twelve hours, as many thousand persons have experienced since his publication."[28] For an additional fee, he also offered advice on how to win at dice, cards, billiards, and E.O.

Hume may well have insisted that the specter of people flocking to urban centers where their lives would be marked by unprecedented forms of sociability would inevitably lead to "*industry, knowledge*, and *humanity*," but for many critics, the extraordinary popularity of dubious instructors such as Katterfelto cast this equation into question. "Every sensible person considers Katterfelto, as a puppy, an ignoramus, a braggadocio, and an imposter," Charles Moritz declared in his *Travels, Chiefly on Foot, Through Several Parts of England in 1782*.[29] William Cowper's account of the "wilderness of strange / But gay confusion" of newspaper ads in Book Four of *The Task* famously singled out Katterfelto "with his hair on end / At his own wonders, wondering for his bread" as the epitome of "the stir / Of the great Babel" known as London.[30] At what point did the ideal of sociability as both an index and an engine of progress collapse into the chaos of modern urban life? A letter to the *Morning Chronicle*, which began by noting that "it has long been justly observed that the English are the most credulous people living," cited as the most damning proof of this credulity the extraordinary success of "the present wonderful, wonder-working Philosopher" whose "pompous, puffing advertisements have induced many thousands to go, hear, and see some of that wonderful knowledge he so lavishly pretends to dispence to the public."[31] Ironically given his own notoriety as a charlatan, Philip Breslaw's *Last Legacy*, whose serious educational purpose he emphasized in his preface and introduction, cited the misplaced enthusiasm with which "the multitude . . . croud so often to see their wonders! wonders! and wonders! as performed, and puffed away by that great philosopher Katterfelto" as the surest proof of Lord Chesterfield's insistence that "mankind are easier deceived than undeceived."[32] For the author of a poem in *The*

Aberdeen Magazine, Katterfelto was so perfect an example of this bastardization of learning that his name could become an adjective for a more general state of intellectual corruption that marked the bankruptcy rather than the strategic value of these sorts of wildly popular attractions as sites of fashionable sociability: "And Katterfelto-like be ev'rything."[33]

For his critics, Katterfelto's intellectual pretensions epitomized the carnivalesque excess and cultural emptiness of the age's associational impulse. "This world is a Fair, where the croud is bent wholly / On gew-gaws and rattles, noise, nonsense and folly," Thomas Holcroft suggested in his comic opera, *The Noble Peasant* (1784), "With wonders! wonders! and wonders! enough to make a blind man stare! / Oh! Don't you think it a wonderful fair?."[34] The predictable answer was no, not everyone was so entranced by this fashionable world of "gew-gaws and rattles." But unlike venues like Astley's or Sadler's Wells, which never seriously claimed to offer anything more than harmless entertainment, "philosophers" like Katterfelto flaunted an Enlightenment rhetoric and exploited the most recent scientific devices, from the air pump to electricity to air balloons, in ways that unsettled the distinction between the pursuit of knowledge and a craving for novelty. For skeptics, the relentless sociability that was so fundamental to modern urban life was productive, not of industry, knowledge, and humanity as Hume had so confidently suggested, but the opposite of all three of these: noise, nonsense, and folly. The ambivalence that animated these accounts of a Katterfelto-like world animated by a fully commodified brand of "wonderful knowledge" raised important questions about the limits of sociability and the point at which what Mee has described as its "conversational" self-image collapsed into the cacophonous "stir of the great Babel" of modern urban life.

Historians such as Simon Schaffer and Jan Golinski have demonstrated the considerable effort that individuals such as Joseph Priestley and Humphrey Davy made to enshrine scientific investigation as an important form of public culture, but the chorus of denunciations about Katterfelto's attractions underscores the difficulty of maintaining any convincing distinction between genuine scientific lectures and those spectacles whose theatricality was a sure sign of their intellectual bankruptcy, and which, therefore, catered to a debased craving for novelty and distraction. Davy's lectures at the Royal Society may have been widely embraced as the antithesis of acts such as Katterfelto, but as Golinski and Jon Klancher have suggested, Davy's flamboyant style and personal charisma echoed Katterfelto's promotional energy, rhetorical flash, and use of visually spectacular demonstrations.[35] Nor was it even a matter of distinguishing between legitimate and relatively trivial phenomena; even the most impressive scientific breakthroughs could be trivialized by opportunistic showmen catering to an undiscerning audience. "Electricity happens at present to be the puppet-show of the English," Moritz declared after his 1782 journey. "Who ever at all understands electricity, is sure of being noticed and successful."[36]

Katterfelto's alignment with the art of deception rather than enlightenment, as well as his mixture of dramatic flair and entrepreneurial savvy, scientific pretensions and occult mystery, linked him in the public imagination with other showmen such as Breslaw, the German conjuror and mind-reader who had been a hit at the Haymarket Theatre in 1781, and James Graham, proprietor of the sumptuously decorated Temple of Health which opened in Adelphi Terrace in 1779 (renamed the Temple of Health and Hymen when it moved to less expensive quarters), home of the famous Celestial Bed which, Graham claimed, had wonderful procreative powers. "The truly divine energy of this celestial and electrical fire, which fills every part of the bed, as well as the magnetical fluid, are both of them calculated to give the necessary degree of strength and exertion to the nerves," Graham promised couples who were desperate enough to pay £50 to spend a night in the Celestial Bed (reduced to £25 when interest began to wane).[37] The Temple's complex status as an explicitly commercial site with paid admission, an institution with pretensions to scientific authority, and more than a whiff of sexual intrigue, highlighted the complex discursive topography of modern urban life. The bed itself was a powerful reminder of the convergence of intensely private and flamboyantly public levels of experience in ways that exemplified the hybridizing effects of commerce generally.

In a kind of parody of the ornate interior of the Pantheon, guests could wander through elaborately decorated rooms breathing perfumed air and listening to music, try their luck at the Temple's gambling tables, or take in Graham's lectures on the benefits of electricity and magnetism. Like so many fashionable attractions, though, Graham's pretensions to genteel metropolitan culture were undercut, not just by the Temple's association with a "heterogeneous jumble" of social classes who were more intent on self-deception than critical analysis, but by connotations of illicit sexual commerce. It was widely acknowledged that the same £50 fee could procure unattached men an opportunity to enjoy the use of the bed with one of the scantily dressed women who posed amongst the Temple's statutes. Shaftesbury's ideal of politeness may, as Klein suggests, have grounded itself in a version of sociability that brought aesthetics into "close congruity" with ethics, but the more fashionable version of sociability on offer at the Temple of Health and Hymen aligned science and aesthetics in the service of more visceral impulses.[38] The question that these sorts of venues raised, was, if their popularity distinguished them as sites of sociability, then what was sociability good for? Or, if sociability was to be aligned with the sorts of virtues that Hume suggested, then did these sorts of attractions still merit the name?

Graham sought to distance himself from the scandalous implications of this sexual commerce in favor of an enlightened rhetoric of fashionable sociability that stressed the edifying and even scientifically ambitious nature of his project. As an ad in the *Morning Post* announced, Graham complemented his medical services at the Temple of Health, which was "now embellished to a degree of magnificence, harmonious flowing elegance, celestial liquid brilliancy, far superior to any theatre, public place, or even perhaps to any royal palace in the world," with "curious, free, and very eccentric lecture[s] on the propagation of the human species ... enriched with reflections political, moral, and philosophical."[39] Like Katterfelto's, Graham lectures seemed to be designed to convince the public of the legitimacy of his claims to scientific authority, even as his description of them burlesqued the very idea of that authority.

The limitations that these sorts of attractions seemed to imply for efforts to equate the proliferation of public entertainments with the triumph of new forms of sociability in any positive sense were most clearly demarcated by critics' reaction to another, equally popular act in these years: the celebrated Learned Pig. Debuting in London in 1785, the Learned Pig created a sensation with what seemed to be its powers of rational thought. Exhibited near Charing Cross, men and women "of the first fashion waited four hours for their turn" to pay the five shillings admission to see its act.[40] As Robert Southey noted in an essay on English credulity, "the learned pig was in his day a far greater object of admiration to the English nation than ever was Sir Isaac Newton."[41] When the Pig moved to Sadler's Wells that summer, it featured as the headline act despite "great objections" from the acrobats and tightrope walkers who had been pushed out of top-billing.[42] "The wonderful learned pig," had become "so popular," *London Unmask'd* declared, "that the proprietor is rapidly amassing a fortune, thro' the sway of fashion, as it would be quite monstrous and ill-bred not to follow the *ton*, and go see the wonderful Learned Pig; it being the trite question in all polite circles, Pray, my Lord, my Lady, Sir John, Madam, or Miss, have you seen the Learned Pig? if answer is given in the affirmative, it is a confirmation of taste; if in the negative, it is reprobated as an odious singularity!"[43]

"Impelled no doubt by an epidemic rage" and "determined not to be out of the fashion," the "sentimental peripatetic" narrator of *London Unmask'd* followed his excursion to see the "dancing, or rather acting, dogs" at Sadler's Wells with a visit to the Learned Pig, which seemed "infinitely to surpass all that I had ever seen or heard before," and which, as a result, enjoyed pride of place in the book's ultimate chapter, entitled "The Prevalence of Novelty."[44] The narrator framed his own spectatorial encounter in terms that aligned the Pig with the ambivalence inspired by Katterfelto's own brand of wonderful knowledge:

> As I was walking to Whitehall, I observed a number of people crowding the passage of a house in that neighbourhood, indicating by their looks, that they waited admission to some curious exhibition. Casting my eye to the front of the house, I observed a board inscribed,
>
> **The Wonderful Learned Pig.**
> Well, thought I, it may be truly said, that wonders will never cease. We may now, with propriety, adopt the language of that pretender of all pretenders, Katterfelto, and exclaim, Wonders! Wonders! and more Wonders! Men have traversed the regions of the air; Horses have fetched and carried, laid down and risen up, nodded the affirmative or the negative, and footed it to given numbers at the word of command. Dogs have aped humanity, and represented various scenes which occur amongst us rationals, with astonishing adroitness, and thereby convinced me there is not that remote distance between instinct and reason, which many have imagined and would suggest.
> But here, in this instance, all former efforts must be outdone. What! can it be possible that the most filthy, sluggish, and gross of all animals, should be rendered tractable, alert, and discerning?[45]

The narrator's admission that he had "indulged our passion for novelty in common with *the herd of fellow-mortals*" registered a darker side of Hume's image of people flocking to the cities in search of sociable interaction. To flock to these venues in too great a number was to risk unsettling the sociable pretensions of these very activities by erasing the distinctions that periodicals such as the *Spectator* had worked so hard to secure between an enlightened public and the "thoughtless Herd."

The *Times* warned that this problem of losing one's sense of individuality amongst the pressures of the crowd was doubled by concerns about the tendency of these sorts of spectacles to exacerbate already dangerous social confusions. Being "as cunning as his sagacious quadruped," the proprietor had "left no stone unturned to attract the notice and money of the curious" including all of the usual "squibs, puffs, and paragraphs," but most objectionably of all, he had lured the servants of the genteel families, and when the coach is ordered out to air the children, away go the cooks, the ladies' maids, the nurses, &c. &c. &c. to Charing-cross, where they are introduced as Mrs, Miss, or my Lady, to the levee of the disgusting beast; and for their complaisance, are, besides their admittance gratis, regaled with cake and gin, in a back room. In the meantime, the canaille both without and within, are impressed with a high idea of the consequence of the animal from the assumed rank of his visitors, by which means their curiosity is prodigiously inflamed, and they flock in crowds to the show. But to imagine that any person of figure or even common decency ever put their foot into the nasty stye, is a most absurd reflection on the [t]aste and delicacy of the age.[46]

These tensions were intensified by the fact that people frequently gathered to view their own fashionable habits, or in other words, the most visible aspects of polite society, performed back to them in ways that recast these markers of distinction as parodic elements of a carnivalesque world of competitive display.

No attraction in this period better dramatized these tensions than the "balloonomania" as Horace Walpole called it, which gripped the entire nation after the first human flights ascended in France in 1783 and then in England the following September.[47] As Thomas Carlyle recognized, in his *History of the French Revolution* (1837), balloons, fantastically buoyant but at the mercy of the winds, were the ideal emblem of the instabilities of a transactional world that had come unmoored from any foundational ideas of value: "beautiful invention; mounting heavenward, so beautifully – so unguidably! Emblem of much and of our Age of Hope itself."[48] Balloons' extraordinary visual splendor raised concerns about the spectatorial nature of modern life generally, while the trend's mix of scientific pretensions and entrepreneurial ambitions encapsulated the tensions that seemed to many critics to be an unavoidable part of sociability in a modern commercial nation.

Like the cases of Katterfelto, Breslaw, and Graham, ambivalent responses to the ballooning craze often focused on the promotional efforts of a showman with an instinct for merging scientific pretensions, philanthropic rhetoric, and self-advancement: Vincent Lunardi, the minor Italian diplomat who rose to fame as Britain's first aeronaut, whose relentless self-promotional efforts exemplify these connections in uniquely powerful ways. Few developments in the age compared with the public impact of the arrival of air balloons. "*Balloons* occupy senators, philosophers, ladies, everybody," Horace Walpole proclaimed.[49] "The term balloon is not only in the mouth of every one, but all our world seems to be in the clouds," *London Unmask'd* agreed.[50] And in England, no one rivaled Lunardi, either in the extraordinary public response which his flights aroused, or, closer to the ground, in the skill with which he manipulated the narratives of these achievements in order to maintain the public's interest. The diverse elements of the public persona that he managed to cultivate in these years reflect the cacophonous world of commercial modernity generally, from the flights themselves to swiftly published autobiographical accounts, public appearances, elaborate indoor shows at the Lyceum and then the Pantheon both before and after his great initial voyage, endless advertisements in leading newspapers such as the *Morning Post* and the *Morning Chronicle*, as well as the fashion trends that quickly developed as a result, from a style of hat dubbed "the Lunardi" to a new color named "Lunardi maroon" to women's garters bearing his name. "The Pantheon seems to have become the fashionable lounging place for all the beauties in town," the *Morning Post* noted just weeks after his flight. "The attractions are considerable: The magnificence of the building, the suspension of the Balloon and Gallery, and tho' the last, yet seemingly not the least in admiration, Lunardi's paying his respects to the chearful crowd for their friendly attention."[51]

Attempting to evoke a genteel spirit of refined sociability, Lunardi's ads were frequently marked by a tone of comically extravagant politeness. "Mr. Lunardi is peculiarly happy in having lately experienced, that the attachment of the Public to him is in unison with feelings and particularity to this Nation," one ad for his exhibit at the Pantheon proclaimed.[52] This emotional reciprocity between an Enlightenment man of feeling and the nation that had embraced him, which found its clearest affirmation in the steady flow of paying customers to his exhibit, was a persistent theme. "As Mr. Lunardi has nothing more at heart than to gratify the public curiosity in the most ample and satisfactory manner, and that to disappoint the general expectation in the smallest particular, would be inexpressibly repugnant to the sincere and grateful feelings he entertains of their past favours," another ad hastened to deny rumours of an imminent flight, and to announce that his exhibit at the Pantheon would remain open, having "spared no pains or cost to render it elegant and magnificent to the eye, and to blend in the numerous parts of his machinery, the ornamental with the useful."[53]

However much he may have presented the exhibit at the Pantheon in terms that reinforced his philosophical pretensions, the exhibits themselves were equally distinguished by the pressures of fashionable display which tended to blur still further the line between science and sociability, curiosity and polite entertainment. In the same ad in which he stressed his gratitude "to a generous and intelligent people, to whom he is bound by obligations which he never can forget, to the latest hour of his life," Lunardi announced that he would mark the imminent closure of his balloon exhibit at the Pantheon (in order to prepare for another flight) with a grand final night combining "his Exhibition" with

> a ball on the said night, at which nothing shall be wanting to render it elegant, brilliant, and accommodating. In addition to the lights of the lustres, part of the Dome will be illuminated. The best Bands of Music that can be acquired for Minuets, Cotillons, and Country Dances, and every other particular that can tend to the entertainment or gratification of the company, shall be provided and attended to, under the management of two Gentlemen who have taken upon themselves to regulate the ceremony of the night with due and proper decorum.[54]

A masquerade at the Pantheon three months later was similarly "elegantly illuminated and embellished with the appendage of *Lunardi*'s balloon."[55] Yet another masquerade four months later combined decorations "representing the Grand Saloon of the Doge of Venice, decorated and ornamented in the most elegant taste" with "the balloon, [which] will likewise be suspended, with the Gallery and the whole of the apparatus."[56] Other ads promised the combined attraction of the balloon with "the musical child," a prodigy who "will perform from Two o'Clock till Four, and though but Nine Years of Age, will take off several of our first Performers, and will Sing and Play at sight."[57]

Between the ballooning demonstrations and these related events, the Learned Pig's performances, Graham's Temple of Health and Hymen, Katterfelto's solar microscope, and Breslaw's conjuring tricks, there was no shortage of public venues for those who like Hazlitt's satirical account of a "lady of quality" and her daughters, wished to frequent "the most fashionable places of resort."[58] But each of these attractions was also evidence of the fact that this sort of fame was as short-lived as it was intense. By the end of the decade, Katterfelto, Breslaw, Graham, and Lunardi had all sunk beneath the horizon of public attention. Ballooning would remain popular but by January 1786, the *European Magazine* could already refer to "the then fashionable rage for ballooning" two years earlier.[59] However opportunistic many of these promotional efforts may have seemed to be, they were little more than reflections of the entrepreneurial energies of their day. It remained open to dispute how much they could be reconciled with the promotion of industry, knowledge, and humanity, but this reservation did little to dampen the popularity of these attractions, or to diminish the promotional power of the rhetoric of sociability as one of their most compelling features. The real lesson, however, may have been the sheer impossibility of imposing any regulating cultural codes that would help to stabilize the forms of prestige that being in the right places, and with the right people, might help to afford. Like the balloons themselves, the potential for important forms of distinction that had once been reliably tethered to particular forms of sociability had floated free from any stable ground, caught up the winds of commercial opportunism, scientific rhetoric, and carnivalesque theatricality that people in this age were coming to recognize as modernity.

Notes

1 Harriet Guest, *Unbounded Attachment: Sentiment and Politics in the Age of the French Revolution* (Oxford: Oxford University Press, 2013), p. 3. I take the Clark reference from the subtitle of his book, *British Clubs and Societies: The Origins of an Associational World* (Oxford: Oxford University Press, 2000).
2 David Hume, "Of Refinement in the Arts," *Essays: Moral, Political, and Literary*, ed. Eugene F. Miller (Indianapolis: Liberty Classics, 1985), p. 271.
3 Ibid., p. 271.
4 John Trenchard and Thomas Gordon, *Cato's Letters, or Essays on Liberty, Civil and Religious, and Other Important Subjects*, ed. Ronald Hamowy (Indianapolis: Liberty Fund, 1995), vol. I, p. 48.
5 Adam Smith, *An Inquiry into the Nature and Causes of the Wealth of Nations*, 2 vols. (Indianapolis: Liberty Fund, 1981), vol. I, p. 26.
6 *European Magazine*, 6 (1784), pp. 17–19.
7 Robert Jones, *Gender and the Formation of Taste in Eighteenth-Century Britain: The Analysis of Beauty* (Cambridge: Cambridge University Press, 1998), p. 33; Jürgen Habermas, *The Structural Transformation of the Public Sphere: An Inquiry into a Category of Bourgeois Society*, trans. Thomas Burger and Frederick Lawrence (Cambridge, MA: MIT Press, 1989), p. 25.
8 Gillian Russell, *Women, Sociability and Theatre in Georgian London* (Cambridge: Cambridge University Press, 2007), p. 9.
9 Robert Miles, *Romantic Misfits* (Basingstoke: Palgrave Macmillan, 2008), pp. 13–8.
10 Deidre Shauna Lynch, *The Economy of Character: Novels, Market Culture, and the Business of Inner Meaning* (Chicago: University of Chicago Press, 1998), p. 222.
11 Lawrence Klein, *Shaftesbury and the Culture of Politeness: Moral Discourse and Cultural Politics in Early Eighteenth-Century England* (Cambridge: Cambridge University Press, 1994), p. 4.
12 Ibid., p. 11, 12.
13 *The Spectator*. Everyman's Library Edition, ed. G. Gregory Smith, 4 vols. (London: J. M. Dent & Sons, Ltd., 1907), vol. I, pp. 38–39.
14 Russell, *Women, Sociability and Theatre in Georgian London*, p. 9.
15 Klein, *Shaftesbury and the Culture of Politeness*, p. 12.

16 *Gentleman's Magazine* 55 (86), 766.
17 Quoted in *European Magazine* 11 (1787), 111.
18 *European Magazine* 1 (1782), 108.
19 *European Magazine* 3 (1783), 13; 4 (1783), 94.
20 Russell, *Women, Sociability and Theatre in Georgian London*, p. 1.
21 *Morning Post*, July 23, 1782.
22 Ibid., July 23, 1782.
23 Ibid., November 18, 1782.
24 *Morning Chronicle*, March 20, 1782.
25 Ibid., July 5, 1782.
26 Ibid., July 3, 1782.
27 Ibid., April 16, 1782.
28 Ibid., July 3, 1782.
29 Charles P. Moritz, *Travels, Chiefly on Foot, Through Several Parts of England in 1782*, Translated from the German, by a Lady (London: Printed for G. G. and J. Robinson, 1795), pp. 88–9.
30 William Cowper, *The Task, A Poem, in Six Books* (London: Printed for J. Johnson, 1785), p. 141.
31 *Morning Chronicle*, October 12, 1782.
32 Philip Breslaw, *Breslaw's Last Legacy; or, The Magical Companion* (London: Printed for T. Moore, 1784), pp. 37–8.
33 *The Aberdeen Magazine*, p. 119.
34 Thomas Holcroft, *The Noble Peasant. A Comic Opera in Three Acts* (Dublin: Printed for J. Exshaw for the Company of Booksellers, 1784), p. 5.
35 Jan Golinski, "Humphrey Davy's Sexual Chemistry," *Configurations*, 7 (1999), 25; Jon Klancher, *Transfiguring the Arts and Sciences: Knowledge and Cultural Institutions in the Romantic Age* (Cambridge: Cambridge University Press, 2013), p. 79.
36 Moritz, *Travels, Chiefly on Foot, Through Several Parts of England in 1782*, p. 88.
37 James Graham, *The Temple of Health, Shewing the Magnetico-Electric Pathway to Elysian Lovemaking*, www.printsgeorge.com/ArtEccles_Temple ofHealth2.htm (n.d.), p. 1.
38 Klein, *Shaftesbury and the Culture of Politeness*, p. 4.
39 *Morning Post*, October 2, 1782.
40 Charles Royster, *The Fabulous History of the Dismal Swamp Company: A Story of George Washington's Times* (New York: Knopf, 1999), p. 308.
41 Robert Southey, *Letters from England. By Don Manuel Alvarez Espriella. Translated from the Spanish* (London: Longman et al., 1808), p. 20.
42 Royster, *The Fabulous History of the Dismal Swamp Company: A Story of George Washington's Times*, p. 308.
43 *London Unmask'd: Or the New Town Spy. Exhibiting a Striking Picture of the World as it Goes.* (London: William Allard, 1785), pp. 141–2.
44 *London Unmask'd*, pp. 141–2.
45 Ibid., pp. 140–1.

46 *The Times*, May 2, 1785. My thanks to David Fallon for bringing this passage to my attention.

47 Horace Walpole, *The Correspondence of Horace Walpole* (London: Oxford University Press, 1937–1983), vol. 25, p.596.

48 Thomas Carlyle, *The French Revolution; a History* (New York: The Modern Library, 1934) p. 42.

49 Horace Walpole, *The Correspondence of Horace Walpole*, vol. 25, p. 449.

50 *London Unmask'd*, p. 137.

51 *Morning Post*, October 3, 1784.

52 Ibid., May 5, 1785.

53 Ibid., March 26, 1785.

54 Ibid., November 24, 1784.

55 Ibid., February 9, 1785.

56 Ibid., June 6, 1785.

57 Ibid., April 21, 1785.

58 William Hazlitt, *The Selected Writings of William Hazlitt* (London: Pickering and Chatto, 1998), vol. 7, p. 107.

59 *European Magazine and London Review* 13 (1782), 7.

PART III

Interior Places

CHAPTER 6

"The place is not free to you"
The Georgian Assembly Room and the Ends of Sociability

Gillian Russell

In 1902 the Hill sisters, Constance and Ellen, made a tour of sites in the south of England connected with the life and fiction of Jane Austen. One of the most evocative of their encounters occurred at the Angel Inn in Basingstoke where the Hills had gone to inquire about the location of an assembly room that Austen had frequented in the late 1790s.[1] The landlord was unable to help them but his wife drew their attention to a large room over the stables at the back of the inn. Then used as a hayloft, this space was the room that the Hills had been searching for. Constance Hill uses the present tense to convey the dramatic immediacy of the discovery: "there are the handsome chimney-pieces, the sash windows and the double-flap doors that mark a reception-room of importance; and when we push aside the litter beneath our feet, the fine even planking of a dance floor appears." The present of 1902 then uncannily gives way to the past as evidence of decay – "the discoloured and mouldering plaster" and the "broken panes . . . all vanish, and we seem to see the room as it appeared in its palmy days when prepared for a county ball."[2]

Kathryn Sutherland has highlighted the importance of the Hills' book in the development in the twentieth century of "heritage Austen," that is, Austen's status as a temporally mobile signifier of both a sentimentalized English past and the recuperability of that past as contemporary fashion.[3] The Basingstoke episode in the Hills' evocation of Austen's "haunts" can also be seen as an example of the enduring importance of the assembly room as a portal into the Georgian past, giving access to a lost world of sociability which persists in manifesting both its spectral and its more concretely material traces. Austen herself inaugurated this trend in her representation in *Emma* of the assembly room at the Crown Inn which attracts the attention of Frank Churchill on his return to Highbury: "its character as a ball-room caught him; and instead of passing on, he stopt for several minutes at the two superior sashed windows which were open, to look in and contemplate its capabilities, and lament that its original purpose should have ceased."[4]

For both Churchill and Constance Hill in 1902, the assembly room compels spectatorial curiosity: it must be looked into. Austen's *Emma* registers how, by 1816, the assembly room and its "purposes," both practical and ideological, were beginning to be used as tropes in prose fiction in terms of a nostalgia or "lament" for an eighteenth-century past. A later example of this trend is the assembly room in Elizabeth Gaskell's *Cranford*, added to the George Inn about "a hundred years before" (i.e. the 1720s): "the old room was dingy; the salmon-coloured paint had faded into a drab; great pieces of plaster had chipped off from the white wreaths and festoons on its walls; but still a mouldy odour of aristocracy lingered about the place."[5] The representation of the assembly room in imaginative literature after 1800 as a specifically Georgian phenomenon in decay is misleading, however: many assembly rooms survived into the nineteenth century and beyond as important multi-purpose institutions of civic life, not only in the British isles but throughout the English-speaking world, including places such as India and Australia. This chapter focuses on the representation of the assembly room in William Godwin's novel *Caleb Williams*, published in 1794 on the cusp of the time the assembly room began to be conceived nostalgically in fiction as emblematic of a lost form of sociality. *Caleb Williams* has featured significantly in discussions of the public sphere in the 1790s as a "crisis" in which the ideals of free exchange – the rational exercise of public opinion in Jürgen Habermas's terms, particularly through the medium of the republic of letters and its institutions – achieved a form of revolutionary realization only to be defeated by the forces of counter-revolution and the public sphere's own internal weaknesses.[6] According to Nicolle Jordan, *Caleb Williams* is the "ur-novel of the public sphere" for its staging of a "confrontation between textual, sociable, and governmental dimensions of that public."[7] However, the specificity of Godwin's exploration of that confrontation in relation to sociability and its material spaces, such as the assembly room, has received very little critical attention. In *Caleb Williams* the assembly room is the venue for the events that ultimately determine the fate of the eponymous hero – Tyrrel's assault on Falkland and the latter's murder of his antagonist, an association which is, I wish to argue, far from accidental. Godwin depicts the model of sociality exemplified by the assembly room as a challenge to the ruling order in its politely civilized (Falkland) and brutally tyrannical (Tyrrel) typologies. The critical neglect of the assembly room episode in *Caleb Williams* is also partly due to the fact that the representation of sociable spaces in eighteenth-century fiction has yet to be significantly explored. The recognition of drama, music, and visual art as aspects of human endeavour worthy of scholarly attention has granted to Georgian theatres, concert rooms and art exhibitions a visibility that spaces devoted primarily to sociability currently lack.[8] Similarly, the perspectives of eighteenth-century social history, shaped as they have been by economic and political history, have meant that the importance of the assembly room – though recognized in the work of Peter Borsay, John Brewer, and others – has been subsumed in synthesizing accounts of the commercialization of culture.[9] The phenomenon of the assembly room has not been systematically studied and historicized in its right.

One of the challenges in attempting such a history is the meaning of assembly itself. All kinds of social, cultural, and political activities, not only in the eighteenth century but also transhistorically, are based on a gathering of a group of people at a particular time and in a particular place – thus a theatre performance before an audience is an assembly, as are a collective act of worship, a political demonstration such as a riot, a sitting of a legislative or deliberative body, a court in session or a mobilized army.[10] While the Georgian assembly room was primarily devoted to the form of entertainment known as an "assembly" – a gathering entailing dancing, conversation, music and the consumption of refreshments – the material space and the practices it housed adumbrated these other connotations of "assembly." In this sense participants were not merely enjoying quadrilles and cake, they were also enacting what it meant for people to join together in an assembly for whatever purpose, making the assembly and the assembly room potentially meta-sociable, a fact which Jane Austen recognized by returning to the assembly room so many times in her fiction.

This chapter makes a preliminary contribution to a study of the Georgian assembly room as a key space of sociability by considering *Caleb Williams* in the context of the history of a particular room, that in Lisburn in the north of Ireland. *Caleb Williams* suggests that William Godwin understood the assembly's distinctive contribution to the evolution of the Georgian public sphere as well as its significance to the crisis of that public sphere in the 1790s. Its "character" as a space "caught him," much as it would later attract the attention of Frank Churchill.

Before discussing *Caleb Williams*, however, I want to outline some of the original "purposes" of the assembly room. The development of spaces outside the home as venues for dancing, card-playing and tea-drinking dates from the early eighteenth century, Daniel Defoe noting in the 1720s the attraction for women of those "assemblies ... lately set up."[11] There

were three main kinds of rooms – free-standing buildings such as Burlington's famous neo-Palladian rooms at York (1730–1732), rooms attached to
inns such as the Angel at Basingstoke, and those that were part of market
houses, usually located on the upper storey. Assembly rooms such as those
of York and Bath consisted of a central space for dancing connected to
rooms for cards and tea-drinking as well as lobbies and cloakrooms. Unlike
the coffeehouse or the theatre, where people mainly sat, the assembly room
was defined by a constant mobility and associated conversation, which
found their focus in the liveliness of the dance floor. The assembly room
was thus as much a temple to social intercourse as comparable, more
celebrated, institutions such as the coffeehouse. This flow of talk and
bodies was bounded by the walls of the assembly room as a whole, making
the entrance door crucially important as a point of access and security.
Assemblies were self-governing voluntary associations, regulated through a
system of paid subscription, supervised by a group of managers with a
master of ceremonies at their head: who had rights to participate was
therefore closely monitored. Like many aspects of civic life, assemblies
were reliant on the paraphernalia of print matter associated with sociability
such as newspaper publicity, tickets, handbill advertisements and printed
rules.[12] This association with print and its institutions was most apparent
in the development of spa towns and seaside resorts in the late eighteenth
and early nineteenth centuries, where the assembly room was often linked
with newspaper reading rooms, stationery shops and circulating libraries.
In Dover, for example, the Batcheller's King's Arms Library where "the
London and county papers, reviews, magazines &c. are constantly on the
table" also had an assembly room located above it for "promenades in the
season" and "quadrille and card assemblies in the winter."[13]

   Within the space of the assembly room, no area was lacking in sociable
meaning: even the stairway could be a place of affective association, and
writing about the assembly room is always attuned to the highly charged
atmospheres of these zones of parasociability. Jane Austen's *The Watsons*,
for example, is meticulous in its depiction of an arrival at a village assembly
as an occasion of sensational excitement. Emma Watson's party exchanges
the "quiet warmth" of "a snug parlour" for "the bustle, noise and draughts
of air of the broad entrance passage of an inn," followed by a climb up a
"wide staircase," to the sound of a "scrape" of a single violin, a passage
along a "short gallery," before a final arrival in the ballroom itself, an
Aladdin's cave "brilliant in lights before them."[14] Assemblies in the provinces were customarily winter affairs, often occurring fortnightly – Thurs-
day was a favourite night – so the contrast between the illuminated rooms

and the darkness without would have been an important dimension of the assembly-going experience. John Marsh, whom I will discuss later, noted how assemblies often took place on moonlit nights when transport was easier.[15]

Assemblies in London took two main forms – long established rooms in the suburbs such as those at Chelsea, Hampstead or Mile End that differed little from comparable venues in the country – and the pleasure palaces of Carlisle House, Almack's and the Pantheon, established in the 1760s and 1770s.[16] The assembly room is, however, a predominantly provincial rather than a metropolitan creation and quickly spread to the British empire as a whole. One of the most striking aspects of eighteenth-century social history is how widespread the phenomenon was, only comparable to the frequency of playhouses. In addition to the famous rooms of York, Bath or Newcastle, there were many more obscure venues such as the rooms on Bush Fair common in the parish of Latton in Essex which had their origin as a "tea booth" built before 1778.[17] The small borough of New Romney in Kent which, according to the 1801 census had a population of 755 people, had one of the longest established assemblies in the country.[18] East Dereham in Norfolk was described in 1822 as having "many good houses; it has assembly rooms, a convenient market-house and a weekly market on Friday." Ulverston in Cumbria similarly had "a neat theatre, assembly rooms, and [a] public subscription library."[19]

Another example of the importance of the assembly room in non-metropolitan contexts is the case of the north of Ireland. There were assembly rooms across the province of Ulster in towns such as New-townards, Enniskillen, Carrickfergus, Newry, and most notably Belfast, where in 1776 Lord Donegall sponsored the construction of lavish rooms, costing £7000, as the second storey of the town's market house.[20] The Lisburn market house, which dated from the seventeenth century, also had an assembly room on its second floor. It was described in 1778 by a writer to *Walker's Hibernian Magazine* as being "fifty feet by twenty-five in the clear," linked to "a drawing-room twenty-five feet by twenty." A "genteel assembly" consisting of "gentlemen, clergy and linendrapers" was held fortnightly there during the winter with "two great balls annually."[21] The room was described in 1837 as being "beautiful," "well lighted by seven large windows" with a "very neat ... gallery, for the music players to sit on," and as having "three handsome chandeliers" and "two fireplaces."[22]

The print genre most closely associated with the assembly room, apart from the newspaper, is that of the tour, such as Arthur Young's *A Tour In Ireland*, which described the assembly room in Belfast as "60 feet long, by

30 broad, and 24 feet high; a very elegant room."[23] Giving specific information about the dimensions, decorations and facilities of an assembly
room was characteristic of commentary on it, partly because assembly
rooms often represented the largest available public meeting space in a
town or community. In delineating the dimensions of the Belfast assembly
room Young was enabling his readers to compare it with others they knew
and also to envisage its potential as an empty space open to sociability. In
the *Tour* Young also mentions the "new assembly-house, built for the
purpose" in Limerick – "Upon the whole, Limerick must be a very gay
place," he observed, "but when the usual number of troops are in town,
much more so."[24] Assembly rooms were constructed partly with this kind
of citationality in mind: they were a way for local elites to advertise and
promote their civility, to put themselves on the map as part of the increasingly global reach of the institutions, practices and media of the public
sphere. This orientation of the assembly room toward publicity or the
stranger was manifested materially through the use of architectural features
such as sash windows, allowing heat to be regulated, and also, through the
illumination of candles, making the sociability within the assembly visible
to those outside.

The Lisburn assembly was at the centre of the town's voluntary associational culture, its balls being the occasion for philanthropic efforts on
behalf of the local infirmary and the poor (Figure 4).[25] In addition to balls,
it was also the venue for concerts, and was reputed to have hosted John
Wesley on one of his tours of the province.[26] The dancing school of a Mr.
Dumont was also based there, and in 1772 Dumont performed "several
Airs on the Musical Glasses" after a ball.[27] Glassware also featured in the
adaptation in 1777 of the space as a saleroom for cut glass, the three
chandeliers reflecting myriadly in a display of "Girandoles, Hall and
Stair-Case Bells, Candlesticks, Decanters [and] Drinking-glasses."[28] The
location of the Lisburn assembly room in the market house, where
animals, foodstuffs and other goods were traded, placed it at the very
centre of the town's commercial life. Like other rooms throughout Britain
and Ireland it served as place where town elites – the professional and
upper merchant classes and the neighbouring lower gentry – could constitute themselves as a public. The assembly room was important as a zone of
encounter outside customary vectors of contact based on class, religious,
political, gender and clientage relationships. It facilitated contact between
town elites and the nobility in which the latter played the role of a guest or
visitor, enabling the exertion of patronage in informal contexts that could
nonetheless be of political value. Lord Osborne in Austen's *The Watsons*

Figure 4   The Lisburn Market House and Assembly Room, as it most likely appeared, after additions of the early nineteenth century.

only goes to the assembly "because it was judged expedient for him to please the Borough."[29] His attendance is an act of condescension and calculated public relations. The assembly was also notable as a space of heterosociability. Like the circulating library or the theatre, it was one of the new commercialized spaces of sociability in which women socialized in public with men and other women outside the boundaries of the household. It was also important as a zone of intergenerational contact and a site of what we might term Georgian youth culture. John Marsh, for example, was initiated into assembly going, and implicitly manhood, when he was fifteen and became a master of ceremonies two years later.[30]

Marsh, who was born in 1752 and died in 1828, is now best known as an amateur composer, musician and concert impresario, activities that were part of a wider commitment to sociability. The son of a captain in the royal navy and a gentlewoman from a leading Kentish dissenting family, he began his career articled to a solicitor in Romsey. He was later able to establish himself as an independent gentleman due to inherited wealth, but was never part of the first circles of society. William Weber describes him as "standing on the boundary between the gentry and the more prosperous

levels of the urban middle class," the zone which the assembly made
visible.[31] Marsh made sociability his career as a way of validating a new
identity for the gentleman based on the assembly room's ethos of polite
heterosocial companionability, untainted by political or religious faction.
The importance to him of sociability as a mode of social identity rather
than mere recreation is indicated by his decision in 1785 to move from
Kent to Chichester. Marsh selected Chichester not only because as a
cathedral town it offered opportunities for music making but also because
the "circle" there was "extensive for us in a manner to be able to chuse our
own society."[32] The opportunity to choose and to be chosen was an
important aspect of polite sociability in provincial towns, the class boundaries of which were never absolutely fixed. The expansion in polite culture
gave people such as the Marshes the chance to determine their own kind
and subscription societies such as the assembly were a model of that
selectivity in action.

Marsh's memoir, entitled "History of My Private Life," the thirty-seven
volume manuscript of which is now in the Huntington Library, tells us a
great deal about the late Georgian provincial assembly. Marsh devoted
much of his time and energy to it, particularly to dancing, assemblies being
a way for him to maintain respectable contact with young women when he
became a married man.[33] As was the case in the north of Ireland, the
assembly rooms frequented by Marsh were used for a variety of purposes,
such as lectures in astronomy, conjuring shows and meetings of the town
corporation.[34] The sociability of the country dance was not the only kind
of gathering to take place in these rooms, the trope of the empty ballroom,
as in *Emma*, suggesting an openness to the manifold meaning of "assembly." In the 1790s the Chichester rooms became a venue for the demonstration of loyalty to the crown, Marsh playing "God Save the King" on
the organ for the mayor and corporation in 1794 as they drank to the
health of George III.[35] In this respect the assembly functioned to reinforce
the political and class authority of Chichester's elites, but Marsh's memoir
also reveals the significance of the assembly as a venue for intra-class
faction, when dissension rather than harmony was the norm and the flow
of bodies and conversation became blocked. It was not uncommon for
assemblies to be scenes of public dispute: in 1769 a conflict between rival
masters of ceremonies in the rooms at Bath led to a pitched battle and the
reading of the riot act.[36] There is nothing as dramatic as this in Marsh's
memoirs but he does give details of two disputes, the first occurring in
1770 when he was a young master of ceremonies at Romsey. Mrs Daman,
the wife of the solicitor to whom he was articled, objected to the

introduction to the assembly of a musician called Mr Day on the grounds that he was a "*shoemaker's son.*" Mrs Daman was anxious that the presence of Day at the assembly would embarrass its noble patron Lord Palmerston and advised Marsh that he should "*turn*" Day "*out*" if he "presum'd to come in." Marsh refused on the grounds that this was not the collective will of the assembly's subscribers: Day was allowed in, probably to the consternation of Mrs. Daman, and Lord Palmerston, according to Marsh, was not "contaminated" by his presence.[37]

A second incident occurred in the Salisbury rooms in 1779 when the MC, a dancing master called Burgat, was assaulted by Captain Mitchell of the dragoons for what the latter took as an impertinence. Burgat was "drag'd out of the room & kicked downstairs," an action which Marsh claimed was resented by many of the subscribers because Burgat had been "appointed . . . as their agent."[38] The affront to Burgat was perceived to be an insult to the assembly's men as a collective body. The dispute was carried on into 1781, when Captain Mitchell attended a violin concerto in which Burgat was playing at the Salisbury catch club and Burgat pointedly hissed at him, leading to a fight between the military man and his friends on the one side, and the dancing master and his supporters, including a French master, "Mr De Hearle" on the other: "a fine hubbub was created, the whole room being now rous'd."[39] As John Brewer has noted, these episodes in Marsh's memoir draw attention to the people on the edges of polite culture such as dancing masters who were often foreigners or pretended to be so.[40] Another possible example of such an individual is Mr. Dumont in Lisburn, the dancing master and performer of airs on glasses. These incidents revealed the capacity of the new culture class of dancing masters, masters of ceremonies, actors, musicians and lecturers to destabilize social distinctions, revealing the porosity and also the insecurity of the assembly. Military men, often itinerant like the dancing master, were similar in their capacity to unsettle families and communities. In spite of its heterosocial character the assembly was as prone as other cultural institutions to the display of tensions between men and the ever present possibility of the eruption of physical violence. The incidents as recorded in Marsh's memoir tested the viability of this self-constituted body as a micro-commonweal or polity. Marsh's defence of Mr. Day in terms of the democratic will of the subscribers and the Salisbury assembly's support of Mr. Burgat because he was their agent were thus forms of political behavior, exploring alternative forms of collective representation and exemplifying the "plural form of performativity" that Judith Butler identifies as characteristic of public assemblies.[41]

These accounts of violence between men in Marsh's memoir provide a context for the confrontation between Falkland and Tyrrel in *Caleb Williams*. The assembly in Godwin's novel is not a fashionable venue such as those of Bath and York but is a small-scale "weekly assembly at the nearest market-town, the resort of all the rural gentry."[42] It is conceivably located, though Godwin does not specify this, in the market house, like the assembly at Lisburn. In this small pond, Tyrrel is able to dominate as an "insolent bashaw," the "grand master" of his own "*coterie*" (pp. 18, 17). The term coterie was of relatively recent coinage, being adapted in the 1760s from the French *côté*, meaning side, to refer to a group of anti-ministerial Whigs: it was later applied to a fashionable gambling club in London known as the Ladies Coterie in the 1770s.[43] By deploying the term in this context, Godwin was suggesting the pretensions of this insignificant rural gathering as well as linking the assembly to a specific historical phenomenon – the mid-century emergence of metropolitan sites such as Carlisle House, the Pantheon and the Ladies Club or Coterie as signs of the generative, transforming power of heterosociability. These sites exemplified the potential of what Habermas termed the "town" or "the market of culture products" as a zone of publicity and critique comparable to those defined by the republic of letters and by the "public sphere in the political realm."[44] As I have argued elsewhere, applications of Habermas's theories of the public sphere have tended to neglect the significance of "the town" in favour of an emphasis on the republic of letters and related spaces such as the coffeehouse. Assemblies and card parties could also have a politics.[45]

Tyrrel's dominance of the assembly is challenged by the arrival of Falkland who, unlike Tyrrel, practices politeness for its own sake as part of his performance of a virtuous, cosmopolitan disinterestedness. Thus Falkland stands aloof from the petty realm of local politics being "occupied in contemplations too dignified for scandal . . . too large for the altercations of a vestry or the politics of an election-borough," and his engagement with Tyrrel is primarily through the rules of the assembly room (p. 22). Their first alteraction occurs when Tyrrel resents Falkland, assuming the former's prerogative by leading Miss Hardingham in a dance: when challenged, Falkland "gently" repels Tyrrel, the first physical contact between them, and appeals to the master of ceremonies as "the proper person to decide in a difference of this sort" (p. 22). Falkland therefore attempts to bolster his authority within the community, implicitly contesting that of Tyrrel, by proclaiming his commitment to alternative modes of social organization based on ideals of civility and the possibility that politeness might be a means of ameliorating difference or conflict.

The other challenge to Tyrrel comes from the return to the community of the poet Mr Clare who, in combination with Falkland, transforms the assembly into a kind of literary salon. It is Clare who, at the behest of a lady, reads to the company Falkland's manuscript poem, an "Ode to the Genius of Chivalry" (p. 25). Godwin's use of "coterie" can be linked with the later applications of the term to models of literary production and literary-related sociability in which women dominated, apparent in works of twentieth-century literary criticism such as Arthur Marotti's *John Donne, Coterie Poet* and Jeffrey Cox's *Poetry and Politics in the Cockney School.*[46] The "coterie" that is created by Clare, the published poet who has achieved national fame, and who mediates the aristocratic voice of Falkland, has the effect of marginalizing Tyrrel who is placed at its "extremity" (p. 25). Falkland's appropriation of the assembly as his own particular sphere culminates in the events that follow the death of Emily Melville, Tyrrel's niece and ward. Tyrrel's cruel treatment of her leads to an implosion of his authority in the community, Godwin stating that his "large estate could not now purchase civility from the gentry, the peasantry, scarcely from his own servants" (p. 92). This response to the death of Emily Melville, galvanising the people as a whole to turn against Tyrrel, is therefore a revolutionary moment.[47] The protocols of the assembly room are used as a means of staging a confrontation between old regime power, embodied by Tyrrel, and the force of public opinion manifested by the assembly, focusing on the possibility that power can be de-legitimated by the public will. Tyrrel is voted out of the assembly, news of which is conveyed to him by letter, but he insists on appearing at the assembly in person, brushing past the master of ceremonies who confronts him at the door in his role as the assembly's gatekeeper. Tyrrel dominates the space by sheer physical force, pacing the room and defying the right of the assembly to "intrude into the concerns of any man's private family" (p. 94). The company is daunted, seeming "to want a leader" and it is at this point that Falkland enters, causing both Tyrrel and himself to blush or "redden" at the sight of each other in a moment of revelatory intimacy (p. 94). Falkland assumes the right to speak on behalf of the assembly, acting in the place of the master of ceremonies by declaring "the place is not free to you" (p. 94). Tyrrel challenges Falkland's speaking position, claiming that he is acting "under shelter" of the assembly, but Falkland insists on the legitimacy of the "public scene" as "the only place where I can have any thing to say to you," before mounting his attack on Tyrrel's character (pp. 94–95). The idea of the assembly as a place of rational communication degenerates into noise as the "general voice" performatively sounds Tyrrel's expulsion

with "hootings, tumult, and a deafening noise of indignation," recalling
Mr. Burgat's pointed hissing of Captain Mitchell in Marsh's journal
(p. 95). Deeply wounded, Tyrrel leaves the room only to return later,
drunk; he assaults Falkland, kicking him to the floor as Burgat had been
kicked and humiliated by his antagonists. The levelling which Falkland
experiences – "with one blow of his muscular arm [Tyrrel] levelled him
with the earth" – is both literal and social (95). Falkland is rendered the
equivalent of an abject dancing master, a humiliation which leads Falkland
to attack Tyrrel later the same evening. Tyrrel is found by "the
company . . . having been murdered at the distance of a few yards from
the assembly house" (p. 96).

I have outlined this episode in some detail in order to highlight the
specificity of Godwin's evocation of the assembly room both spatially and
in terms of its sociable protocols. This specificity is inextricably bound up
with the significance of the assembly as a space of social and personal
transformation, apparent, for example, in its status as a site of heterosexual
romance. The assembly is where Emily Melville first begins to dream of an
alliance with Falkland – "the civilities, that had once or twice occurred in
the bustle of a public circle, the restoring her fan which she had dropped,
or the disembarrassing her of an empty tea-cup, made her heart palpitate,
and gave birth to the wildest chimeras in her deluded imagination" (pp.
41–42). Emily's dreams are still-born but are nonetheless expressive of the
political romance of the assembly as a whole. That romance is the ideal of
civility as a universal, incorruptible value and a defence against tyrannical
power and violence, a reason why the door can be shut against that power.
The assembly represented the possibility of men and women being able, as
Marsh had done, to choose their own society, and the conflict between
Tyrrel and Falkland dramatizes both the potential and the limits of that
romance.

Tyrrel's status in the assembly is less ambiguous than that of his
antagonist: he concedes no authority to it and insists on its irrelevance to
the private affairs of his family. His authority within both his household
and the assembly are synonymous – he has no separate public identity in
the space of the assembly because he has no need for one. Falkland's status
in the assembly is more equivocal, however. His commitment to the ideals
of civility and his endorsement of the assembly as the only valid "public"
place in which he wishes to engage with Tyrrel means that he in effect
authorizes himself to speak on its behalf, as the spokesman for the "general
voice." However, as a gentleman visitor, of the same social status as Tyrrel,
he is not fundamentally *of* the assembly, in the same way as he does not

properly belong to the literary coterie but must speak through Mr. Clare. As Tyrrel asserts, Falkland acts "under shelter" of the assembly. It is the front which disguises his identity as someone who does not need to seek collectivity in order to acquire political status: he already has it in his own courtly person, "the publicity of representation inseparable from the lord's concrete existence, that, as an 'aura,' surrounded and endowed his authority," as Habermas explains.[48] The fact that Tyrrel and Falkland "redden" at the sight of each other is a sign of their mutual recognition as being of the same political kind, as belonging to what Habermas terms the "Sphere of Public Authority" consisting of the state and the court as opposed to the "Private Realm" to which the public sphere of the assembly belongs.[49] Both men are engaging in a performance of power before the audience constituted by the public sphere of "the town." Godwin thereby explores the potential of sites such as the assembly to produce a crisis of publicity for the old regime: Falkland is exposed for what he is in an experience of abjection reminiscent of, on the one hand, Burke's warning in *Reflections on the Revolution in France* about the consequences of stripping away the mystique of monarchy and, on the other, Thomas Paine's emphasis in *Rights of Man* on the need to expose the sham theatricality of the monarchical system. This humiliation also explains why Falkland kills Tyrrel in the parasociable space close to the assembly room: in a sense Falkland is also trying to annihilate the assembly itself as the space in which his masquerade of civility has been shown to be impossible.

Godwin's representation of the assembly room thus recognizes the potential of that space as a laboratory of sociality that could expand the boundaries of social and gender distinction and express the capacity of the urban middle class and lower gentry to embody the "general voice" against the operations of elite power. However, *Caleb Williams* also suggests why such a potential could never be realized. The master of ceremonies is unable to resist Tyrrel and his voice is easily appropriated by Falkland who, as we have seen, essentially masquerades as a member of the assembly. The model of literary culture that the assembly practices is also shown to be weakly imitative of courtly society; literally it is his master's voice. Like Emily Melville's dreams of Falkland, the romance of civilized social intercourse as a means of ameliorating social difference and as a counterforce to tyranny is shown to be "deluded," because, as Godwin suggests through the dyad of Tyrrel and Falkland, the elite are incapable of genuinely participating in the public sphere of the town without comprising the substance of their authority. There could be no coming together in sociable harmony of rulers and ruled, thereby disqualifying the assembly room as a potential model for Thomas Paine's idea of representative government as an "open theatre of the world," inspiring a "language, that, passing from heart to heart, is felt and understood."[50]

A version of the potency of assembly sociability and also its weakness is also apparent in the history of the Lisburn assembly. The associational culture created by the Georgian urban renaissance – the development of clubs and societies, of circulating libraries, coffeehouses, theatres and assemblies – was instrumental in the growth of republican radicalism in Ireland that culminated in the 1798 rebellion. One of the leaders of the United Irishmen in the north, who led their forces at the battle of Ballynahinch, was the Lisburn linendraper, Henry Munro. After the rebels' defeat Munro was captured, tried and hung. His head was cut from his body and displayed outside the Lisburn market house.[51] As a linendraper Munro belonged to the class of merchants who were the main subscribers to the assembly: if he did not dance there he would certainly have known of its existence. The display of Munro's head outside the windows of the assembly room was a repudiation of the politics of an enlightened civilized sociability. It demonstrated that the desire to choose your own society was a deluded one and also that genteel civility was incapable of sequestering itself, of keeping itself safe from the wider world. Like the glasses on which Mr. Dumont played his airs the mini-commonweal of the assembly was fragile and easily shattered. After the failure of the 1798 rebellion a number of assembly rooms were appropriated to act as courts in which United Irishmen were tried: in July 1798, the Rotunda assembly room in Dublin served as a military barracks. The Rotunda remained "dark" for nearly four years, the *Belfast News-letter* reporting on July 11 1802 that "nearly all the temporary barracks in the metropolis had been abandoned by the military . . . as to the Rotunda, its inmates will 'to their innocent sports again.'" The Addisonian model of polite sociability was developed in the early eighteenth century as a way for gentlemanly elites to negotiate the problem of factional or sectarian conflict. It was a means of managing but not necessarily eliminating dissensus. The capacity of the Belfast assembly rooms and the Dublin Rotunda to change from places of "innocent" amusement to a court room or a military barracks (and back again) is an indication of the closer proximity of the public sphere as it developed in Ireland in the eighteenth century to what that sphere was defined against – the alternative grotesque sociality of war. Thus the Irish case is an important framework for understanding the assembly room as a colonial and imperial transnational phenomenon, as well as one which was local and national. Such a case informs Godwin's *Caleb Williams*, as much as Godwin's novel universal-izes spaces such as the Lisburn assembly room.

Henry Munro's dead gaze into the assembly room thus contextualizes the ambivalence of the assembly in *Caleb Williams* in a particularly acute way, testifying to its potential as a site of resistance to power and why that resistance would never be properly realized. If not endorsing Godwin's politics, Austen's *Emma* nonetheless also obliquely registers the signifi-cance of the assembly room as a model of a more open social order, less anxious and inward-looking than that represented by Highbury. The foregrounding in Austen's novel of the heterosexual romance narrative that Godwin marginalizes in his story of the assembly room signifies the emergence and the effectiveness of another element of the Habermasian public sphere – the literary one of the republic of letters, specifically the novel, that constituted a public primarily in terms of affective reading relations and the mystification of the political order in such terms. Both Godwin and Austen acknowledge that the more expansive literary public sphere of the novel with its potential to imagine publics into being was deeply invested in the historical experiment of institutions of the town such as the assembly room. This indebtedness also has a formal dimension, the novel, like journals such as Marsh's, the newspaper and the mass of printed ephemera that enabled and documented assemblies, being a gen-eric correlative of the assembly as a space in which quotidian sociality could be enacted and, temporarily, reimagined. The fictions of Godwin and Austen thus register both the dreams and the disappointments of the assembly room by reworking it as a space in which, as Bakhtin claimed of his theory of the chronotope, time "thickens."[52]

Many examples of Georgian assembly rooms continue to be used in the twenty-first century as leisure centres, venues for weddings and afternoon teas, and in the case of the magnificent York assembly rooms, an Italian restaurant. Sociable chatter endures long after Godwinian rational inquiry has gone silent. The Lisburn assembly rooms survive as part of the town's museum, though their history after 1798 continued to be shadowed by violence. On the morning of Sunday, August 22, 1920, a policeman, District Inspector Oswald Swanzey, was shot by an IRA hit squad as he was leaving the town's cathedral in the market square, just a few yards away from the assembly rooms. Swanzey had been involved in the extra-judicial murder in Cork of Tomàs MacCurtain, the lord mayor of Cork and commanding officer of the first IRA brigade, and had been moved to the largely protestant town of Lisburn at the other end of the country in the north. The killing was notable not only for its audacity but also for what happened afterwards: in the days that followed, the protestant population of Lisburn exacted revenge by attacking their Catholic neighbours, driving them out of the town and leaving it a wasteland; over 400 buildings were burned to the ground, leading some to compare Lisburn with the ruined towns of Flanders.[53] The contiguity of sociability and violence, instantiated in 1798, therefore never went way, never became "history," and it was repeated when the "Troubles" were renewed in the 1970s. We tend to regard concrete material structures as more enduring than the evanescent social life that occurs within them but the history of Lisburn, the very name of the town derived from one of its periodic destructions, is testimony to the insubstantiality of the places that house us and the persistence of violence and faction which always haunt the ideal of sociability as a civilizing force. In the early 1980s, the Georgian features of the Lisburn assembly room were renovated as part of the town's museum (Figure 5). This "reconstitution" as the town's historian put it, included the restoration of the entrance to the assembly room, similar to the kind of doorway which the master of ceremonies in *Caleb Williams* would have guarded and which Tyrrel was able to enter nonetheless.[54] This doorway is exemplary of how the assembly room is embedded in the fabric and the imaginary of British and Irish civic life. Assemblies can be seen as

Figure 5   The eighteenth-century door case of the Assembly Room, as restored in 1980.

laboratories of social change that explored the possibilities of both inclusion and exclusion in limited but significant ways: this doorway persists in sequestering those possibilities, trying to keep them safe, as much as Godwin's novel and the history of Lisburn suggest that closing the door against the violence that shadowed such a space was ultimately impossible.

Notes

1 Jane Austen, *Jane Austen's Letters*, ed. Deirdre Le Faye, 3rd ed. (Oxford: Oxford University Press, 1995), e.g. pp. 20, 22, 27.

2 Constance Hill, *Jane Austen: Her Homes & Her Friends* (London: John Lane, 1902), pp. 53, 54.

3 Kathryn Sutherland, *Jane Austen's Textual Lives: From Aeschylus to Bollywood* (Oxford: Oxford University Press, 2005), pp. 10–11.

4 Jane Austen, *Emma*, ed. Richard Cronin and Dorothy McMillan (Cambridge: Cambridge University Press, 2005), p. 213.

5 Elizabeth Gaskell, *Cranford*, ed. Elizabeth Porges Watson (London: Oxford University Press, 1972), pp. 85–86.

6 See Andrew McCann, *Cultural Politics in the 1790s: Literature, Radicalism, and the Public Sphere* (New York: St Martin's Press, 1999), esp. chapter two, 'William Godwin and the Pathological Public Sphere: Theorizing Communicative Action in the 1790s'; see also Paul Keen, *The Crisis of Literature in the 1790s: Print Culture and the Public Sphere* (Cambridge: Cambridge University Press, 1999); for the wider context of Godwin's relationship to the conversable public sphere in the 1790s see Jon Mee, *Conversable Worlds: Literature, Contention, and Community 1762–1830* (Oxford: Oxford University Press, 2011), pp. 137–67.

7 Nicolle Jordan, "The Promise and Frustration of Plebeian Public Opinion in *Caleb Williams*," *Eighteenth-Century Fiction* 19: 3 (2007), 251.

8 An important strand of popular antiquarianism in the eighteenth century was the documentation of a wide range of forms of sociability, including that of assemblies, pleasure and tea gardens, lectures, exhibitions, ballooning etc., through the collection of printed ephemera. These collections constitute a record of contemporary public culture that was the basis for subsequent histories such as Richard D. Altick's *The Shows of London* (Cambridge MA: Belknap Press, 1978). For an account of this tradition, see my *The Ephemeral Eighteenth Century: Sociability, Print, and the Cultures of Collecting 1640–1860*, in preparation. For an account of social dancing, see Cheryl A. Wilson, *Literature and Dance in Nineteenth-Century Britain: Jane Austen to the New Woman* (Cambridge: Cambridge University Press, 2012).

9 Peter Borsay, *The English Urban Renaissance: Culture and Society in the Provincial Town 1660–1770* (Oxford: Clarendon Press, 1989); John Brewer, *The Pleasures of the Imagination: English Culture in the Eighteenth Century* (London: HarperCollins, 1997), Amanda Vickery, *The Gentleman's Daughter: Women's Lives in Georgian England* (New Haven, CT: Yale University Press, 1998), p. 42.

See also Helen Berry, "Creating Polite Space: The Organisation and Social Function of the Newcastle Assembly Rooms" in *Creating and Consuming Culture in North-East England 1660–1830*, ed. Helen Berry and Jeremy Gregory (Aldershot: Ashgate, 2004), pp. 120–40.

10 For an account of assemblies as forms of 'performative action' see Judith Butler, *Notes Toward a Performative Theory of Assembly* (Cambridge MA: Harvard University Press, 2015).

11 Daniel Defoe, *A Tour Through the Whole Island of Great Britain*, ed. P. N. Furbank, W. R. Owens, and A. J. Coulson (New Haven, CT: Yale University Press, 1991), p. 88.

12 See for example, the archives of the Tunbridge Wells, bookseller, and printer Jasper Sprange in the Tunbridge Wells Museum for printed ephemera in relation to assemblies; also the archives of the proofs of the printer William Davison of Alnwick, in the Northumberland Record Office.

13 William Batcheller, *A New History of Dover and of Dover Castle* (Dover: William Batcheller, 1828), p. 341.

14 Jane Austen, *Later Manuscripts*, ed. Janet Todd and Linda Bree (Cambridge: Cambridge University Press, 2008), pp. 93, 94.

15 John Marsh, *The John Marsh Journals: The Life and Times of a Gentleman Composer (1752–1828)*, ed. Brian Robins (Hillsdale, NY: Pendragon Press, 1998), p. 592.

16 On Carlisle House, Almack's, and the Pantheon, see Gillian Russell, *Women, Sociability and Theatre in Georgian London* (Cambridge: Cambridge University Press, 2007).

17 "Latton," *A History of the County of Essex: Volume 8* (1983), pp. 186–95. URL: www.british-history.ac.uk/report.aspx?compid=63852&strquery=Latton Date accessed: April 15, 2014.

18 Alan Everitt, *Landscape and Community in England* (London: Hambledon Press, 1985), p. 179.

19 *Paterson's Roads: Being an Entirely Original and Accurate Description of All the Direct and Principal Cross Roads in England and Wales*, 16th ed. (London: Longman et. al. 1822), pp. 323, 496. There is a need for an historical topography or atlas of the assembly room not only in the British Isles but also in the Georgian Anglophone world as a whole, a project which the digitization of printed sources and capacity for searching makes potentially more realizable than ever before.

20 C. E. B. Brett, *Court Houses and Market Houses of the Province of Ulster* (Belfast: Ulster Architectural Heritage Society, 1973), p. 44. See also Maurice Craig, *The Architecture of Ireland from the Earliest Times to 1880* (London: Batsford, 1982), p. 202; Gilbert Camblin, *The Town in Ulster* (Belfast: Wm. Mullan & Son, 1951), pp. 86–87; T. C. Barnard, "The Cultures of Eighteenth-Century Irish Towns," in *Change, Convergence and Divergence: Provincial Towns in Early Modern England and Ireland, Proceedings of the British Academy 108*, ed. Peter Borsay and Lindsay J. Proudfoot (Oxford: Oxford University Press for the British Academy, 2002), pp. 195–222; *Two Capitals: London and Dublin*

1500–1840, Proceedings of the British Academy 107, ed. Peter Clark and Raymond Gillespie (Oxford: Oxford University Press for the British Academy, 2001). For the development of associational culture in Georgian Ireland see e.g. *Clubs and Societies in Eighteenth-Century Ireland*, ed. James Kelly and Martyn J. Powell (Dublin: Four Courts Press, 2010); *Associational Culture in Ireland and Abroad*, ed. Jennifer Kelly and R. V. Comerford (Dublin: Irish Academic Press, 2010).

21 *Walker's Hibernian Magazine* 8 (May 1778), 268.

22 Quoted in Brian Mackey, "The Market House and Assembly Rooms, Lisburn," *Lisburn Historical Society Journal* 6 (1986), 46.

23 Arthur Young, *A Tour in Ireland: With General Observations on the Present State of that Kingdom*, 2 vols., second ed. (London, 1780), vol. I, p. 166.

24 Ibid., vol. I, p. 366.

25 *Belfast News-Letter*, February 1, 1771; *Belfast News-Letter*, June 11, 1771.

26 Mackey, "The Market House and Assembly Rooms, Lisburn," p. 47.

27 *Belfast News-Letter*, March 24–28, 1775; *Belfast News-Letter*, November 3, 1772.

28 *Belfast News-Letter*, May 30–June 3, 1777.

29 Austen, *Late Manuscripts*, pp. 96–97.

30 *John Marsh Journals*, pp. 42, 69.

31 William Weber, "The Fabric of Daily Life and the Autobiography of John Marsh," *Huntington Library Quarterly* 59:1 (1989), 149; see also Brewer, *The Pleasures of the Imagination*, pp. 531–72.

32 *John Marsh Journals*, p. 350.

33 E.g. "On Tuesday 10th. [November 1795] I went to the 3d. Assembly & danced with Misses Garthwaite Cope Diggens & Peckham": *John Marsh Journals*, p. 590.

34 Ibid., pp. 134, 142.

35 Ibid., p. 556.

36 See e.g. *London Chronicle*, April 13–15, 1769.

37 *John Marsh Journals*, pp. 73–74.

38 Ibid., p. 207.

39 Ibid., p. 233.

40 Brewer, *Pleasures of the Imagination*, p. 550.

41 Butler, *Notes*, p. 8.

42 William Godwin, *Caleb Williams*, ed. David McCracken (Oxford: Oxford World's Classics, 1982), p. 17. Subsequent references are to this edition, and are included in parentheses in text.

43 Russell, *Women, Sociability and Theatre*, p. 71.

44 Jürgen Habermas, *The Structural Transformation of the Public Sphere: An Inquiry into a Category of Bourgeois Society*, trans. Thomas Burger and Frederick Lawrence (Cambridge, MA: MIT Press, 1989), p. 30.

45 Russell, *Women, Sociability and Theatre*.

46 Arthur Marotti, *John Donne, Coterie Poet* (Madison, WI: University of Wisconsin Press, 1986); Jeffrey N. Cox, *Poetry and Politics in the Cockney School: Keats, Shelley, Hunt and their Circle* (Cambridge: Cambridge University Press, 1998).

47　See also Jordan, "The Promise and Frustration of Plebeian Public Opinion in *Caleb Williams*": "the text delivers retribution in terms that emphasize the power of public opinion to defeat the privilege of status" (260).

48　Habermas, *Structural Transformation*, p. 7.

49　Ibid., p. 30.

50　Thomas Paine, *Rights of Man, Common Sense and Other Political Writings*, ed. Mark Philp (Oxford: Oxford World's Classics, 1995), p. 235.

51　Mackey, "The Market House and Assembly Rooms, Lisburn," p. 47.

52　M. M. Bakhtin, *The Dialogic Imagination: Four Essays*, ed. Michael Holquist, trans. Caryl Emerson and Michael Holquist (Austin, TX: University of Texas Press, 1981), p. 84.

53　The Swanzey assassination and its aftermath have recently featured in two post-Troubles memoirs, Glenn Patterson's *Once Upon a Hill: Love in Troubled Times* (London: Bloomsbury, 2008) and Patricia Craig, *A Twisted Root: Ancestral Entanglements in Ireland* (Belfast: Blackstaff Press, 2012).

54　Mackey, "The Market House and Assembly Rooms, Lisburn," p. 48.

CHAPTER 7

Unconventional Calling
Godwin, Women and Visiting in the 1790s
Mark Philp[1]

This is a paper about a quintessential mode of sociability in radical circles in the 1790s – visiting and calling on friends and acquaintances, primarily in each other's homes. It centers on William Godwin (1756–1836), philosopher, novelist, and literary figure, husband of the now more famous Mary Wollstonecraft, and thereby father to the still more famous Mary Shelley. Godwin rose to public prominence in the opening years of the French Revolution with his magnum opus, *An Enquiry Concerning Political Justice* (1793), but his career was a major casualty of the backlash against radicalism after 1798. Godwin made and received a lot of visits – hundreds each year. Although scholars have often referred to his carefully kept diary, their use of it has been relatively impressionistic. In this chapter I want to explore more systematically some of the complexities of domestic visiting, drawing on the digital edition of Godwin's diary.[2]

Godwin attached considerable philosophical importance to visiting, its norms, and its possibilities. He was not an informal man; he came from a strict Calvinist background and was originally a dissenting minister. Yet, as his thinking developed – and somewhat under the influence of Rousseau's critique of contemporary manners and politeness, coupled with his dissenting commitment to candour and sincerity – he came to see many of the conventions of society as restraints on the development of mind and the free communication of truth through discussion. Indeed, he predicted a future in which conventional restraints would disappear and benevolence and virtue would triumph under the direction of people's rational capacities.

This radical vision, powerfully expressed in his *Enquiry*, brought Godwin widespread fame. But the vision was accompanied by considerable caution. He feared that precipitate action would produce chaos and delay the advance of humanity. As John Thelwall pointed out: Godwin's "visionary peculiarities of mind," which "recommend the most extensive plan of freedom and innovation ever discussed by any writer in the English language . . . ," were coupled with a conviction that it was necessary "to reprobate every measure from which even the most moderate reform can rationally be expected."³ Thelwall had a point. There was, however, one area in which Godwin's practice did seem to answer to his speculation: his relationship with Mary Wollstonecraft (almost certainly his first affair) was not conventional. They married when she was several months pregnant – and he did that with some philosophical embarrassment. When she died he wrote an extremely frank *Memoir* of his wife detailing her love affairs (including their own). It became a major target for the anti-Jacobin and loyalist press. Southey said: "he stripped his dead wife naked." Godwin's relationship with Mary Jane Clairmont, who became his second wife some four years after Wollstonecraft's death, was similar; it too involved pre-marital pregnancy. This was unconventional behavior, but it was linked to a set of alternative standards by which Godwin sought to regulate his conduct in the 1790s and that he applied in his intimate friendships and relationships. Yet this was not just a matter of personal conduct in private domestic space; these spaces and the relationships formed in them were subject to powerful social norms and expectations that touched and influenced the behavior of a wide range of people with whom Godwin interacted.

Although visiting was deeply imbedded in eighteenth century practices, it was also something on which the radical literary culture of the 1790s reflected critically, in their novels, letters, and practices. In his *Enquiry*, Godwin inveighed against the practice of making servants tell visitors that the individual or family was "not at home" when they did not wish to see the caller (a phrase that Godwin reduces to "nah" and which crops up frequently in the diary). For Godwin, such conventions prompted dishonesty, violated duties to candour, truth, and utility, and taught servants to be even more mendacious than their position ordinarily led them to be.⁴ They also represented an unwillingness to be candid about the distribution of our cordiality and esteem – and they preserved the rich and the powerful from the interpolations of the rising middling orders.

In some contexts, Godwin was powerless over these conventions. When gentlemen with whom he had animatedly conversed at Debrett's or elsewhere the evening before ignored him in the street the following day, he could not make them respond. And the diary shows that in his connections with men of quality, none violated the implicit norms for domestic visiting: he called on them; they did not call on him. If they wished to see him, they summoned him. Even the apparently "radical" John Horne Tooke set his relationship with Godwin in traditional terms: from 1792 Godwin dined at Tooke's very regularly and was keen to have

Tooke call, and to be the person to introduce him to Thomas Lawrence the painter, but Horne Tooke did not call on Godwin until 1799, (when he dined), and 1800, (when he called on him). But these are two out of the 122 contacts over fifteen years – so the norms were essentially maintained – yet Horne Tooke was not a conventional man.

It was norms such as these that Godwin wanted to jettison among like minds and in the 1790s and early 1800s he found considerable openness and egalitarianism in many of his relationships – where this implied that the relationship was not a relationship of supplication and patronage but involved an equality of access and exchange between people sharing in the pursuit of truth. Godwin found this with his contemporaries – such as Joseph Fawcett, Thomas Holcroft, James Marshall, and William Nicholson – but he also sought it more especially in his relationships with younger pupils, acolytes, and friends, such as Thomas Cooper, Willis Webb (both relatives), and then George Dyson, Joseph Gerrald, Basil Montagu, John Stoddart, Ralph Fell, John Arnot, Thomas Turner, Patrick Patrickson, Percy Shelley, and so on. The open character of these relationships emerges in the often very frank debates and arguments he had with so many. When he struck gold he said so: in January 1796, after he met John Stoddart, a lawyer some seventeen years his junior, he wrote:

> I indulge with some impatience the hope that you will repeat your visit to me before you leave town. I do not recollect any instance of a total stranger having won so much of my esteem in a single interview, as you have done. I want to know whether in exhibiting so many excellencies you have put a deception on me; or whether, as I like to believe, I have found a treasure. This is an inquiry with which I am not often disposed to trouble a man upon so short an acquaintance. [5]

This was characteristic: Godwin sought to dispense with formality when he met those whom he considered to be talented and worthwhile men. He wanted to engage them in conversation and debate – he sought the clash of mind on mind. This was a central part of Godwin's "Conversable World," as Jon Mee has called it: a world in which mutual expectations about interpersonal conduct and civilities were actively reworked by participants in the 1790s.[6]

Nonetheless, these partly public/partly domestic spaces had their tensions, dangers, and possibilities for transgression. There were many boundary problems for Godwin in relation to those whom he welcomed so wholly into his society. He wanted to challenge the norms of domestic sociability for philosophical purposes – but the practices of his acquaintances did not always meet his expectations. For example, consider the case of the writer

Ralph Fell whom Godwin met in 1797 and saw very frequently until 1804, when the relationship foundered because Godwin was unable to repay a debt.[7] Fell was friendly with Godwin's only sister, Hannah, but his involvement with Godwin's domestic circle became troubled at the end of 1799. Hannah Godwin was a single woman and a Mantua maker in London. She visited Godwin regularly, calling occasionally in the company of girls apprenticed to her business. In August 1798 she introduced her apprentice, Sarah Carey/Karre to Godwin, and he met the two women with Ralph Fell in August and again in November 1799. In November 1799, Fell wrote to Godwin referring to his getting married (to Carey). Godwin was clearly angry about the relationship, suspecting that his sister was using his philosophical "salon" as a means of securing husbands for her apprentices. His wrath is clear from the note he sent Hannah:

> I am extremely mortified at your conduct in what has lately passed between Miss Carey and Mr Fell. You must have known, if you were capable of any accurate judgment, that it was the case of a young man of superlative talents and promise throwing himself away, from the most puerile, or rather the grossest motives, upon a creature comparatively worthy only of a dunghil. You ought, if you had any propriety, immediately to have consulted me on this subject. But I bear you no resentment. As I have said, I am only mortified, but not surprised by your conduct.[8]

His draft to Fell was equally unrestrained: "But my judgment is clear: I will never see Miss Carey, as Miss Carey, so long as this business is in hand: if she should ever become Mrs Fell, I will treat your washerwoman with respect under that character, and will allow myself no retrospect to what is irremediable."[9] Fell married Sarah Carey/Karre on July 5, 1800, at St Dionis Backchurch with James Marshall and Hannah Godwin as witnesses.[10]

Fell's marriage to Carey, followed by the marriage of another young friend and acolyte, Henry Dibbin to Louisa Jones (Godwin's housekeeper) in May 1801 (at which Hannah Godwin was again a witness), led to a serious cooling in Godwin's relationship with his sister. Their relationship may have been additionally complicated by Hannah's intimacy with Godwin's amanuensis James Marshall. In the 1790s, she seems to have been very close to Marshall, and the evidence suggests that she fell out with him in 1800 partly over Fell. Prior to this, their relationship was such that Godwin's mother expressed concern about it in a letter to Godwin: "your poor sister is I fear a bad oeconermist her heart too generous for her comings in . . . , many people think her carrector injured by Marshal a married man, who I suppose dines with her on Sundays, is it not so, do you commend her, tell me freely, or advise her against it yourself, she will hear you sooner than any body else . . ." [11] To our knowledge Godwin did not advise against it – perhaps assuming that Marshall was philosophically above reproach. Yet it is clear that there were a number of secrets being kept from Godwin even in his most intimate visiting circles: Godwin believed that it was George Dyson who had married Louisa Jones (when in fact he was only a witness to the wedding), and he reported as much to his young friend the traveller John Arnot, who was himself in love with Jones. It is unclear when Godwin found out the complete truth, but his reaction to Jones's marriage was uncompromising: she was forbidden to see the children again.

This was clearly treacherous social terrain – protégés, acquaintances, friends, and family, clearly failing, on Godwin's view, to act according to his expectations. The exact nature of his expectations with respect to personal relationships are unclear, but seem to have concerned the furthering of intellectual development and of capacities for contributing to the broader world; and they seem to have required affinities of mind between partners – promising a companionate, mutually educative, progressive, and philosophical, not just a social or sexual partnership. Or at least, that was the case when he was (as he saw it) defending his friends against the attractions of Hannah Godwin's young apprentices.

It is worth emphasizing how judgmental and intolerant Godwin could be, especially in very close relationships. Indeed, friendships break down because of his strictures (derived from strict philosophical principle). By 1805, he and Hannah had little contact – indeed, he included her in a list of "amis perdus" drawn up (probably) in around 1812; a list that names many of his former and younger friends – Dyson, Montagu, Stoddart, Arnot, Dibbin, and Kearsley – and a number of other women – Inchbald, Gisbourne/Reveley, and Amelia Opie/Alderson. [12] Many on the list are people who became alienated from Godwin in part because of the problems of policing the boundaries of these public and private spaces and connections. Dyson, Dibbin, and Arnot were linked through Louisa Jones, Godwin's housekeeper; Godwin alienated Reveley by proposing to her too soon after the death of her husband in the summer of 1799 (despite their secret assignation of 1795); [13] Inchbald froze Godwin out after his marriage to Wollstonecraft; and Amelia Alderson's earlier intimacy with Godwin cooled on her marriage to Opie. The list testifies to Godwin's misjudgements and mismanagement of the expectations of others, and his overstatement of his own claims with respect to them. But it also speaks eloquently to the complex character of personal relations in the radical culture of sociability, conversation, and candour in London at the end of the eighteenth century, and to the difficulties of living in the light of one's private judgment in ways that are necessarily partly public, even if conducted in domestic space.

The dramatic misjudgement Godwin made in publishing his *Memoirs* of Mary Wollstonecraft suggests that he was largely unaware of the very limited public tolerance for his unconventional behavior (or that he was too distraught to be cautious). At the same time, his behavior with respect to Fell looks stultifyingly conventional, and it is clear that there are other cases in which he found himself acting in ways that to the external observer look identical to the classic position of the outraged patriarch of eighteenth century fiction.[14] There are then two contrasting sides – seemingly conventional opprobrium for some of his friends and their choices – and his own very unconventional relationships – not just with Wollstonecraft and Clairmont, but also, less intimate but not necessarily wholly intellectual, with a number of others including Elizabeth Inchbald, Maria Reveley, Amelia Alderson, but to whom we might add, Sarah Anne Parr,[15] Nan Pinkerton, Mary Robinson, and Mary Hays. This list is rather impressionistic. Little exists to allow us firmly to determine Godwin's intentions, these women's expectations, or the precise character of their relationships, but there is a clear sense in many cases that those who called on him, and on whom he called, were looking for at least a kind of intense intellectual relationship with him that was far from conventional, and that the boundaries of their relationships with Godwin were not well-defined, and could generate difficulties and misunderstandings.

Godwin certainly invited a degree of unconventional behavior. On September 26, 1798, just over a year after Wollstonecraft died, and after Harriet Lee, the headmistress of a Bath school for girls, gave a decisive, final rejection to Godwin's proposal of marriage, he met a "miss Kinsman" with John Philip Kemble, in Watford.[16] Godwin had previously encountered her brother Henry on a visit to the Wedgwoods in 1794. The day after they met, Godwin wrote to her. He began:

> As I did not say to you the things that I ought when I saw you I feel myself prompted to say them to you now on paper. You overstepped the dull rules of old fashioned etiquette and ceremony by the action that gave me the pleasure of conversing with you, I therefore make no apology for the liberty I take in addressing you . . .

Apologizing for not having responded equally openly and unreservedly, Godwin went on:

> I ought to have said to myself when a spirited conduct on your part so extraordinarily introduced you to me this morning, accident has thrown

this lovely girl in my way, I ought to use the moment she affords me, in encouraging her virtue, in blowing the flame of her spirit, &endeavouring to render, as far as my powers may extend, the excellencies she now possesses as lasting as her life. This you had a right to expect from me, and I did nothing of this. Your accosting me as you did persuades me on reflection that you have a mind / capable of rising much above the vulgar of your sex. But you must treasure this gift, it is a talent that you may not neglect with impunity.[17]

Godwin addressed his letter to "Miss Kinsman," not realizing that Emily was the youngest of three daughters. The letter clearly caused consternation in the household and was answered, rather stiffly, by her brother. But the family had made an impact, and Godwin called on them at their home in King's Langley, Herts, in May 1799. E. Kingsman also appears in Godwin's "1796 List" (which identifies the year in which he met people who have some special significance for him) for the year 1798, and D (orothea) Kingsman for the year 1799! If he was not spontaneous in practice, Godwin was clearly willing to respond to unconventional initiatives – given a little time, some ink, and some paper. We have to rely on our imaginations to tell us how the family responded to Emily.

Although this is just one incident, there are a lot of visits to and from women in the diary, and the diary's digital edition allows us to look more systematically at the pattern of visits that Godwin paid, or was paid, enabling us to deduce something about the norms that operated in his circles. I want to focus my remarks on the occasions on which Godwin saw women alone either at his home, or in theirs – something that he did to some degree, although much less commonly than was the case for his contacts with men.

I take the significance of them being "alone" to be as follows. The reputation of women (in relation to men) was socially policed in this period. There were norms of conduct. Of course, people bent and broke them, but in doing so they risked their reputation, and that could lead to them being cut, ostracized from various circles, and could diminish their respectability and, for some, their consequent (marital) prospects. The costs to men were substantially fewer – the point of having a past was, in part, to have something to put behind you! But for women these norms were powerful and responsible men would have had some concern for the reputational risks run by their female friends (although see Godwin's striking letter to Maria Reveley when he courts her (too) soon after the death of her husband beginning "How my whole soul disclaims and tramples upon these cowardly ceremonies. Is woman always to be a slave?").[18]

Most women sought to avoid providing food for gossip and speculation; many were also concerned not to be associated with women whose reputation might produce collateral damage; and many might be anxious, especially following Godwin's *Memoirs* of Wollstonecraft, not to be seen as intimate with him. Radical women (that is, women who had sympathies with the reform movement and sought to challenge the polite conventions by which they were constrained) might or might not bend or break these rules; they might also be less judgmental about those they associated with; but in neither case could they expect to do so wholly without cost. Wollstonecraft was certainly concerned about such issues. When she returned to London from Paris she presented herself as Mrs Imlay and was taken by many to be exactly that. Indeed, Godwin, prior to the commencement of their affair, despite referring to her throughout the diary as Mrs. Wollstonecraft, referred to her as Imlay in an unconscious reflex on the first occasion that he included her in a dinner party with his respectable friends (April 22–23, 1796).

Godwin was often unconventional – in whom he saw, how he saw them, and in his attitude to propriety and social norms. He married after the fact, not before; he exhorted Wollstonecraft the day after the diary entry "chez moi toute" – "Humble! for heaven's sake, be proud, be arrogant!"[19]; in his many relationships with women he talked to them as a philosopher, irrespective of convention or offence; and he was friendly with several women who were in various ways "unrespectable" (such as Mary Robinson, formerly mistress to the Prince of Wales and subsequently to Col. Tarleton). But that meant that the women he met had to consider how to respond to such an unconventional man (especially after the *Memoirs*). Above all, they were probably wary of being seen to be intimate with him.

Nonetheless, between 1791 and 1801 (in the December of which Godwin married Mary Jane Clairmont) there were many occasions on which Godwin recorded visits to or meals with women where no one else was recorded as present. Some can be eliminated because they involved domestic help. Others, although by no means all, were instances where Godwin (and his visitor/hostess) were not behaving strictly within the norms of propriety. For the historian the central issue is how these might be differentiated: not just by us, but also by his contemporaries. How might others have seen these calls as something other than evidence of scandal? One principle that is likely to have operated in Godwin's circles is that people would have been concerned only where there was a *consistent* pattern of compromising behavior. Also, married women might have had a degree of licence that single women did not – especially eligible single women. Older, well established women may similarly have had this.

There were four main possibilities for Godwin seeing a woman on her own – the "place" would either be his or her domestic space; and it might be a call, or might involve a meal. Some categories are harder to establish than others. Godwin lists "calls" to him in a way that does not make clear whether people are calling together or separately. For example, on August 29, 1800 he records "Curran, Taggart, A Walker, Ht & Phebe G call." Whether this is one or four calls (or something in between) is just unclear (they were probably four separate calls – Phebe G is Godwin's niece). Our coding treats these as single calls, but we emphasize that caution should be attached to that judgment and to this category.

We also do not know whether a "call" or "dine" where no one else is recorded really is a case of Godwin meeting the person alone. Godwin identifies housekeepers and servants in the diary only exceptionally, and on many occasions when it appears that Godwin was alone, servants may have been in attendance. Servants could be a mixed blessing: they could hold one's reputation in their hands, and they could conspire for or against their mistress or master, so that people may often have needed to maintain appearances in front of them as well.[26] Moreover, what matters reputationally is not whether two people were actually alone – but whether others assumed that they were.

If we set some of these concerns aside for a moment and look at the broader picture, we can recognize the following patterns. If we take the occasions on which Godwin recorded seeing women on their own and look at the busiest years, it is striking how far a single person accounts for around half of all such contacts. In 1793, 1794, and 1795 this was Elizabeth Inchbald; in 1796 and 1797 this was Wollstonecraft (the numbers hold up despite the fact that Godwin ceased to list Wollstonecraft in the diary after their marriage in March 1797); in 1798 this was Charlotte Smith; in 1799 and 1800 this was Sarah Elwes; and in 1801 this was Mrs. Clairmont. In terms of total contacts across these years, there are 135 with Inchbald; 168 with Wollstonecraft; 28 with Smith; 116 with Elwes; and 56 with Clairmont. At this point, before leaping to conclusions, we might want more granularity.

Visits by Godwin to women when no other person is recorded as present were paid most often in 1793, 1794, and 1795 to Inchbald; in 1796 and 1797 to Wollstonecraft; in 1798 there was a cluster of women (Smith, Hays, Christie, and Lee) each of whom was seen slightly fewer than ten times; in 1799 and 1800 it was Elwes; and in 1801 no one stood out.

Visits by women to Godwin when he was alone are far fewer. The only people who visited more than 10 times in a year on their own were Wollstonecraft and Elwes. In 1797 and 1798, in the aftermath of Wollstonecraft's death, Maria Reveley was also a frequent visitor, ostensibly to help care for the children, but her visits caused her husband sufficient disquiet that she stopped them. Reveley was a married woman; no single woman could have acted in this way without cost.

Meals that Godwin had at a woman's home on their own are in similar numbers to solo calls on Godwin. But even fewer people account for a very substantial proportion of such calls: Wollstonecraft, Smith, Elwes, and Clairmont received Godwin more than ten times – and they account for a substantial proportion of such events. Finally, meals taken alone with Godwin is the most exclusive group – only Elwes and Clairmont appear more than ten times. Moreover, of the 40 such occasions between 1798 and 1801, Elwes accounts for 20 and Clairmont for 14.

The years 1797 and 1798 were slightly odd because from March 1797 Godwin continued to see Wollstoncraft, but no longer recorded her: also, from March he had a family home changing the salience of several of the conventions; and from September 1797 he was desperate for help with his family in the aftermath of Wollstonecraft's death. 1798 clearly involves several people who were supporting Godwin, such as Eliza Fenwick and Mrs. Christie.

Nonetheless, there is clearly a growing intimacy as we move through these categories – "calling" probably had components that were not fully registered in the diary, such as leaving a card, paying respects, etc., which conformed to social manners. Also, while young women in particular might not have done much receiving of young men without supervision, it was not necessarily inappropriate to do so (as Fanny Burney's novels suggest). Women may also have been able to control the situation, through the proximity of family, servants or maids, and thus to minimize their exposure. "Mrs Perfection," as Wollstonecraft called Inchbald, clearly maintained control of Godwin's intimacy with her by restricting it to calls on her – of her 135 solo contacts with Godwin, all but five were calls he made to her. Charlotte Smith also saw a lot of Godwin, especially in 1798, when she was in London a good deal but she was married with ten children and, again, the vast majority of contacts took place at her home, with Godwin calling on her or, more usually, taking tea with her.

Those most at risk of accusations of impropriety were those who frequently called on or dined alone with Godwin, or with whom he dined alone. There are three such people who stand out: Wollstonecraft, Elwes, and Clairmont. We know a good deal about Wollstonecraft, and we have discovered a good deal recently about Mary Jane Clairmont.[21] Sarah Elwes has, thus far, been largely unnoticed and unidentified, but she offers us an especially interesting perspective on the problems that attach to encounters in private spaces.

Sarah Elwes was married to John Elwes, who was the youngest of the two illegitimate sons of John Elwes senr, renowned as the meanest man in Britain on his death on November 26, 1789 (in Dickens' *Our Mutual Friend* Mr. Boffin reads Edward Topham's *Life of Elwes* (1790) to train up as a miser). Sarah and John Elwes married on December 23, 1789. John may have been re-marrying, he had a son by Margaret Olley Elwes in 1788 (but his will suggests that this son did not survive).[22] It was Sarah's second marriage, her first husband (probably from 1785) was Captain Thomas Haynes, who died on December 26, 1788.[23]

In October 1793, Sarah and John Elwes separated and in 1794 John Elwes brought an action in the Court of the King's Bench, against a Mr George Samuel Harvey for criminal conversation with his wife dating from 1791. Harvey was approximately 22 years of age. Mrs Elwes was described as being between 30 and 35 years of age (John Elwes was 42).[24] The case cited another young man, Jasper Egerton, a lawyer who had acted as Mrs. Elwes's representative and lawyer in the months leading up to the criminal conversation case.[25] The case against Harvey was based on the testimony of various servants employed by John Elwes, who filed reports of lewd and intimate behavior occurring in the back sitting room of the house (which was the main reception room) on various occasions; of Mrs. Elwes's maid letting in Harvey (or Egerton) without the other servants' knowledge; of her having taken the carriage with, or gone riding with one or other of the named gentlemen, to Kensington Gardens, "and there quit her horses, and desired the same to be put up at some Inn or Public House in the Neighbourhood, and would remain in the said Gardens for several Hours together, and till after it was dark, and was almost constantly, at such Times, met either by Mr Harvey or Mr Egerton, and they used to retire into the most private and unfrequented Parts of the Garden, and remain there so long, that the Gate-Keepers have frequently taken Notice of it to the Servant waiting for her."[26] Moreover, the claim was that "Mrs Elwes used very frequently to call upon Mr Egerton at his Chambers in Gray's Inn and on Mr Harvey as his Chambers in the Temple, and at other times, in the Absence of her Husband, used to invite, sometimes the One, and sometimes the other of them home to her House, in Weymouth Street, and remained alone with them for a considerable Time."[27] Reports of behavior in the back sitting room came from the groom who could see into that room from the loft of the stables (and from other servants whom the groom encouraged to join him in his observations). Another detailed servant's report describes his mortification at accompanying Mrs. Elwes in public when she and her sister-in-law were in the carriage, drawing attention to themselves by boisterous behavior.[28]

The court found for the plaintiff and awarded 100 guineas damages against Mr. Harvey (taking into account his age and lack of resources). John Elwes followed up this case with a suit against his wife for an Ecclesiastical divorce or "separation from Bed and Board and mutual cohabitation by reason of adultery," heard in the Consistory Court at Doctor's Common, in which both Harvey and Egerton were named.[29] The Court found against her on July 13, 1796.[30] She immediately appealed against the judgment and the case was assigned to Sir William Wynne, Bishop of London, in the Arches Court of Canterbury.[31]

Her appeal denied the items of the libel entered against her, pleading that the two visits of Mr. Harvey were in fact made not to her, but to her sister-in-law Amelia/Emily Elwes, who used the house in Weymouth Street to entertain friends when her husband was absent, and that Harvey's visits were on matters of business. She claimed she consulted Egerton as a lawyer because of her husband's behavior; that "for a considerable time previous to the institution of the present suit, and from the beginning of 1791 [John Elwes] declared to several Persons he was tired of his wife, and was determined to get rid of her at all Events, and should be obliged to any Man to enable him to get rid of her"; and that John Elwes had used an intermediary, William Hayward, to offer to John Gray, a former servant of Elwes, a considerable sum of money if he could persuade Mrs. Elwes to lie with him, or "if he would at least put himself into, or under the Bed of his Mistress, in order that he might be detected in that Situation." She also alleged that witnesses subpoenaed in the cause of Mr Harvey, and ready to rebut and falsify the claims of the chief witnesses used by Mr Elwes, had not been called in his defence in the original court hearing, to the injury of Mrs. Elwes and expressly contrary to assurances to her by Mr Harvey, and that the costs and damages awarded to Mr Elwes by the court had not been paid by Mr Harvey, or if they had been paid, that had been returned (suggesting they had conspired against her).

The Arches Court of Canterbury declared in favour of John Elwes on November 6, 1797. Notwithstanding, Sarah launched a further appeal, heard by the High Court of Delegates, which pronounced sentence on June 26, 1798, affirming the judgments of the lower courts.[32] There was no higher court of appeal. Either John Elwes feared he had insufficient evidence to go to the House of Lords and move from an Ecclesiastical divorce to a civil divorce, or he may have had enough of the institution of marriage. Sarah Elwes continued in her status as a wife, separated for matters of bed, board, and accommodation, but still using the name and title of Mrs. Sarah Elwes. In 1800 – while Godwin was on a trip to Ireland – in a case prosecuting Elizabeth Scoltock for stealing clothing from her, she testified "I am the wife of John Elwes." [33]

This is not a paper about scandal but about Godwin's unconventional relationships and the spaces in which they took place. Sarah Elwes is especially interesting because Godwin's early friendship with her runs parallel in the early months to his friendship with Fell and the tensions introduced by his relationship with Miss Carey. Sarah Elwes's history is also important because of how she was represented by others, and because, when she began to see Godwin, a number of features of their behavior, on the basis of the details in the Diary, replicated the conduct of which her husband accused her. A fortnight afterward Godwin first recorded calling on her for tea (May 3, 1799), having already seen her twice more, the entry reads: "Ride with mrs Elwes, Highgate, Hornsey & Hampstead: mrs Elwes calls."[34] He dined with her, apparently alone;[35] she called on him; they went to the theater together early in June; four days later they walked together. On a handful of occasions he met her with Jasper Egerton, but for the vast majority of their meetings, they were alone. There was a break in their relationship briefly when Godwin turned to Maria Reveley after the sudden death of her husband, but by October they were seeing each again frequently. On November 26, Godwin's entry was: "Post, w. S E; dine at Salt Hill; sleep." (Salt Hill is near Slough). Godwin called on Charles James Fox and Mrs Armistead (at St Anne's Hill, nr Chertsey) the next day, but returned that night to Salt Hill to dine and sleep. No further mention is made of Sarah Elwes on this trip and there is no other similarly cryptic entry.[36] These last events are within days of Godwin's dramatic expostulations with Fell.

Godwin was clearly attracted to Sarah Elwes. Newspapers reported that Erskine (who acted for the prosecution in the Criminal Conversation case, and again for her husband at the High Court of Delegates, alongside William Garrow) said that she was an extremely beautiful woman, and Godwin clearly enjoyed her company.[37] Indeed, although his relationship with Elwes collapsed after he began seeing Mary Jane Clairmont, he made several efforts to bring her back into his society and she became a family friend and regular visitor from 1812 until her death five years later (and she

bequeathed both of them items and some money in her will).[38] There is little
to suggest Elwes pursued Godwin, and much to suggest that she stood back
from the relationship at points when he turned to Reveley and later to
Clairmont. They were clearly at an impasse. She could not marry, and had
she set up house with him, or flagrantly cohabited, she would have lost her
financial settlement.[39] Although Elwes had been concerned to limit his
wife's claims on him, the settlement was significant. Correspondence in
1794 indicates that when she was dismissed from the house by her husband
he agreed to allow her £40 per month for her maintenance and support (the
naval pension she lost on marriage to him was worth about £45 p.a.), which
he then suspended in July 1794 on her application for alimony, on the
grounds that he had been paying the sum on the understanding that she
would not do so.[40] The outcome of the disagreement in July 1794 is unclear,
but on the commencement of the case in the Consistorial Court, Judge
Scott allotted £550 annually to Mrs. Elwes, for the duration of the suit.[41]
Whether this changed subsequent to the finding of the High Court of
Delegates is unclear. However, when Sarah Elwes died in 1817 her moveable
property was valued at some £400, and she bequeathed 2300 pounds in 3
percent consolidated annuities and 600 in the 5 percent, which suggests the
alimony was maintained.[42]

Godwin too was stuck. He wanted a wife, both for companionship and
as a mother for Mary and Fanny. And he probably sought to avoid the
further controversy (following the furor over the *Memoirs*) that cohabiting
would have produced. For her part, Sarah Elwes had much to lose
financially, and she probably did not want to gain responsibilities for
two young children in a household of uncertain income.

Was Godwin a hypocrite in denouncing Fell's object of choice and
himself consorting with Elwes? My sense is that he was not. His and
Elwes's relationship does seem to have been in part about intellectual
companionship – of the sort he had experienced with Wollstonecraft. It
was in the wake of his relationship with Wollstonecraft that he wrote his
idealized portrait of companionate love, both in his *Memoirs* and subsequently, in his second major novel, *St Leon*, half of which was written
during his friendship with Elwes. If he was not being hypocritical, it is
because he saw himself and Sarah Elwes as having something like this sort
of relationship. This may be why he was so attentive in his attempts to
draw her back into his life later on – because he saw her as a woman of
abilities and talents who had been exploited by and had fallen foul of the
masculine world. Part of that later "courting" may have been motivated by
the difficulty such women had in gaining acceptance in any form of

society – and, as in the 1790s, Godwin would not let a woman's reputation trump his own judgment of her worth. But other women behaved differently: it is striking that Godwin does not record meeting any single woman on any occasion on which he saw Sarah Elwes between 1799 and 1802 (and only two married women are mentioned, both of whom Godwin meets through her). Indeed, Godwin's later despair over the behavior of his daughter Mary and step-daughter Jane with Shelley and Byron arose from his fear that they were exposing themselves to abandonment and rejection by society. The apparent inconsistency of being concerned about the costs of questioning convention, despite his intellectual commitment to doing so (because it allowed people to realize goods, values, and activity of mind that the conventions of their patriarchal society precluded) simply underlines his recognition of the scale of those costs.

Godwin's relationship with Sarah Elwes captures several aspects of his unconventional and conventional character, and something of the difficulties of the norms and conventions governing sociability in domestic space. Each of the three central women in his life had experienced the injustices of the patriarchal order in which they lived. All were abandoned by previous partners in ways that rendered them vulnerable to the respectable world (in Elwes case it is difficult to believe that her husband did not frame her to at least some extent). They were all attractive women;[43] and Godwin seems to have recognized them as victims and actively disdained the ordinary conventions that relegated them firmly to the private world. In keeping with his judgment on Mrs. Fell, he responded to people's minds and their qualities, not to their reputations or superficial attractions. And, in the case of these women, he did partly re-establish them – bringing them into his circles (and joining theirs), challenging conventions, and doing so with a degree of confidence and pride. But in each case, these women indicate how powerful the established norms were. Most of Godwin's female acquaintance (for all their attractions to radicalism and the new philosophy) did not do what these women did, they were much more careful about the proprieties, more conscious of their reputations, more aware (than Godwin) that they would pay costs for being seen as associating with him in particular ways (and places) or, indeed, for associating with his other women friends (the diary suggests very low levels of interaction between these women and most of Godwin's other female friends). Godwin wanted to challenge convention, he wanted meetings of mind with mind, he wanted candour and engagement – and he got these things from his male friends. But he also wanted something similar with the women he met – and therein lay the problem. Few were unconventional enough.

It is also true that those who appeared less conventional – such as Sarah Anne Parr, Maria Reveley, Nancy Pinkerton, Amelia Alderson, and Emily Kingsman – were able to discomfit him. We do not have his replies to Anne Parr's letters but they would discomfit most men: "Oh thou unfeeling, cruel, insulting, barbarous man, or to sum up thy iniquities in one word, thou philosopher – art though not ashamed, of conduct so atrocious,? I am so angry that I wou'd marry thee in downright spite, if I did not hold sacred the oath I swore six years ago never to marry – a wise man –"[44] It is also hard to believe that Mary Robinson was not teasing him a little when she started a letter to him the day after he had stayed with her (when she was in extremely poor health): "I was extremely sorry, my dear philosopher, when I opened my eyes this morning, that you had kept your word and departed without your breakfast."[45] And Mary Hays' awkwardness in explaining that when he called she was in the process of dressing and that she is not yet so Frenchified that she could admit him – seems similarly coy.[46]

One central relationship for Godwin was that with Maria Reveley – but again, there was some misconnect – they seem to have been deeply attracted to the other, and utterly unsure of how to behave about it – as suggested by the sequence of entries in the diary following an assignation at Greenwich with her (entered in the diary just as "Greenwich"): January 12, 1795. "sup at Reveley's, courir dehors"; January 19, "sup at Reveley's l'eternal"; January 24, "tea Reveleys t.a.t., l'imposteur." In an extraordinary undated letter to Maria Reveley, after her husband's death (July 6, 1799), Godwin rehearses their relationship in some detail, giving some idea of its complexity, and the difficulty involved in sustaining it given the prevailing norms, concluding, in frustration, that "If you are all at once become so thoroughly the slave of miserable etiquette that you must not even risk seeing me alone, you may dine here with my sister . . . or order me to invite Mrs Fenwick; where the heart is willing, such trifles are easily adjusted."[47]

Godwin was philosophically committed to being unbounded by convention – yet he often failed to be so. Moreover, that commitment made it harder for him to read these more challenging women's behavior. It seems clear that he was unsure how far to treat them unconventionally and he found negotiating an alternative standard of appropriateness difficult; and even when committed to following through his unconventional conduct, he could see that it was something that should be kept from his friends and acquaintances' inquiring surveillance. But an additional difficulty for Godwin in being unconventional for principled reasons was that he found it hard to judge how far those whose behavior bent, played with or violated the conventions, were acting from similarly praiseworthy motives. So Godwin's apparent inconsistencies and oddities were partly of a function of his desire for non-conformity and of the difficulty he found in responding to it.

I have tried to suggest some of the complexities of innovation in an age when social conventions governing conduct were deeply rooted and powerful – perhaps less so in London's radical metropolitan culture than in country seats but, nonetheless, still an issue for members of Godwin's social and intellectual circles. Godwin was concerned to jettison convention as an irrational constraint – but that was easier said than done, for others but also for him, especially with respect to women. The result was a complex interaction around calling and dining, above all around being known to spend time alone in domestic space with others. The diary shows that, despite his and his friends' radicalism, these norms were widely shared and complied with by most people, and their transgression was clearly thought to be (and was) socially punished. There were margins for experiment, but these could not be breeched – unless you had nothing to lose, or were prepared to take the chance that the anonymity of the city (or an excursion outside it) would provide protection. There is more research to be done – especially over who would not associate with whom – but I hope to have shown that the Diary gives us access to Godwin's world of political and literary radicalism in the 1790s in a way that allows us to uncover some of the intricacies of the conventions that governed people's sociability, especially in domestic spaces, and that framed their friendships, intimacies, and occasional unconventional transgressions.

Notes

1 My thanks to Adam Obeng who worked on turning Godwin's diary into harder quantitative data; and especially to Edward Pope, who has explored some aspects of these relationships of Godwin in ways that he has generously shared. For details of his work see www.edpopehistory.co.uk/. Thanks also to Gail Bederman, Sarah Lloyd, Rebecca Probert, and my fellow contributors for their comments on earlier drafts.

2 *The Diary of William Godwin*, ed. Victoria Myers, David O'Shaughnessy, and Mark Philp (Oxford: Oxford Digital Library, 2010), http://godwindiary.bodleian.ox.ac.uk. Hereafter cited as Diary.

3 John Thelwall, *Tribune*, 3 vols. (London, 1796), vol. 2, p. vii.

4 William Godwin, *An Enquiry Concerning Political Justice* (London, 1793), IV, iv, appendix II, "Of the Mode of Excluding Visitors."

5 MS. Abinger c. 53, fol. 19r.

6 Jon Mee, *Conversable Worlds: Literature, Contention, and Community 1662–1830* (Oxford: Oxford University Press, 2011).

7 Fell wrote *A Tour through the Batavian Republic during the Latter Part of the year 1800: Containing an Account of the Revolution and Recent Events in that Country* (London, 1801), and *Memoirs of the Public Life of the Late Right Honourable Charles James Fox* (London, 1808).

8 MS. Abinger c. 17, fol. 9r-v. See HG's spirited replies MS. Abinger c.5, fols. 14–17, and Godwin's subsequent responses MS. Abinger c. 22, fols. 127–30.

9 It seems likely that he sent a toned down version; see *The Letters of William Godwin, Volume II: 1798–1805*, ed. Pamela Clemit (Oxford: Oxford University Press, 2014), 111–12.

10 The certificate suggests that Godwin's references to Miss Carey involved a consistent misspelling of Sarah Karre.

11 MS. Abinger c.3, fol. 64v (May 3, 1797).

12 See my "Preaching to the Unconverted," *Enlightenment and Dissent* 28 (2012), 73–88.

13 *Diary*, January 9, 1795.

14 In 1804, he was involved in proceedings to rescue his niece Harriet who had runs off with Thomas West, a married man; and his reaction in 1814 to his daughter Mary's love for Shelley and their subsequent elopement seems very conventional. National Archive KB 1/32/2f.107.

15 See forthcoming work by Gail Bederman.

16 In fact, Miss Emily Kingsman – the spelling is corrected in the later entry.

17 MS. Abinger c. 17.

18 MS. Abinger c. 22 fols 117–18.

19 MS. Abinger c. 40, fol 30.

20 See, for example, Amelia Opie's *Adeline Mowbray* (1805) for problems with servants.

21 See http://somerset-cat.swheritage.org.uk/records/DD/DP/17/11, Papers of Dodson and Pulman, Solicitors of Taunton, Lethbridge estate papers (correspondence concerning Mary Jane Vial) and the transcription of this correspondence. at https://sites.google.com/site/maryjanesdaughter/the-dodson-and-pulman-papers.

22 National Archive PROB 11/1591:129/110–12. Despite Scott's instruction at the Consistory Court that John Elwes should live chastely, he had at least one other child in 1804/5, John Meggot Elwes, *Derby Mercury* May 1, 1817.

23 Although it is difficult to be certain, it seems likely that Sarah's maiden name was Allen, and that she married Thomas Haynes in June 1785 in the Parish of Winsham in Dorset.

24 The register of marriage for Sarah Allen and Thomas Haynes identifies Allen's date of birth as November 22, 1761, meaning that she would have been thirty in 1791.

25 Egerton clearly remained associated with Elwes; he was named as the executor of her will.

26 See Sarah Lloyd, "Amour in the Shrubbery Reading the detail of English Adultery Trial Publications of the 1780s," *Eighteenth Century Studies* 39, 4 (2006), 421–42.

27 High Court of Delegates Judgment National Archive Del 7/1, p. 2

28 London Metropolitan Archive DL/6/662/179/3; DL/C/0562/177–79.

29 Lambeth Palace Archives D675 and D 676, case number 3111; National Archive DEL 670 v. 2.

30 *Morning Chronicle* July 14, 1796, Law Intelligence.

31 DL/C/562/177/2. National Archive DEL 1/670 v. 1; Lambeth Palace Archives G 155/18; G 155/79; G 153/89; E45/100; G155/79; MS Film 104, 105; Process books D 675, D 676.

32 DEL 1/670 v.i, ii; The formal, printed declaration of High Court of Delegates verdict is at Del 7/1. See also Del 5/35; and Del 6/52.

33 *Old Bailey Online*, Case 489, July 9, 1800.

34 May 18, 1799.

35 In the first hearing, under the 8th Article of her evidence, Elwes was concerned to insist that she had not dined alone with Harvey on August 18, 1793 and that they "never did dine alone together." National Archive DEL 1/670, v. 1

36 Elwes may have been starting a longer journey: after this entry Godwin writes to her on December 6 but she calls on him only on the 14th.

37 *Morning Post and Fashionable World*, July 18, 1794.

38 Only one letter to her survives (identified by Pamela Clemit: July 31, 1810, MS Abinger. c. 21 fols. 24–25) – although several were clearly written. This strongly suggests the elimination of papers by Mary Jane and/or Mary Shelley.

39 Susan Staves, *Married Women's Separate Property in England, 1660–1833* (Cambridge, MA., Harvard University Press, 1990); Joanne Bailey, *Unquiet Lives: Marriage and Marriage Breakdown in England, 1660–1800* (Cambridge: Cambridge University Press, 2003); and Rebecca Probert, Julie Shaffer, and Joanne Bailey, *A Noble Affair: The Remarkable True Story of the Runaway Wife, the Bigamous Earl and the Farmer's Daughter* (Brandram: Kenilworth, 2013).

40 DL/C/0562/178.

41 Lambeth Palace, Process Books D 675, fol 38.

42 National Archive Prob 11/1600 113r–4v.

43 See Mary Jane's complaint in MS. Abinger c. 11, fol. 50r.

44 MS. Abinger c. 2, fol. 88v.

45 MS. Abinger c. 6 fol. 41r.

46 *The Correspondence of Mary Hays, British Novelist,* ed. Marilyn L. Brooks (Lampeter: Edward Mellon Press, 2004), 444, March 10, 1796.

47 MS. Abinger c. 17, fol. 93r–v. See also Edward Pope's discussion paper at www.edpopehistory.co.uk/.

PART IV

Traveling Sociability

CHAPTER 8

Sociability among the Ruins
The Colosseum by Moonlight, circa 1820

Christopher Rovee

Staring at the freckles on your knees,
I missed the whole Colosseum!

Daniel Hughes, "A Roma"[1]

The conventional fiction of the romantic ruins-viewer is the fiction of aloneness – of being the Last Man, standing heroically alone with one's deep thoughts and at a distance from the contemporary. But "melancholy among the ruins," Jean Starobinski's well-known phrase for the solitary pleasures of the *sentiment des ruines*, is a strange and contradictory enterprise, deeply rooted in, and fostered by, the very forms of sociability that it wants to reject.[2] Such is the paradox of the Colosseum by moonlight, which rapidly transformed, in the decade or so after Waterloo, from an exclusive destination for foreign travelers who prided themselves on being in-the-know into a locus of conventional touristic practice. In the following pages I train attention on this late-romantic "sociable place," situating the genesis of the moonlight tour amidst the shifting topography of social class that was integral to the early history of mass tourism. I focus on written accounts produced primarily by British travelers during the period when the Colosseum emerged as a prominent scene of traveling sociability – most clustered around 1820, in which year alone more than a dozen Italian "tours" went into print. By defamiliarizing "the Colosseum by moonlight" (as contemporaries termed it), we can understand it less as a site for the revelation of autonomous subjectivity than as a place where enlightenment and early-romantic sociability attuned itself to a range of middle-class touristic practices belonging to the realm of modern, commercialized leisure.

"Travel," writes Arjun Appadurai, implies "motion of the free, arbitrary, adventurous sort associated with metropolitan behavior," and the Colosseum by moonlight was, for the late-romantic traveler, a place where this "adventurous" mobility manifested in all its contradictoriness.[3] On one hand, postwar British tourism entailed the translocation of behaviors and the reproduction of social practices. "Go where we may – rest where we will," joked Thomas Moore in *Rhymes on the Road*, "Eternal London haunts us still."[4] Yet the "full moon" in Rome facilitated release from this constrictive world; it "made everything a fairyland," as Goethe marveled.[5] Touring the Colosseum beneath that moon was part of an increasingly desperate effort, on the part of the post-Grand Tour, post-aristocratic traveler, to claim snatches of experience apart from history and class politics. At the farthest extreme it meant casting off the world of verifiable coordinates and disconnecting from the circuit of time itself. The Colosseum at night was, in essence, a sociable place whose appeal was that it seemed no place at all, and the accounts that define its emergence as a "must-see" for foreign travelers suggest the desirability of disconnection and dislocation as well as the impossibility of sustaining an authentically detached aesthetic perspective in the commercial sphere of modern tourism. Even the reproducible Byronic pose, which James Buzard posits as a means of claiming something "special about one[…]'s tourism," became eventually a vitiated and compulsory identity for the moonlight tourist, a nearly mandatory performance through which one marked one's individuality in the very act of submitting to a routinized social practice.[6]

There is, to be sure, a longer history of viewing the Colosseum by moonlight. In the sixteenth century, the sculptor Benvenuto Cellini went with a necromancing Sicilian priest in hopes of raising demons, and throughout the eighteenth century various travelers admired its appearance under the moon's soft illumination.[7] Lady Phillipina Knight writes of amusement-filled evenings at the French Ambassador's residence in Rome in the 1770s, with fine dining, music, *boccetta*, and frequently topped off with visits to the moonlit Colosseum – nocturnal entry being a privilege enjoyed by élites of the city.[8] Goethe, too, records frequent nighttime visits in his *Italian Journey* (1786–1788), though his interest is spurred less by custom than by a philosophical preoccupation with the aesthetics of vision; indeed when he first stumbles upon the ruin during an evening stroll, he flatly observes that "It is closed at night."[9]

The Colosseum by moonlight may have been, to Goethe, "a marvellous sight," but it was not yet a *site*.[10] In *Corinne; ou, L'Italie* (1807), Madame de Staël, inspired by Chateaubriand, kindled the romantic vogue: "You cannot know the feeling aroused by the Colosseum if you have seen it only by day," she writes; "the moon is the star of ruins."[11] A decade later, Lord Byron molded the moonlight tour for generations of travelers, representing it as an "exhaustless mine of contemplation" where one stood apart from history and alone with one's deep thoughts. His evocative depictions gave license to the many travelers who followed in his footsteps and established the terms in which they wrote about the experience. The account in *Manfred*, one of the very first we have of the arena's interior by moonlight, recalls the effusive colloquys of the self with nature in Coleridge's conversation poems. "The stars are forth, the moon above the tops / Of the snow-shining mountains. Beautiful!" the tortured hero exclaims, standing – to a middle-class reader in 1817, rather uniquely – "within the Coliseum's wall" at night. There is nobody to intrude, nobody to spoil the rapture of the arena's ruins, viewed by the light of the quietly shining moon:

> The trees which grew along the broken arches
> Waved dark in the blue midnight, and the stars
> Shone through the rents of ruin; from afar
> The watch-dog bay'd beyond the Tiber; and
> More near from out the Cæsars' palace came
> The owl's long cry [. . .]
> And thou didst shine, thou rolling moon, upon
> All this, and cast a wide and tender light,
> Which soften'd down the hoar austerity
> Of rugged desolation, and fill'd up,
> As'twere anew, the gaps of centuries;
> Leaving that beautiful which still was so,
> And making that which was not, till the place
> Became religion, and the heart ran o'er
> With silent worship of the great of old![12]

Here Byron recalls the Colosseum not as a restricted, localizable place but as part of a wild expanse, as if it were continuous with all of nature and empty of all people. This convention of representation features in J. M. W. Turner's moody sketch of the ruin beneath a silver half-moon (Figure 6), and it reappears in countless later writers, including Henry James, who in 1909 compared the arena to "the depths of some Alpine valley."[13]

Byron returned readers to the moonlit Colosseum a year later, this time through his recurrent hero, Childe Harold. With Rome's streets and *piazze* once again lit up by "flickering candles or oil lamps" set before the thousands of shrines on or in the city's walls – sources of illumination that had been snuffed out during the French occupation[14] – the natural light of the moon must have made the Colosseum a rare urban locale where, by night, one could escape the visible modernity of the city. Byron, accordingly, figures the moonbeams as the arena's "natural torches":

Figure 6   Joseph Mallord William Turner, *The Colosseum, Rome, by Moonlight*,
from *Rome: Colour Studies Sketchbook*, 1819

Arches on arches! as it were that Rome,
Collecting the chief trophies of her line,
Would build up all her triumphs in one dome,
Her Coliseum stands; the moonbeams shine
As 'twere its natural torches, for divine
Should be the light which streams here, to illume
This long explored but still exhaustless mine
Of contemplation[.] [15]

More than merely natural, the moonlight is, in the full romantic sense,
divine. Towering upward and threaded by the moonbeams, the "Arches on
arches!" symbolize the sublimity of Rome's history, but the real object of
lunar illumination is a mindscape, in recession from its physical surroundings, which is every bit as sublime as the "exhaustless" Roman arches and
Roman past.

This inward turn would come to define the Byronic traveling persona,
particularly in the moonlit Colosseum. The posturing of canto 3 – "in the
crowd / They could not deem me one of such – I stood / Among them, but
not of them" (III: 1053–55) – marks the oppositional stance of a man in
retreat from the "rank breath" of "the World" (III: 1049–50) and frames

Harold's subsequent, self-aggrandizing depiction at the darkened arena. "There is that within me," Byron memorably writes,

> which shall tire
> Torture and Time, and breathe when I expire,
> Something unearthly, which they deem not of,
> Like the remembered tone of a mute lyre[.] (IV: 1229–32).

This unnameable "something" offers him a companion there, and he turns toward this "dread power" in an apostrophe that reaffirms his difference from the crowd:

> Now welcome, thou dread Power
> Nameless, yet thus omnipotent, which here
> Walk'st in the shadow of the midnight hour
> With a deep awe, yet all distinct from fear:
> Thy haunts are ever where the dead walls rear
> Their ivy mantles, and the solemn scene
> Derives from thee a sense so deep and clear
> That we become a part of what has been,
> And grow unto the spot, all-seeing but unseen. (IV: 1234–42)

This declaration of the self's specialness, of the autonomy of a romantic subject whose inner depths are immune to the tainting effects of the violent and base crowd, belongs uniquely to "the shadow of the midnight hour" in this most desolate of urban ruins.

While earlier travelers than Byron clearly admired the Colosseum by moonlight, and while novels such as *Corinne* conditioned even his admiration, the full efflorescence of the moonlight tour belonged to this postwar moment, when *Manfred* and *Childe Harold's Pilgrimage* helped transform it from a romantic fancy into a touristic practice. Byron's mass appeal effectively suffused the site in what Joseph Roach calls the "It-Effect": a magical quality that emerges at the interface between a captivating figure like Byron and pervasive cultural fantasies like those associated with continental travel and the *sentiment des ruines*, and with the Colosseum in particular. It is not that Byron "invented" the moonlight tour (surely, when he went to Rome in 1816, he was himself dipping into an embryonic vogue) but rather that he culled widespread recognition for it as a distinctive touristic attraction, helping to make it an appealing and chic thing to do.[16]

In the half decade or so that followed, a nighttime visit to the Colosseum became a routine stop on the continental itinerary and a standard ingredient in Roman travelogues. Its emergence was marked by the proliferation of the very phrase, "the Colosseum by moonlight," which came in these years to describe a recognizable cultural attraction. The phrase is ubiquitous in post-Napoleonic travel writing, and while Byron himself passed on it, his influence in shaping this signature romantic experience is everywhere apparent. Practically all visitors to the Colosseum after 1817 begin with Byron; by the Victorian period allusions to his works were tired clichés. "There are few travellers who do not visit this spot by moonlight in order to realise the magnificent description in 'Manfred,' writes the guidebook-producer and publisher of Byron, John Murray, in his *Handbook to Central Italy* (1843), shrewdly exploiting mass tourism to advertise his own author.[17] Murray effectively advised readers to join the crowd – a crowd that, Nathaniel Hawthorne would later remark consisted largely of English and Americans "exalting themselves with raptures that were Byron's, not their own."[18] The *Handbook*'s readers thus involved themselves with a kind of serial crowd, made up of travelers past and travelers still to come. And yet, standing amidst so many notional visitors, they could – with Byron's literary assistance – turn inward and become, themselves, notional romantic solitaries.

Such was Byron's influence that he became a part of the moonlight tour's conventional infrastructure, his anti-sociability a key element in the touristic practice of the moonlight tour, a way of "being there" to which nearly all subsequent visitors aspired. "No one acquainted with our language, or capable of appreciating our poetry," claimed Marguerite Gardiner Blessington, "can ever visit the Coliseum without remembering [his] verses, and feeling their truth."[19] To visit the Colosseum by moonlight was an experience inextricable from Byron's poetry – indeed with Murray inserting extracts from Byron in his various Italian handbooks, the poetry became in time an indispensable component of such a visit.[20] He was part of the Colosseum's resonance, integral to its prestige as a scene of romantic reverie. "'Have you seen the Coliseum by Moonlight?' is one of the first questions among the visitors here," writes a correspondent for the *Free Church Magazine*; "'You must certainly go to-night, and read Byron's description of it.'"[21] Few moonlight tourists were sufficiently confident in their own powers of description to pass up the opportunity to quote him. "I saw [the Colosseum] for the first time by moonlight," reports Selina Martin in 1819, "and must refer you to Lord Byron's description, to give you an idea of the effect."[22]

Martin quotes *Childe Harold's Pilgrimage* to give readers a feel for her two-hour ramble through the ruin's porticos and arches; Henry Mathews, who traveled to Italy on his doctor's advice and came to be known in the

British press simply as "the Invalid," turned instead to *Manfred* for descriptive support:

> Drove at midnight to see the Coliseum by moonlight; – but what can I say of the Coliseum? It must be *seen;* to describe it I should have thought impossible, – if I had not read Manfred. To see it aright, as the Poet of the North [Sir Walter Scott] tells us of the fair Melrose, one must "Go visit it by the pale moonlight." The stillness of night, – the whispering echoes, – the moonlight shadows, – and the awful grandeur of the impending ruins, form a scene of romantic sublimity, such as Byron alone can describe as it deserves. His description is the very thing itself; – but what cannot he do on *such* a subject, the touch of whose pen, like the wand of Moses, can produce waters even from the barren rock![23]

Mathews performs a full-scale submission to Byron's powers of depiction, deferring his own experience to that of the poet's literary proxy. Not only does the legibility of the experience depend on Mathews' having read *Manfred*, but that reading substitutes – redundant intensifers and all – for his own experience. To write about the moonlight tour at all, he insinuates, is to reproduce Byron, whose poetry functions as "the very thing itself."

Access to this famous ruin at night thus doubled as access to the quasi-literary sphere of travel narration. Undertaking a nocturnal tour of the ruin was inseparable from the act of writing about it, and even for non-writers the literary experience of a Childe Harold or Corinne was a necessary precedent. These were "the best guides and companions of a visitor to Rome," according to the traveler Marianne Colston, and they helped establish the sociable practices that governed tourists' visits, even provided the script for visitors to follow and for travel-writers to reproduce.[24] That script crucially entailed the elision of any visible sociability, and the moonlight tour has in turn come down to us in verbal representations whose precondition is their fictionality: to write about "the Colosseum by moonlight" is to bypass the social element that is essential to a tour there.

Byron may have provided nighttime visitors a script, even "a full-dress traveling persona" that could be donned "with the smallest gesture or quotation," but the consolidation of the moonlight tour as a conventional touristic practice was left to the numerous, ordinary travelers, women and men alike, who drew on the vocabulary he helped to popularize.[25] The quiet removal of the spirit of sociability marks account after account of "melancholy among the ruins." This verbal performance of counter-sociability, paradoxically made possible by being shared, assists particularly with what seems to have been the primary threat facing the romantic

tourist in Rome: the presence of other tourists. Narrations of the moonlight tour of the Colosseum are an essential staging-ground for the concept
of "anti-tourism," coined by Dean MacCannell and elaborated by Buzard
as "a symbolic economy in which travelers and writers displayed marks of
originality and 'authenticity' in an attempt to win credit for accultur-
ation."[26] The occlusion of social life from some accounts may have had
practical explanations; as Rosemary Sweet explains, "there was no point in
regaling one's mother" in a letter home "with a summary of what one had
been told by the *cicerone* at the Coliseum," just as it was "probably best not
to inform one's father of the full scale of sociability which had been
indulged in" there.[27] But more often, in published travel narratives and
in poetic accounts, the elision of sociability is simply a convention aligned
with anti-touristic romanticism and with a "poetry of ruins" that blooms in
the soft-dying day. Rejection of the social might have been the most social
thing about visiting the Colosseum by moonlight.

As one readily sees in the elegiac rhetoric repeatedly invoked there, the
moon's soft beams helped to domesticate a massive, crumbling edifice that,
in another light, could be seen as subject to "HORROR'S mad control" (as
William Parsons puts it in 1785, in his "graveyard-style" elegy on the
Colosseum).[28] But less apparently, it also obscured the all-too-visible signs
of contemporary life. For continental travelers triumphant in their physical
mobility and confident in the economic might that authorized it, the
taming of a foreign landscape was akin to taking imaginary possession of
that landscape, and while moonlight visitors to the Colosseum seized upon
the symbolic goods that tourism so readily promised, they did so under a
sacralizing cloak of darkness that gently erased potentially debasing realities – from intractable poverty, to politically charged excavations, to the
visible presence of other travelers.

Travelers in Rome had long focused so intensively on the classical
history as to negate the existence of the living culture (Joseph Addison is
a seminal instance) but this habit of denial was severely challenged by the
increasingly mixed settings of the modern city.[29] When the artist Henry
Sass, echoing Bellay, declared that "ROME NO LONGER EXISTS" in
a section-heading of *A Journey to Rome and Naples, Performed in 1817*,
he simultaneously lamented the decline of an idealized ancient world and
triumphs as a modern Briton over the fall of imperial Rome, all
while explicitly denying the complicated, distinguishing realities of the
city's political present.[30] These realities would have been hard for a
sophisticated visitor to overlook. Against the common view of Italy as
"a dream-like haven for the male northern traveller," the Colosseum held

symbolic "pride of place" both for Papist and nationalist forces following the Napoleonic occupation of 1806–1814.[31] Without ever setting foot in Rome, Napoleon made archaeology a central part of his political program, and though Pius VII re-filled the Colosseum and restored the Stations of the Cross, the scars left by the excavations conveyed a modern political story that was difficult to shunt aside.[32] Moonlight, however, mitigated their appearance and thereby camouflaged the Colosseum's contemporary significance. As darkness transformed its vast skeleton into an ideal object of pleasure for the romantic traveler, it gently erased not only these complicated visual signifiers, but also the sight of beggars sleeping in the crumbling vaults, and of rival groups setting out on their nocturnal tours.

This last erasure was especially significant, for if the actuality of modern Rome could unsettle the British leisure-traveler's confident sense of belonging, so too was the simple fact of his or her tourism. Stendhal famously complained that "The moment other people enter the Coliseum, the pleasure of the traveller almost entirely disappears," and sightseers allergic to the distracting bustle caused by other sightseers would have found an evening visit to the Colosseum less crowded, and more conducive to focused attention.[33] The view that the continent was overrun by foreigners was already active when the exiled Byron described Rome as "pestilent with English, – a parcel of staring boobies, who go about gaping and wishing to be at once cheap and magnificent."[34] However exaggerated such claims may have been, the rise of disposable incomes and quent upsurge in middle-class tourism nevertheless contributed to the prominence of foreign travel in a competitive cultural marketplace. It was not enough for the socially ambitious tourist simply to go to bustling Rome. For Brits like Mathews, the "silent solitude" of the Colosseum by moonlight offered a haven from the "uproar" of "the noisy crowd"; it promised the "dose of *difference*" that the socially mobile sightseer wanted.[35]

Such solitude was often figured as a gendered alternative, a manly respite from the tourist crowd's association with female consumerism: "A man," Mathews writes, "should go *alone* to enjoy, in full perfection, all the enchantment of this moonlight scene." The "moonlight scene" was a place where the natural emotions associated with Edmund Burke's ideal of English manliness could prosper: "if it do not excite in him emotions, that he never felt before," Mathews adds, "let him hasten home, – eat his supper, – say his prayers, – and thank Heaven that he has not one single grain of romance or enthusiasm, in his whole composition."[36] Mathews embraces a solitary, nocturnal visit to the arena as a masculine counter to the "effeminacy" of mass tourism. The fact that so many female travelers, from Charlotte Eaton to Jane Waldie to Selina Martin, draws on a similar vocabulary goes to show how readily these gendered concepts, which governed the economy of prestige within which the moonlight tour was enmeshed, could be appropriated or performed.

A major element in this vocabulary involves a stylized dialectic between small sonic effects and profound silence. Harriet Morton, who visited under "a brilliant moon" in 1826, accents her account by noting "a solitary bird" that "sent forth a long and piercing note," and contrasts to this "the shouts of the multitude" in times past.[37] William Sotheby's long 1828 poem *Italy* relegates the Colosseum by moonlight to a timeless, ahistorical dreamscape where "Eternal silence dwells" in spite of the presence of actual sounds, such as those emitted by a "solitary pilgrim" who "breathes [his] pray'r," by his "grey-stol'd brethren" who "chant the deep-ton'd rhyme," or by "tempestuous whirlwinds" that alternately "sweep / Thro' chasms yawning wide" and "mingl[e] with the murmur of the air."[38] The restriction of sound to human prayer or natural phenomena, which intensifies the sense of quiet emptiness, is also a feature of the Scottish landscape painter Hugh William Williams's *Travels in Italy, Greece, and the Ionian Islands* (1820). Williams, whose account made a minor splash when it appeared, is struck dumb in the darkened Colosseum, feeling deeply "how utterly inadequate my powers are to the subject." His conventional claim of speechlessness licenses an intertextual habit centered, yet again, on Byron, though here he refrains from quotation: "We walked by the pale beams through all the witchery of the place; silence and uncertainty prevailed; and a single drop of water, falling from a vaulted roof, was heard at a great distance." The emphasis on the singularity of certain sounds – here the "single drop of water," later a "single sentinel's tread, and the ticking of our watches" – lends a certain preciosity to the tourist's experience.[39]

The silent "witchery of the place," which brings the intimidating enormity of the Colosseum into line with the tendency to regard modern Rome in feminine terms, is so overdetermined that it summons its opposite, the haunting presence of others in this otherwise desolate solitude. Staël's Corinne rejoices in the absence of others, employing terms that would resonate in later accounts: "'Solemn place,' cried Corinne, 'where, at this moment, no living being exists with me, where my voice alone responds to my voice.,"[40] Nighttime is the right time for apostrophe, as this and nearly all subsequent accounts of the moonlight tour make clear, and the audible presence of the traveler's body in addresses to the

Colosseum hints at a strangely displaced version of sociability endemic to the figure. In *Rome in the Nineteenth Century* (1820), Charlotte Eaton enters the dim building with a single companion only to be greeted by the sounds of their bodies: "No sound met our ear but the measured tread of our own footsteps, and the whispered murmurs of our own voices."[41] As in Wordsworth's "Lines Written a Few Miles above Tintern Abbey" (1798), another lyric meditation among ruins, the sociability suppressed in apostrophe performs an uncanny return.

This is in keeping with the structural dependence of the romantic ruins-meditation on an occluded sociality, "a social investment," as Susan Wolfson puts it, "if only on a minimal level of imagining audition by another."[42] For Wordsworth, social investment is revealed by his sister's voice, quickly assimilated as "the language" of his "former heart," and as "the shooting lights" of her "wild eyes," which figure her silence even as they embody her authorizing presence as interlocutor. The moonlight tourist, who calls out to nobody in particular, instead hears in reply the eerie sounds of purely physical phenomena (dripping water, breezes), of non-human interlocutors (lone birds), or, uncannily, of their own bodies (echoed footsteps, breaths, whispers). Culler, who has written influentially about both apostrophe and tourism, finds something "embarrassing" in both of these concepts. The embarrassment of apostrophe is its "embodiment of poetic pretension": "the *O* of apostrophe refers to other apostrophes and thus to the lineage and conventions of sublime poetry."[43] Analogously, tourism "constitutes an embarrassment" because it focuses attention on the pretensions of the modern traveler. The "ferocious denigration of tourists," which Culler considers "integral to [tourism] rather than outside it or beyond it," is, he says, "an attempt to convince oneself that one is not a tourist."[44]

Be it Stendhal lamenting the disenchanting appearance of fellow travelers in the Colosseum, or Marguerite Gardiner Blessington recalling the "discordant . . . feeling" of sharing Rome with a "gay throng" who were "insensible" to the city's "solemn associations," the denigration of other tourists seems practically prerequisite to the enjoyment of the Eternal City.[45] At the moonlit Colosseum, however, anti-tourism expresses itself subtly. The frequent mention of guards in various accounts, for instance, quietly underscores an infrastructure for travel that was evolving, during the Papal restoration, out of its original function of protecting antiquities from vandals. "The Coliseum at night would be a cut-throat place but for the guard, which turns out for the protection of visitors after sun-set," writes the Swiss-American traveler Louis Simond of his visit in late 1817;

"There are sentinels besides in several places among the ruins, by whom you are challenged, and the *chi viva!* the gleaming of steel, the very clatter of iron shod boots on the ancient pavement, served as picturesque touches to the scene, for imagination, like a child, feeds on empty nothings such as these."[46] Mariana Starke, whose guide-books for travelers originated in the late 1790s and were in nearly continual reissue after the war, comments in her first post-Waterloo edition on the presence of soldiers "constantly stationed here" whose purpose was not merely "to guard the edifice from mischief" but "also to protect Travellers, who may wish to examine this stupendous pile by moonlight."[47] And in the popular stories that Constantine Henry Phipps, Marquise of Normanby, collected in *The English in Italy* (1825), the "papal sentinel established there" was "all too well accustomed to the strange freaks and whims of Englishmen." The guard's chief purpose, Normanby wrote, was to collect money from "those who loved to view it 'by the pale moonlight.'" The allusion to Scott's *Lay of the Last Minstrel* defines such visitors as modish types, who tote their literary experience about with them like a high-end accessory. In this story, those types are embodied by the "gay party, chiefly of ladies," who "alit from a carriage, at the entrance of the Coliseum," flung a few francs to the guards, and – practically parodying the work ethic of the modern tourist – "commenced their work of contemplation and admiration."[48]

The "work of contemplation" disturbs the escapism involved in traveling. John Urry has described tourism as "a leisure activity which presupposes its opposite, namely regulated and organized work"; to "go away" is to seek temporary refuge from the run-of-the-mill, to remove oneself from ordinary social life and from the workaday world of industrial society.[49] The appeal of the Colosseum by moonlight is its provision of a site for just such a vacation (or more accurately, perhaps, a vacation within a vacation). However, as a conventional touristic practice the moonlight tour comes to be governed, as we see here, by a set of expectations that unsettle the attractive dilution of fixed identities associated with "home" and "work," "here" and "there."

Given verbal form, the "work" of the moonlight tourist typically invokes the opposition between solitude and sociability. Throughout postwar representations of the Colosseum, countless descriptions conjure the noise and crowdedness of the building's ancient past only to deepen the crystalline quiet of the present scene. "What a contrast to this death of sound!" exclaims Hugh William Williams, invoking the "unnatural shouts of applause called forth by the murderous fights of the gladiators."[50] As far back as 1705, comparison of the empty present with the thriving social life of ancient times had served Joseph Addison, and during the decade or so when the moonlight tour became a prestigious undertaking, one struggles to find accounts that don't mobilize this contrast.[51] "It must have been a noble sight," writes the "Invalid" Mathews, "to behold this vast Amphitheatre filled with spectators."[52] Williams personifies the ruin, comparing its "open arches" to "the eyes of past ages," exemplifying the tendency among travel writers to displace the sociability of the contemporary scene onto the ancient past.

A more complex instance occurs in Eaton's *Rome in the Nineteenth Century*, where the author and her companion inhabit a "deep solitude and silence" which, in combination with "the immensity" of the place, seems to make all traces of history fall away. In Stephen Greenblatt's terms, the Colosseum's "resonance," its imbrication in histories both ancient and modern, gives way to "wonder," an all-encompassing response to an object that cancels external considerations, allowing for no thought or sensation apart from the experience of the thing itself.[53] But in a curious twist, wonder in Eaton's account turns back on itself, and rather than eliminating the possibility of a resonant response, the awesomeness of the Colosseum by moonlight serves as a provocation: "The ruin of the great fabric that surrounded us," she reports,

> filled our minds with awe; and as we caught the view of the stars appearing and disappearing through the opening arcades, marked the moonbeams illumining the wide range of these lofty walls, and raised our eyes to the beauty of the calm, clear firmament above our head, – we could not but remember that, many ages past, these eternal lights of heaven had shone on the sloping sides of this vast amphitheatre when they were crowded with thousands of human beings, impatient for the barbarous sports of the rising day, – where now, only the wild weeds waved as the night-breeze passed over them.[54]

The darkness of evening enables a strange interpenetration of past and present, which is reinforced by a footnote that tacitly places Eaton and her companion among the spectacle-seeking commoners of ancient Rome, who arrived at the arena overnight so as to secure their spots for the next day. But if Eaton presents herself as helpless to recall the ruin's deep history ("we could not but remember . . ."), she comes eventually to rest in a more comfortable, stylized comparison of present with past – the "thousands of human beings" eager for blood-sport having been replaced by something like Wordsworth's "crowd of dancing daffodils," here the alliterative "wild weeds" that "waved" in "the night-breeze."

Eaton bids farewell to Rome with her visit to the Colosseum by moonlight, thus tapping the strong sense of an ending encoded in its history of representation. To say farewell to Rome by night at the Colosseum is to follow an emotionally potent classical script, whose first actor was Ovid. "[H]ow could I fail to remember the elegy of Ovid, the poet who also was exiled and forced to leave Rome on a moonlit night?" asks Goethe, peering into the arena's interior while indulging a last nighttime walk through the city. It is not merely Goethe's evening walk that is cut short at this moment; the *Italian Journey* as a whole swiftly concludes in the midst of this contemplation: "I tried to recite his poem to myself and parts of it came back word for word, but the only effect of this was to confuse and frustrate my own composition, and when later, I tried to take it up again, I could get nowhere with it."[55] The narrative – in what would later become another highly conventionalized aspect of the moonlight tour – then concludes not in the writer's own words, but with an extended quotation from Ovid. Thus does Goethe enact a peculiarly writerly loss-of-self, giving way to quotation as he gives over his speech to a literary precursor. The writer at the end of history (or after history's end) finds no setting more suited to that endemic belatedness than the silent, unpeopled Colosseum, haunted by echoes of the ancient world and emptied, by the obscuring effects of darkness, of both recent history and contemporary realities. To commit one's moonlight tour to words is almost by necessity to position oneself in epilogical terms: how could such a visit be positioned anywhere else than at a narrative's end?

For the British traveler abroad around 1820, the allure of an evening visit to the Colosseum was its paradoxical status as both a modish locale and as a stage where visitors could undertake an impossible performance of fashionable and prestigious solitude. It comprised a simultaneously novel and conventional element of touristic practice for those who otherwise considered it their "unhappy lot" to be forced "to move amidst and in the wake of tourists."[56] With its promise of silence and solitude, the moonlit Colosseum gave relief from the press of the crowd, affording travelers in the post-Grand Tour era a civilized respite through which they could separate themselves from an unprecedented influx of British tourists in Italy. Yet the rapidity with which this fashionable haven, initially borne of the anti-touristic impulse was folded into the practice of modern tourism, is a testament to the late-romantic sociability that thrived there. At the decade's onset, even Edward Burton, writing less as a tourist than as a guide to antiquities, notes the essentially social quality of a moonlight visit. "In exploring the ruins at night," Burton warns, "it is absolutely necessary for a party to keep together, or they may be lost in the different windings." While Burton mentions only the "soldiers [. . .] constantly stationed there" and "a solitary friar," stock characters of such accounts, other travelers found the dimmed arena rather more lively.[57] Anna Jameson hilariously records a visit spoiled by a pair of *"smoking, spitting, and spluttering"* young men, whose "tasteless and misplaced flippancy" persuaded her that "nothing should induce me to visit the Coliseum by moonlight again."[58] And on a "warm moonlight evening" soon afterward, the American artist Rembrandt Peale reports being joined by several "parties of pedestrians" and "eight carriage loads of company."[59] The Irish diplomat Thomas Wyse, perhaps embittered by his contentious marriage to Letizia Bonaparte, goes so far as to describe the Colosseum at night as a site of mixed-sex sociability, full of peril for the wealthy but incautious foreigner: "What shall I say of a visit to the Colosseum, by moonlight? Nothing now; but thus far only: that *it is worth four thousand pounds of dowry* to a good manoeuvress, if properly managed."[60]

This contradictory image of the moonlit ruin, as site of solitary rumination and of touristic sociability, is crystallized by Simond, whose *Travels in Italy and Sicily* appeared in the same year as Chateaubriand's iconic account of a twilight meditation there. It is "the fashion to go to the Coliseum by moonlight," Simond remarks, though he then qualifies the claim:

> and although fashions when generally adopted become like proverbs, trite and vulgar, yet as the very currency either of a proverb or of a fashion was originally owing to some degree of merit, in respect to convenience, beauty, or wisdom; it would be more unreasonable still to abstain from doing or saying any thing, simply because it had been often done or said before, than because it never had been done or said at all.[61]

Simond escapes the rhetorical knot in which he ties himself by ending on a simpler and more straightforward note: "We certainly found it well worth while to go and see the Coliseum by night during a full-moon." But the hedging and self-justification nonetheless affirm precisely what he seeks to deny: that the Colosseum by moonlight, despite the fashionable mythology of silence and solitude that enveloped it, was always already a sociable place. Even at its inception as a prestigious touristic practice, it was on the verge of becoming commonplace as a proverb, "trite and vulgar."

Merely to be acknowledged as "the fashion" is in a sense already to have outlasted the rationale for such eminence, and it is the transience of the prestige associated with the late-romantic moonlight tour that is its indispensable quality. References to visiting the Colosseum by moonlight (as opposed to stumbling upon it during an evening walk, or viewing it from the outside at night) are rare indeed prior to Byron; in 1802 the

Pennsylvanian Joseph Sansom was deemed so suspicious for loitering there late at night that he was forcibly confined in the guard-house until early the next morning.[62] After 1817, it metamorphosed with striking alacrity from the distinctive elegiac experience outlined by Byron into a normative undertaking that promised certain rewards to the traveler discerning enough to undertake it. Soon enough it would be only too common in travel accounts, to the point that by 1870 even "Mrs. Brown," the working-class Cockney who features in George Rose's satires of British tourism, makes the visit: "I never did see such a tumble-down old place," she complains of "the Collyseum," "full of 'oles, as is 'ighly dangerous, partikler for parties as goes to see it by moonlight, as Mrs Maltby she persuaded me to, tho' I told her as the night-air were treacherous with the moon near the full."[63]

Byron, so allergic to the sight of English abroad, could hardly have wished himself muse to a "Babel" of British tourists, yet this is the situation outlined by the *Free Church Magazine* in 1851, in an account that begins by detailing the social pressure to read Byron amidst the Colosseum's moonlit ruins. But a less enchanted vein ultimately prevails:

> The night was splendid, and ideality all alive for the treat. What was my disappointment, then, to find at least twenty carriages there, and a crowd of rough fellows near the entrance, enjoying moonshine and liberty songs to the top of their bent. The arena, too, was lively as the Tuileries. Such a Babel of tongues could probably be heard nowhere else; for all nations seek Rome, and all must see the Coliseum by moonlight. English, however, was the noisiest tongue here, as it generally is, where there's any sentiment to be spoiled.[64]

As mass tourism took hold in the mid-nineteenth century, the Colosseum was overrun with noisy English travelers and, eventually, became host to expensive light shows for those who could afford the steep price. When William Dean Howells called it "that battered old coquette [. . .] which so many emotional people have sighed over, kissing and afterwards telling," thus extending a familiar trope of anti-tourism, he was merely elaborating what had begun as an element of a late-romantic sociable practice.[65]

Notes

1 Daniel Hughes, *You are Not Stendhal: New and Selected Poems* (Detroit, MI: Wayne State University Press, 1992), p. 133.
2 Jean Starobinski, "Melancholy among the Ruins," in *The Invention of Liberty, 1700–1789*, trans. Bernard C. Swift (Geneva: Skira, 1964), pp. 180–81.
3 Arjun Appadurai, "Putting Hierarchy in its Place," in *Rereading Cultural Anthropology*, ed. G. E. Marcus (Durham, NC: Duke University Press, 1992), p. 35.

4 Thomas Moore, "Extract IV" of *Rhymes on the Road* (1819), in *The Poetical Works of Thomas Moore* (Paris: A. and W. Galignani, 1829), p. 175.

5 Johann Wolfgang von Goethe, *Italian Journey [1786–1788]*, trans. W. H. Auden and E. Mayer (Harmondsworth: Penguin, 1970), p. 348. The untranslated German emphasizes this fictional quality: "Es war ein schöner klarer Himmel und der Mond voll, dadurch ward die Erleuchtung sanfter, und es sah ganz aus wie ein Märchen."

6 James Buzard, *The Beaten Track: European Tourism, Literature, and the Ways to Culture, 1800–1918* (Oxford: Oxford University Press, 1993), p. 34.

7 Benvenuto Cellini, *Memoirs of Benvenuto Cellini: A Florentine Artist* (c. 1558–1563), ed. T. Roscoe, 2 vols. (London: Henry Colburn, 1823), vol. II, p. 237–38.

8 *Lady Knight's Letters from France and Italy, 1776–1795*, ed. Lady Elliott-Drake (London: Arthur L. Humphreys, 1905), pp. 60–61.

9 Goethe, *Italian Journey*, p. 168. Though not published until 1816–1817 (in German, as *Italienische Reise*), when it was likely crafted as a novelization of the original, Goethe's reminiscences nevertheless indicate some of the distinctive qualities of Rome in the late eighteenth century. See Hans Erich Bödeker, "German Travellers to Italy in the Eighteenth Century: Motives, Intentions, Experiences," in *Unravelling Civilization: European Travel and Travel Writing*, ed. Hagen Schulz-Forberg (Brussels: Peter Lang, 2005), pp. 213–16.

10 Attending an evening function at the residence of a Senator of Rome, Goethe observes that "the view of the Colosseum and its surroundings from the Senator's windows was magnificent" but resists its powerful allure: "I could not give myself up to it without seeming to show a lack of manners and respect for the society which had assembled there." Such resistance in the name of politeness would have seemed odd when the *Italian Journey* was finally published three decades later, at which time giving oneself up to the arena's nocturnal magnificence was becoming de rigueur. Goethe, *Italian Journey*, p. 476.

11 Mme. de Staël, *Corinne, or Italy* (1807), trans. Sylvia Raphael (Oxford: Oxford University Press, 2009), p. 276.

12 Lord Byron, *Manfred* (1816), III. iv. 12–39.

13 Henry James, *Italian Hours* (Boston and London: Houghton Mifflin, 1909), p. 201. For a reading of this scene as a fleeting evasion of "rigidly exclusive interiority," see A. Elfenbein, *Byron and the Victorians* (Cambridge: Cambridge University Press, 1995), p. 38.

14 Susan Vandiver Nicassio, *Imperial City: Rome under Napoleon* (Chicago: University of Chicago Press, 2009), p. 91.

15 Lord Byron, *Childe Harold's Pilgrimage*, Canto IV (1818), 1153–60.

16 Joseph R. Roach, *It* (Ann Arbor, MI: University of Michigan Press, 2007). For the appropriation of Byron by later readers, see also Buzard, *The Beaten Track*; Tom Mole, *Byron's Romantic Celebrity: Industrial Culture and the Hermeneutic of Intimacy* (New York: Palgrave Macmillan, 2007); and Susan J. Wolfson, *Romantic Interactions: Social Being and the Turns of Literary Action* (Baltimore,

MD: Johns Hopkins University Press, 2010), pp. 253–90. For the claim that
the moonlight tour preceded the romantics, see Robert Casillo, *The Empire of
Stereotypes: Germaine de Staël and the Idea of Italy* (New York: Palgrave
Macmillan, 2006), 3.

17 *Handbook for Travellers in Central Italy, Including the Papal States, Rome, and
the Cities of Etruria* (London: J. Murray and Son, 1843), p. 296.

18 Nathaniel Hawthorne, *The Marble Faun; or, The Romance of Monte Beni*
(Boston: J. R. Osgood, 1876), p. 196. For Murray's marketing of Byron, see
Peter J. Manning, "Childe Harold in the Marketplace: From Romaunt to
Handbook," *Modern Language Quarterly* 52 (1991), 187.

19 The Countess of Blessington [M. Gardiner], *The Idler in Italy* (Paris: Baudry's
European Library, 1839), p. 233.

20 Barbara Schaff, "Italianised Byron – Byronised Italy," in *Performing National
Identity: Anglo-Italian Cultural Transactions*, ed. Manfred Pfister and Ralf
Hertel (Amsterdam: Rodopi, 2008), pp. 111–12.

21 "A Letter from Rome," *The Free Church Magazine* 8 (1851), 270.

22 Selina Martin, *Narrative of a Three Years' Residence in Italy, 1819–1822*
(London: J. Murray, 1828), p. 111.

23 Henry Mathews, *The Diary of an Invalid: Being the Journal of a Tour in Pursuit
of Health in Portugal, Italy, Switzerland and France in the Years 1817, 1818 and
1819* (London: J. Murray, 1820), p. 155.

24 Marianne Colston, *Journal of a Tour in France, Switzerland, and Italy, during
the Years 1819, 1820, and 8121*, 2 vols. (London: G. and W. B. Whittaker, 1823),
vol. II, p. 199.

25 Buzard, *The Beaten Track*, p. 35.

26 Ibid., p. 6. See Dean MacCannell, *The Tourist: A New Theory of the Leisure
Class* (Berkeley, CA: University of California Press, 1976).

27 Rosemary Sweet, *Cities and the Grand Tour: The British in Italy, c. 1690–1820*
(Cambridge: Cambridge University Press, 2012), p. 18.

28 William Parsons, "Elegy on Visiting the Coliseo, or Amphitheatre, by Moonlight, Written at Rome in the Year 1785," *Travelling Recreations*, 2 vols.
(London: Longman, Hurst, Rees, and Orme, 1807), vol. II, p. 2.

29 Joseph Addison, *Remarks on Several Parts of Italy &c. (1705)*, second edition
(London: J. Tonson, 1718).

30 Henry Sass, *A Journey to Rome and Naples, Performed in 1817* (London: Longman, Hurst, Orme, Reese, and Brown, 1818), p. 101. For the motif of "Rome is
no more," see Joachim du Bellay, *The Ruins of Rome* (1588).

31 Alison Chapman and Jane Stabler, "Introduction," in *Unfolding the South:
Nineteenth-Century British Women Writers and Artists in Italy*, ed. Chapman
and Stabler (Manchester: Manchester University Press, 2003), p. 4.

32 Carolyn Springer, *The Marble Wilderness: Ruins and Representation in Italian
Romanticism, 1775–1850* (Cambridge: Cambridge University Press, 1987), p. 82.
See also Nicassio, *Imperial City*, and R. T. Ridley, *The Eagle and the Spade:
Archaeology in Rome during the Napoleonic Era* (Cambridge: Cambridge Uni-
versity Press, 2009).

33 M. de Stendhal, *Promenades dans Rome*, 2 vols. (Paris, 1829), vol. I, p. 28–29. See Chloe Chard, *Pleasure and Guilt on the Grand Tour: Travel Writing and Imaginative Geography, 1600–1830* (Manchester: Manchester University Press, 1999), p. 228.

34 Thomas Moore, *Life of Lord Byron; with his Letters and Journals*, 6 vols. (London: J. Murray, 1854), vol. III, p. 361.

35 Mathews, *Diary of an Invalid*, pp. 155–56; Buzard, *The Beaten Track*, p. 104.

36 Mathews, *Diary of an Invalid*, pp. 155.

37 Harriet Morton, *Protestant Vigils; or, Evening Records of a Journey in Italy, in the Years 1826 and 1827*, 2 vols. (London: R. B. Seeley and W. Burnside, 1829), vol. I, p. 68.

38 William Sotheby, *Italy, and Other Poems* (London: J. Murray, 1828), p. 34.

39 H. W. Williams, *Travels in Italy, Greece, and the Ionian Islands*, 3 vols. (Edinburgh: A. Constable, 1820), vol. I, p. 300.

40 Staël, *Corinne; or Italy*, p. 276.

41 [C. Eaton (née Waldie)], *Rome in the Nineteenth Century; Containing a Complete Account of the Ruins of the Ancient City, the Remains of the Middle Ages, and the Monuments of Modern Times. . .in a Series of Letters Written during a Residence at Rome, in the Years 1817 and 1818*, 3 vols. (Edinburgh: A. Constable and Co., 1820), vol. III, p. 421.

42 Wolfson, *Romantic Interactions*, p. 1.

43 Jonathan Culler, "Apostrophe," *Diacritics* 7 (1977), 63.

44 Jonathan Culler, "The Semiotics of Tourism," *Framing the Sign: Criticism and its Institutions* (Norman, OK: University of Oklahoma Press, 1986), p. 153, 156.

45 The Countess of Blessington, *The Idler in Italy*, pp. 231.

46 L. Simond, *A Tour in Italy and Sicily* (London: Longman, Orme, Brown, and Green, 1828), p. 176–77.

47 Mariana Starke, *Travels on the Continent: Written for the Use and Particular Information of Travellers*, 2 vols. (London: J. Murray, 1820), vol. I, p. 240.

48 [C. H. Phipps (1st Marquise of Normanby)], *The English in Italy*, 3 vols. (London: Saunders and Otley, 1825), vol. II, p. 83–84.

49 John Urry, *The Tourist Gaze: Leisure and Travel in Contemporary Societies* (London: Sage, 1990), p. 2.

50 Williams, *Travels in Italy, Greece, and the Ionian Islands*, vol. III, p. 301

51 Addison, *Remarks on Several Parts of Italy*, p. v.

52 Mathews, *Diary of an Invalid*, p. 157.

53 Stephen Greenblatt, "Resonance and Wonder," in *Exhibiting Cultures: The Poetics and Politics of Museum Display*, ed. Ivan Karp and Steven D. Lavine (Washington and London: Smithsonian Institution Press, 1991), pp. 42–56.

54 Eaton, *Rome in the Nineteenth Century*, vol. III, p. 421–22.

55 Goethe, *Italian Journey*, pp. 497, 498.

56 James Buzard, "The Grand Tour and After (1660–1840)," in *Cambridge Companion to Travel Writing*, ed. Peter Hulme and Tim Youngs (Cambridge: Cambridge University Press, 2002), p. 49.

57 Edward Burton, *A Description of the Antiquities and Other Curiosities of Rome* (Oxford: J. Parker, 1821), p. 350.

58 [A. B. Jameson], *Diary of an Ennuyée* (London: H. Colburn, 1826), pp. 143–44.

59 Rembrandt Peale, *Notes on Italy, Written during a Tour in the Years 1829 and 1830* (Philadelphia: Carey and Lea, 1831), p. 189.

60 Dr. A. Eldon [pseud. Sir T. Wyse], *The Continental Traveller's Oracle; or, Maxims for Foreign Locomotion*, 2 vols. (London: H. Colburn, 1828), vol. I, p. 225.

61 Simond, *A Tour in Italy and Sicily*, p. 177.

62 Joseph Sansom, *Letters from Europe: During a Tour through Switzerland and Italy, in the years 1801 and 1802* 2 vols. (Philadelphia: A. Bartram, 1805), vol. I, pp. 511–14.

63 A. Sketchley [pseud. G. Rose], *Mrs. Brown on the Grand Tour*, 2 vols. (London: G. Routledge and Sons, n.d. [1870]), vol. I, pp. 61–62.

64 "A Letter from Rome," p. 270.

65 William Dean Howells, *Italian Journeys*, 2 vols. (Edinburgh: D. Douglas, 1883), vol. II, p. 119.

CHAPTER 9

Sociability by the Sea Side
Margate before 1815

Harriet Guest

In 1764, Thomas Gray spent his summer touring the south coast of England. He wrote grouchily that his health was "much improved by the sea; not that I drank of it, or bathed in it, as the *common people* do: no! I only walk'd by it, & look'd upon it."[1] He acknowledged that the place – indeed the sea itself – was good for him, but he also felt polluted by the proximity of "*common people*," and disturbed by the possibility that his pleasure in the distant prospect might be subverted by the commonality of the element, the physical intimacy of the briny deep consuming and consumed by holiday-makers. Two years later, after exposing himself to the hazards of Margate, he dismissed his experiences there with the remark that the place was "Bartholomew fair by the sea side"; London's East End in its most anarchic and carnivalesque mode, magically transposed to a fishing village in the Isle of Thanet as though it had, he wrote, "flown down from Smithfield in the London machine."[2] But despite his apparent distaste he continued to make tours and trips to the seaside, visiting but holding himself apart in the stance of horrified fascination which seaside jollities seemed to exert on so many metropolitan and educated spectators.

Gray's identification of Margate and Bartholomew Fair is a useful shorthand, for many of the characteristic forms of representation that are applied to the resort before about 1815 employ the kinds of inversions and confusions that characterize discourses on the Fair; and the sense in which Margate was seen as London's East End by the sea, or more specifically as Smithfield, Billingsgate, or Wapping, is reinforced by the parallels between the two sites. Accounts of Margate repeatedly marvel at the sheer quantity of people who visit the resort in the summer season, when twenty thousand additional residents (rising to thirty thousand by the end of the period), crowded in on a permanent population of less than a third that size.[3] Margate is in all of these accounts identified as the chosen "place of recess of the London merchants and traders, where they enjoy themselves free from restraint."[4] But they emphasize the overall social diversity of the transient population, all promenading on the pier together of an evening in what one commentator concluded was "a more heterogeneous group than at any place in England."[5] William Robinson's *A Trip to Margate* of 1805 provides a typical sample of how this heterogeneity is represented:

> To the pier you go,
> And there a strange and motley crew you see,
> Compos'd of every trade, and each degree
> Up to nobility, of which a few
> Are sprinkled now and then among that crew.
> The rest made up of male and female cits;
> Loungers in Bond-street, looking for their wits:
> Some macaroni-fops from God knows where,
> And some coarse clowns bred up in vulgar air ... [6]

The list continues with trades and professions – solicitors and lawyers, surgeons and doctors, undertakers, brokers, Jews, money-scriveners, barbers, tailors, slopsellers, butchers, bakers and tea-dealers, each type linked with its characteristic attribute in a potentially endless itemisation of occupational diversity.

The heterogeneity of Margate sociability on which these accounts insist, however, has the effect of blurring differences of identity, an effect seen as rich in comic potential. In the crowded hubbub of the resort, the variety Robinson's poem iterates in this long list of trades and professions accumulates to achieve a sense of ubiquitous, almost homogenising, eccentricity, which leads the poet to remark:

> How are all these distinguished? By dress?
> Far from it. In so great promiscuous press
> Of varying visitants, let him who can
> By dress announce the class of man from man,
> Or of one female from another. There
> Confounded are all orders, all appear
> As if alike in rank.[7]

In this poem, the assumption is that holiday dress makes servants as fine as their employers, a confusion that is central to Robert Cruikshank's humorous print, published by Laurie & Whittle in 1803, titled *A Meeting at Margate, or a Little Mistake* (Figure 7). The print depicts the meeting on Margate sands between two couples, and the caption narrates the exchange between the men: "Lord. *'Sir your face is quite familiar to me, I must have seen you somewhere before, will you do me the honor to tell me your name.'* Taylor. *'Yes my Lord, I have had the honor – I – I – I made your Breeches.'* __ *'Oh! Oh! Major Bridges, I am very happy to see Major Bridges.'*" The peer's

Figure 7   Robert Cruikshank, *A Meeting at Margate, or a Little Mistake*
(London: Laurie & Whittle, January 1, 1803).

self-assurance makes it impossible for him to suspect that his ears have misled him and that he does not inhabit as tightly exclusive a social bubble as he might like. Both couples are well dressed, and both men are tall and well built; the similarity is perhaps great enough to cause the spectator a second's hesitation in distinguishing the tradesman from his customer. But the person viewing the print could quickly regain their sense of social competence by noting the roman profile and officer-class military bearing of the man on the left and the hint of apology in the gesture of the man opposite, or the contrast between the willowy sensibility of the young lady with the parasol and the stouter girth and determined air of the woman on the right, and registering the tell-tale body language of class difference. There is a later print of this joke, published in 1827 with the title *Measure for Measure*, which lacks any seaside reference. It depends more heavily than had the Margate satire on the humor of the caption, for in this version the Lord resembles George III, whereas the tailor is unmistakably characterized by his servile cringe. As Hardwicke Lewis, the sentimental novelist, remarks on shopmen by the seaside, he is recognizable as one of those "who have not yet commenced gentlemen, haughtily throwing the head backwards, through the dread of being thought to have contracted a sneaking stoop behind the counter."[8]

Versions of the Major Bridges joke were clearly familiar to the poet of the *Trip*, who remarks that

> Perhaps the clerk
> Is neater than his master . . .
>   and whether worse in blood,
> Or not, the maid at Margate is as fine
> As any mistress. Few indeed decline
> To dress more shewey, and perhaps more odd,
> In that strange place than at their home they wou'd.[9]

Repeating what is clearly a familiar and enjoyable tale of the puncturing of social pretensions, the *World* newspaper in 1793 gossiped that at a Margate dance attended by "a mixture of all kinds of people, from the *Duchess* down to the *Dust-Man's Wife*," a young lady "danced with an *apprentice to a Pastry Cook* from Cornhill, whom she took for Lord —'s son," and had been "very *unwell* since the *shocking mistake*."[10] Peter Pindar's *Tales of the Hoy* (1798) summarized the transforming powers of Margate:

> Whate'er from dirty THAMES to MARGATE goes;
>   However *foul*, immediately turns *fair!*
> Whatever *filth* offends the LONDON nose,
>   Acquires a fragrance soon from *Margate Air*.

In the purifying air of the resort, Pindar wrote, trades-people forget "whate'er remembrance shocks," and the tailor "struts a LORD."[11] Margate sociability seems to share with Bartholomew fair the sense that the press of the crowd dissolves order and regulation, but in these accounts this seems largely a source of humor and pleasant amusement, distasteful though it might have been to a poet of Gray's fastidious tastes. Perhaps any holiday destination – fair, spa or seaside resort – might share some of this effect of blurred social differences, as everyone might dress fine and behave foolish in their time off. What distinguishes Margate is the combination of the strange and familiar; the recognizable London faces and figures transposed into unknown shapes.

Visual representations of summer visitors arriving at Margate suggest that all comers arrive in a degree of disarray that dissolves any pretentions to social superiority. The paired prints by Charles Ansell, for example,

Embarking at Dice-Quay for Margate, and *Landing at Margate* (both published by S. W. Fores on June 29, 1793), show the smartly dressed company
who leave Wapping reduced to dishevelled distress by the time they land at
the resort.[12] Ansell's arrivals, like most holidaymakers, did not arrive by
Gray's flying London machine but via the river Thames on board a Margate
Hoy – one of the sloop-rigged vessels resembling the traditional Thames
barges (still seen on the river) which transported goods between East
London and Thanet. The supposed convenience in terms of cost and speed
which this method of transport offered was the foundation for the resort's
popularity with Londoners. The journey initiated the "promiscuous press"
that was essential to the holiday mood, and that informed Gray's association
of Margate with Bartholomew fair. As the Guide of 1763 gleefully pointed
out, "The Hoy, like the Grave, confounds all Distinction; high and low, rich
and poor, sick and sound, are all indiscriminately blended together."[13]
Carey's *Balnea,* with rather more mordant humor, compared the hoys to
"small, much crowded, and moving jails" whose captain and crew "assimi-
late much in their manners, and in their language, to the keepers of
Newgate." He warned his polite readers that a willed numbness was necessary to survival: "you must shut your eyes from seeing indecent scenes, your
ears from indecent conversation, and your nose from indelicate smells."[14]
The journey could take from a few hours to three days, during which the
passengers, "a Mecca caravan, of all nations," had to "pig together" in close
confinement.[15] Caricatures dwelt on the mixed character of the passengers,
and the physical intimacy the voyage imposed on them, dissolving the
distances required by propriety and usually also the boundaries of physical
definition. Charles Catton's print of *The Margate Hoy* (1785) is the earliest
example I have found of a number of similar images showing a characteris-
tically diverse company on the deck (Figure 8). Only the seasoned sailor at
the tiller, and his colleague bringing up another pail from below decks, seem
at ease. Around them the assorted polite and vulgar passengers fling themselves into extravagant attitudes of distress, clutching their stomachs, their
mouths, their heads, or in the case of the matron on the right her bottle,
while the Jewish peddler raises his arms in dismay as his goods scatter around
him. In the well of the vessel a stout woman who might be a respectable city
matron or a Billingsgate fishwife – she sits next to a basket of fish – clutches
her partner, who is perhaps a city merchant or alderman, and who seems to
be praying fervently. The humor of the print depends on the perception that
the passengers are unable to assert their social identities, for they all seem
quite unaware of anything but the discomfort they or their immediate
companions suffer.

Figure 8   Charles Catton, *The Margate Hoy* (London: William Hinton, August 19, 1785).

The *Attic Miscellany* for 1791 published a humorous verse epistle on "Landing at Margate" which turns on similar themes. The narrator details the extensive preparations he and his friend make for an elaborate picnic aboard the hoy, fitting out a hamper more suited "for an East India trip," but when they reach the choppier waters of the Nore, where the Thames meets the North Sea, and where they had intended to begin their feast, "As if on a word of command from Old Nick, / We all on a sudden together turn'd sick." This communal experience of seasickness leaves all the passengers at the mercy of the watermen's demands when they finally reach Margate.[16] Allan Brodie and Gary Winter note, in their authoritative study of *England's Seaside Resorts* (2007), that by the early nineteenth century, charges for different degrees of comfort meant that the passengers were no longer united in common misery, and the introduction of the steam packet in 1815 made the journey altogether less demanding, but the print attributed to the novelist Frederick Marryat of *A Margate Packet. The Effects of a Squall, or a Sudden Shift of Ballast* (1821) still resorts to the convention that the voyage is the site of disappointed expectations of ease and pleasure. The print is unusual in showing an interior scene, where the splendor of holiday feasting on roast ham and pies is jumbled up with the desperate abandon of sea-sickness in a topsy-turvy and very crowded mess, which indicates that the steam packet continued to be redolent of the comedy and disgust the hoy had evoked.[17] In this image, as in so many earlier prints, what seems required of the viewer is an uneasy combination of sympathy and a more distanced curiosity that might mock or disdain the plight of the passengers.[18] Seen as a group, prints of the hoy certainly suggest that contemporary spectators took some delight in either viewing the sickness and discomfort of others, or perhaps remembering their own and celebrating their release from it.

The confusion of bodily definition that is a feature of representations of the voyage is echoed in the way the sea and land, hoy and pier, are represented almost as interchangeable, generating similar confusions. In the verse epistle from the *Attic Miscellany*, the hoy has its "motley live cargo," and the bathers are equally diverse – "Fat, thin, male and female, black, sallow, and fair," and "All higgledy piggledy mixed in the water."[19] The powers of the sea are similarly motley and mixed, at once the source of health and disease, of purification and contagion. Robinson's *Trip* dwells with disturbing zeal on the pollution of the bathing water off the beach at Margate, where the "effluvia of the town" are discharged, and with knowing wickedness he both soothes and alarms his readers in offering the reassurance that the sea with "wonderful and mighty filt'ring pow'r / Doth analyze, digest, disperse each thing," so that

> Those who drink
> The waters of that bason need not think
> Of aught that can their nicest sense molest,
> Tho' scores of lepers there together press'd
> Had wash'd their limbs, and scores of those who're sent
> For gen'ral cure to that salt element.[20]

Thomas Rowlandson's images of bathers, with their combination of innocence and mildly smutty prurience, suggest a similar mood of gentle mockery. They exemplify the convention that female bathers (though not usually male ones) are represented naked, like Venus (Figure 9).[21] The sea and land are significantly distinct, so that the sea is at once a place of licensed nudity, and also apparently the scene where Edward Thurlow, Lord Chancellor till 1792 (and a keen frequenter of seaside resorts) could be seen bathing in his black frock coat. But nevertheless the hoy and the Pier attract similar representational tropes of crowding, physical confusion, and the indiscriminate mingling of diverse social groups.[22] An account first published in 1801 claimed that the small pier frequently held "upwards of a thousand persons of all distinctions, indiscriminately blended together,"

Figure 9   Thomas Rowlandson, *Salt Water* (London: R. Ackermann, March 25, 1800).

and concluded that the "humours of such motley groups ... baffle all possibility of description";[23] echoing precisely the phrases which in the guidebook of 1763, described the hoy itself.[24]

The resort is perceived to lack any internal principle of order; to lack, in effect, a middle class substantial enough to impose regularity on the inhabitants or summer visitors, in the absence of a formal structure of government. What was distinctive about Margate was its relation to London, and the sense that what could be seen as the precisely demarcated and discriminated social topography of the metropolis was transposed and transformed by the small scale of the resort, which forced closeness and confusion on groups which in London could keep their distance, or know their place. It jammed Wapping up against Whitehall, Billingsgate against Brooks's. Momus, who wrote a regular column on the Margate season of 1777 for the *St. James's Chronicle*, lamented that Margate society was dominated by the "two extremes of very rich and very poor," who were "equally indecent and vulgar," and could be differentiated only by dress. "True decency and politeness," he concluded, "are to be found only in middle life."[25] Holiday licence in Margate was perceived to exceed that of other resorts because of the ease with which rich and poor Londoners could travel there, and because of the similarities of their manners, or lack of them: their apparently shared love of dressing up and promenading on the pier, making a spectacle of themselves in their holiday finery. And Margate accommodated the excesses of their holiday revels. Hardwicke Lewis, in his *Excursion to Margate* of 1787, noted disapprovingly that the "government of this place is loose, and the people of course dissolute." Momus, a decade earlier, thought criminality was ingrained, noting that the people of Margate seemed to be "kneaded with smuggled dough," and were all, without exception, "occupied in some contraband or illegal practice."[26] The resort was historically a lawless place, under the remote and apparently lax jurisdiction of the port of Dover, about twenty miles distant. The suggestion of pervasive and imminently criminal dissolution is not restricted to the permanent inhabitants. Margate supplied the London newspapers with regular and quite elaborate stories of violent, sometimes drunken clashes – such as the duel of Mr. McCarthy and Lieutenant Leeson in 1790.[27] Behavior there seemed as a matter of routine to exceed the bounds of propriety, and to disrupt the self-discipline of the polite and civilized.

In the face of this apparently overwhelming disorder and dissolution, a degree of order is maintained by the imposition of what seems to be an exceptionally rigorous and uniform regime of types, which seems to grow up almost with the growth of the resort itself. The same cast of characters appears again and again in representations of the resort, solidifying as they achieve formal recognition in plays and songs, the most ubiquitous of which is Charles Dibdin's the *Margate Hoy*, first performed in 1795. There are at least two overlapping sets of characters, one more closely associated with the hoy and the other with the public rooms and meeting places of the resort. They include the alderman and his large wife, the military officer (usually Irish) in regimentals, the flirtatious daughter and foppish son, the Jewish merchant with his box, the hen-packed husband, invalids, and hearty sailors, but most ubiquitous of all are the large women. Their presence, as a sign of the comic inversion of gendered authority, is closely identified with the seaside throughout its history. Several of these character-types appear in Catton's *Margate Hoy* of 1785, and reappear in varying extremities of sea-sickness in Isaac Cruikshank's, *Voyage to Margate* (1786) (Figure 10), Piercy Roberts's, *Sketch on Board a Margate Hoy*

VOYAGE TO MARGATE

Figure 10   Isaac Cruikshank, *Voyage to Margate* (London: William Hinton, January, 1786).

(probably after 1795), and John Fairburn's *Scene Aboard a Margate Hoy* (1804). Samuel Forres reprinted a slightly altered version of Catton's satire in 1795 which Rowlandson probably had a hand in producing.[28] Rowlandson certainly used Catton's print when, early in August 1789, he sketched the King and his family being transported out to the 32 – gun frigate "*Southampton.*" The *Southampton* had been made available to the King and his family during their tour of the southwestern counties, and Rowlandson's image alludes to newspaper reports of one of their less enjoyable sailing ventures. The King and Queen and the three princesses are not as conspicuously ill as the guards in the well of the boat, but they certainly look queasy, and to any viewer familiar with Catton's *Margate Hoy*, the implied comparison with what were by then familiar characters aboard the hoy would have added bite to the satire on royal family's claims to respect.

Other seaside resorts, and perhaps especially those on the south coast, are populated with characters similar to those who people representations of Margate, and suggestions of physical excess, display, and disarray are common. But the strategy does seem particularly rigid and particularly well-policed at Margate, and this regularity extends into less obviously comic and more elevated genres. Seaside resorts are repeatedly represented in paired views of the front from either side of the town, view which are differentiated most obviously by that architectural process of rebuilding the town so that it turns gradually away from the land and toward the sea that Austen points out as a feature of the development of Sanditon. In Philippe de Loutherbourg's watercolor, reproduced as an aquatint in 1801, showing the arrival of the hoy – disappointingly without the press of thousands the guidebooks promised – central to the image are the unmistakeable stout figures of the alderman or city merchant and his wife, as well as the invalid on his crutches, the boisterous sailors, and flirtatious women. Joseph Smith's sketch of the *Margate Hoy* (1807) has a similarly familiar cast of characters, and though there are signs of sea-sickness it shows a peaceful and pleasant excursion rather than comedic mayhem.[29] Rowlandson's quartet of prints of the *Pleasures of Margate* (1800) has more satirical edge, and (perhaps as a result) approximates most closely to an accurate visual summary of the narrative that dominates accounts of visitors to the place once they have escaped from the hoy (Figure 11). It shows the gouty

Figure 11   Thomas Rowlandson, *The Pleasures of Margate* (London: R. Ackermann, 1800).

alderman and his overdressed family consuming to excess at every opportunity, apparently ripped off by the notoriously rapacious Margatians. In
the afternoon the family drive on the sands, the wife confidently taking the
reins as her husband dozes off his lunch, and in the evening they repair to
the library, where the matron irascibly domineers over the gambling table
to the amusement of the watching men while the daughter flirts, apparently with the inevitable uniformed fortune hunter, and the husband –
who seems to become more diminutive as the day progresses – continues
to snore.

   The final image of Rowlandson's quartet, showing the library, is reminiscent of a theatre stage in its simple use of foreground characters framed
by structures reminiscent of proscenium arches. A similar sense of theatricality is still more marked in Georgiana Keate's watercolor of Hall's
Library at Margate, which the librarian had published as an engraving by
Thomas Malton in 1789 (Figure 12). There are more children in Keate's
painting, and the scene is laid out as a series of groups across the page, but
a number of the figures – the gamblers on the right, the uniformed men in
conversation with the stout gentleman on the left – are strongly reminiscent of the characteristic types I have mentioned. George Carey observed
that though Margate has a fine theatre, its productions were not always
well attended – the theatre was increasingly driven to hosting masquerades
and ticketed balls in order to pay its way – and he put this down to the
theatricality every visitor could enjoy in the Assembly Rooms and libraries
of the town, and the "multiplicity of dice-boxes which are generally
rattling" in them, observing that "at the raffle-board every one is an actor;
and . . . the spirit of gambling infuses itself into the hearts and minds of
men, with a much stronger and more interested propensity than the lines
of Shakespeare or the notes of Handel."[30] Raffles, at which the various
libraries of the town disposed of goods ranging from silver ware to
"jewellery, Tunbridge ware, toys, muslins" at vastly inflated prices, were
a hugely popular form of entertainment at Margate – indeed satirists
suggested that they were the main attraction of the resort.[31] Central to
their Margatian character, and to their allure, was the opportunity they
offered to enjoy the pleasures of company without the restrictions of
precedence and politeness which Assembly Rooms required. Raffles provided occasions at which social distinctions and the niceties of deference
and condescension they demanded could apparently be forgotten in the
excitement felt by "ladies of all descriptions and dimensions, crouding,
squeezing, forcing, laughing, squabbling, grumbling, and gambling, over a
half-guinea raffle, for a silver tea-equipage."[32]

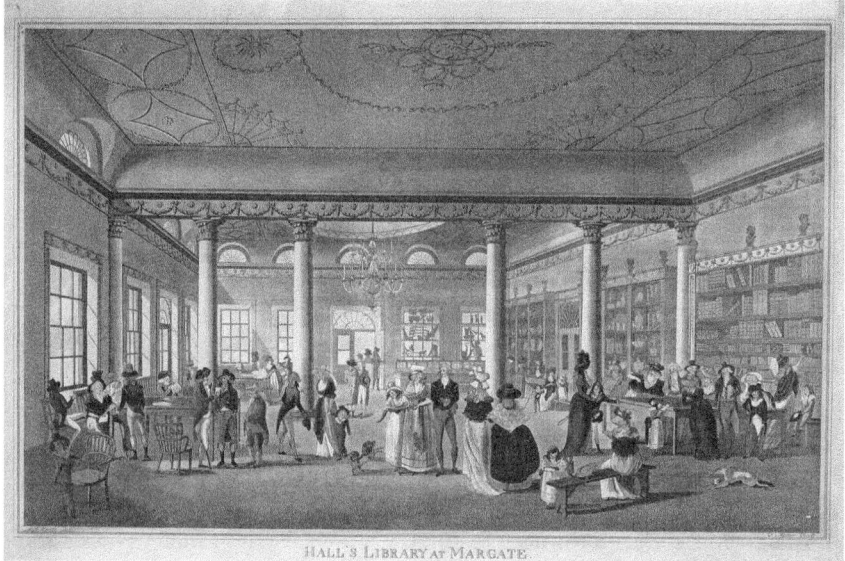

Figure 12   Thomas Malton after Georgiana Keate, *Hall's Library at Margate*
(London: J. Hall, 1789).

Margate could perhaps be thought of as in this sense an exemplary
tourist site. What it offers to the always astonished eye of the commentator
is an extraordinary heterogeneity, a chaotic assemblage of differences that
explodes the boundaries between ranks, races, and persons, and inverts the
hierarchies of the workaday world. Here, as various visitors in different
decades remark, the citizens of London's East End come to "throw about
their money," while the "*nobility* . . . come hither to retrench," and women
tower over puny men. But this remarkable display of diversity is represented as a sight that apparently confirms and consolidates what those who
view it have in common. As they gaze in fascination at its grotesque
multiplicity as it is represented in satirical prints, or read of its social
incongruities in picaresque tales, or more or less skillful couplets, or newspaper gossip columns, they should find themselves coalescing into a
uniform body. And there is perhaps some sign of this in the nature of
the interest that the metropolitan reader or spectator was invited to take in
viewing Margate.

These viewers continually remind themselves of the sense in which
Margate was not remote from their knowledge at all. The loyalist landscape painter and diarist Joseph Farington, who spent the summer of

1804 at Broadstairs – which was by this time becoming a more polite holiday destination than Margate, rather than a dingy little fishing harbour barely capable of accommodating the overflow of its popular neighbour – reported the disgusted comment of one of his companions, that "Margate ... is London – Cheapside, Wapping."[33] The characters who appear so repeatedly in caricatures of the resort are themselves Londoners, familiar figures who could be seen, and represented in image or text, by polite and cultivated visitors such as these on any day of the week. Yet the distance of Margate from everyday life seems necessary to bring these characters into focus; to make them worth looking at or considering at all. Margate offers a canvas for re-imagining and reconfiguring the metropolitan crowd.

An example of this process is provided by one of the more successful poems about Margate, Zechariah Cozens's lengthy descriptive poem *The Margate Guide*, published with extensive "elucidatory notes" in 1797. Cozens was Master of the Margate Charity School, and (from 1799) Steward of the Sea Bathing Hospital.[34] He was a competent poet and determined propagandist for Margate, and had first published a detailed antiquarian survey of the Isle of Thanet in 1793. His guide is explicitly and sometimes fulsomely loyalist; he emphasizes, for example, the loyal enthusiasm with which the "honest tars" of Margate greeted the Duke of York when he landed there on his return from his disastrous Flanders campaign of 1793–1794, though many held him responsible for the loss of life it had incurred. He combines this conservatism with a celebration of the libraries, at whose raffles and assemblies he claims, "every idea of precedency appears to be thrown aside" as "Dukes and Earls, and lords, and Yeomen, join / With humble Cits." He sees in this the epitome of "that fam'd equality, / Which Britons prize, but Frenchmen ne'er shall see," and in what seems to be a thinly veiled reproof to government policy he argues that this equality is based in the rights of "ev'ry Briton" to "freedom of the mind, / Freedom of speech, and freedom of the pen," and to "the judgement of their peers," or trial by jury.[35] But his reassuring conclusion is that any reform of government might threaten to "make distinctions void" and reduce British society to the desperate condition of France. The distinctions necessary to social order, he points out, are in fact reinforced by their temporary suspension in the libraries, where fortune alone governs the raffles, and only the library owners win.

Charlotte Smith's novel of 1796, *Marchmont,* includes an episode set in Margate which exploits the sense in which the social hierarchy of the metropolis is apparently reconfigured there. The mother and daughters of the impoverished Marchmont family open a shop at the resort, and the heroine, Althea, decides to join them in running it. The shop is represented as a genteel "little repository," offering "some little elegant articles of their own ingenious works, which their situation made it convenient to dispose of," but the Marchmont women, as members of a family historically distinguished but debt-ridden as a result of its support for the Jacobite cause, are well aware that the venture will damage their social standing. It would have been safer for them to adopt the alternative course of "creeping through a vegetative sort of life in a cheap country town," dependent on the generosity of their more affluent relations, as the Dashwoods intend in *Sense and Sensibility*, or as Miss Bates does in *Emma*. The Marchmonts console themselves for the difficulties of their chosen situation with the reflection that the merit of securing "the humblest independence" by their own efforts should outweigh the sacrifice of "family pride." But the shop necessarily exposes them to Margate society, and to different and less generous interpretations of their social mobility.[36]

The shop attracts little notice during the height of the Margate season, but once the company starts to thin, idleness and curiosity drive remaining female visitors to their door. These women patronize the Marchmonts "without any feeling for the reduced circumstances of the persons to whom they spoke," and treat them "as they would the tradespeople they commonly dealt with, and sometimes even with less ceremony." The younger Marchmont daughter does not feel humiliated by this treatment. Smith writes that she "sometimes was even amused with the applications from which her sister shrunk with disgust," because she "had at an earlier period of life learned the necessity there was for combating the pride of family, so importunately uneasy to the poor." Her amusement derives from her "conscious superiority of talents and understanding," rather than family pride. She apparently thinks of herself as one of "the poor" to whom pride is inconvenient, but the loss of economic status that makes family pride a hindrance reinforces the value of cultural capital, which enables her to pity the "idle and ignorant children of unenjoyed prosperity."[37] She is still able to feel superior to the people who think their circumstances dictate their status; she is able, in the terms of Cozens's poem, to preserve her distinction in the social mix of Margate while acknowledging the change it involves.

Alluding to the spate of bankruptcies since the onset of the war with France, Smith notes that the downward social mobility of the Marchmonts from gentility to the need to "procure a subsistence" is not unusual – "so many examples had occurred within a few years, that the attraction of novelty was not added to the claims of compassion." The instability of social status that characterizes Margate is here made to seem a paradigm for the economic distresses of the war, which are a major theme of the novel. But the apparently corrosive effect of Margate society on social status has different implications for Althea. As the daughter of a baronet, her presence behind the counter is more remarkable, and the narrator comments that it becomes "a sort of fashion to call at the house in the expectation of seeing this indiscreet young woman of fashion." She finds herself subject to the curiosity of women she regards as her inferiors: a foolish and vulgar woman whose social status is based on wealth unsupported by merit or education, and the demirep wife of a man preoccupied with political intrigue. These women treat Althea as though she had willingly abandoned not just the consequence of her rank, but the propriety it entails – the demirep woman imagines, for example, that Althea shares her delight in making "honest matter-of-fact folks stare." Althea and her friends are dismayed to find that their desire for independence is mistaken for a pleasure in scandalous singularity. As soon as they are able, they abandon their attempt at independence, accepting the charity of an anonymous "woman of high rank," and return to their former way of life.[38]

The Margate episode in *Marchmont* might seem to resemble Cozens's *Margate Guide* in suggesting that the resort works as a site of temporary and licensed disarray which reconfirms the order it seems to challenge. Margate might seem to be the place where Londoners can escape from their workaday identities to play out their fantasies of independence and freedom; where they can achieve an equality that recognizes no distinctions of rank and upsets or inverts distinctions of gender. But it is also of course only London transposed, Bartholomew fair flown down from Smithfield in the miraculous London machine, and it reconfirms and reinstates the differences it seems to elide. In Cozens's poem "The Rights of Man". he celebrates turn out to involve no reform but a conservative resistance to change, and in Smith's novel the women's position seems to be unchanged by their experience of the Margate shop. They went to the holiday resort to leave their pasts behind but found them waiting for them when they got there. But the implications of the shop episode in *Marchmont* also point to a different conclusion. The politics of the novel are complex, informed by Smith's liberal reformist sympathies, and by the disillusioned pessimism of 1796, as well as by the caution necessary to commercial success. Broadly speaking, the alliance of the progressive-minded heroine with the Marchmont family signals an attempt to yoke together disavowal of the mistaken loyalties of the Jacobite past, and an agenda of limited legal and social reform; positions brought together by their common opposition to the corruption and greedy self-interest of modern loyalism. The Marchmonts' plan to support themselves by opening the shop allows them to make their own a language of virtuous independence similar to that which, for example, the heroine wishes for in Mary Hays's *Memoirs of Emma Courtney* (also published in 1796). The fact that the women feel they need to abandon the plan because they are being treated as a spectacle has some resonance with the plight of Hays's heroine, who finds that for women the claim to independence seems inevitably scandalous rather than virtuous. But in Smith's novel the representation of Margate draws on the resort's reputation for unconventional sociability, so that despite the unhappy conclusion of the heroine's experiences there it emerges as a site of the potential for social change which the novel explores. Margate offers the opportunity, even the encouragement, to think differently about the social world from which it presents itself as a temporary reprieve.

Notes

1 Thomas Gray to Norton Nicholls, Monday November 19, 1764, Letter 397, in *Correspondence of Thomas Gray*, ed. Paget Toynbee and Leonard Whibley, with corrections and additions by H. W. Starr, 3 vols. (Oxford: Clarendon Press, 1971), vol. II, 1756–1765, p. 852.

2 Letter to Dr. Wharton of August 26, 1766, in *The Poems of Mr. Gray. To which are added memoirs of his life and writings, by W. Mason, M.A.*, 4 vols. (York and London: Ward, Dodsley, Cadell, 1778), vol. IV, p. 135.

3 See John K. Walton, *The English Seaside Resort: A Social History, 1750–1914* (Leicester: Leicester University Press, 1983), p. 49.

4 *The New Margate and Ramsgate Guide in Letters to a Friend. Describing the Accommodations and Amusements of Those Delightful Watering Places in Prose and Verse* (London: H. Turpin, [?1780]), p. 40.

5 George Saville Carey, *The Balnea: or, an Impartial Description of all the Popular Watering Places in England* (London: J. W. Myers, 1799), p. 9.

6 William Robinson, *A Trip to Margate: With a Description of Its Environs, Written in the Year 1805* (London: H. D. Symonds, [1805]), pp. 16–7.

7 Robinson, *Trip*, pp. 18–9.

8 Hardwicke Lewis, *An Excursion to Margate, in the Month of June, 1786: Interspersed with a Variety of Anecdotes of Well-known Characters* (London: J. French, 1787), p. 26. See George Hunt after M. Egerton, *Measure for Measure* (London: Thomas McLean, 1827), in British Museum Collection Online, at www.britishmuseum.org/research/collection_online/search.aspx

9 [?Robinson], *Trip*, p. 19.

10 *World*, September 27, 1793.

11 Peter Pindar [=John Wolcot], *Tales of the Hoy; Interspersed with Song, Ode and Dialogue* (London: W. Richardson [1798]), pp. 7, 9, 8.

12 See British Museum Collection Online. A good collection of images can be found at Anthony Lee's site, "Margate in Maps and Pictures," at www.margate localhistory.co.uk/Pictures/Prints-London_Publishers-2.html.

13 T. G., *A Description of the Isle of Thanet, and Particularly of the Town of Margate; with an Account of the Accommodations Provided There for Strangers* (London: J. Newbery and W. Bristow, 1763), p. 15. *The Margate Guide. Containing a Particular Account of Margate, with Respect to Its New Buildings, Assemblies, Accommodations, Manner of Bathing, and Remarkable Places in Its Neighbourhood* (London: T. Carnan and F. Newbery, 1775), p. 23. The *Margate Guide* reprints the content of *Isle of Thanet*.

14 Carey, *Balnea*, p. 35.

15 Lewis, *Excursion*, pp. 3, 4.

16 "Landing at Margate. An Epistle from Quintus Quoz, esq. to his uncle," in *The Attic Miscellany; or, Characteristic Mirror of Men and Things* (1789), Vol. 1 of 1, no. XII, pp. 441–3.

17 Allan Brodie and Gary Winter, *England's Seaside Resorts* (Cambridge: English Heritage, 2007), p. 22. For the attribution to Marryat, see British Museum Collection Online.

18 See for example Isaac Cruikshank, *Voyage to Margate* (London: William Hinton, 1786), Piercy Roberts, *Sketch on Board a Margate Hoy* (London: Piercy Roberts, probably after 1795), John Fairburn, *A Scene Aboard a Margate Hoy, as described by Dibdin* (London: John Fairburn, June 2, 1804).

19 "Landing at Margate," pp. 441–2.

20 Robinson, *Trip*, p.10.

21 See, for example, Rowlandson's *Bathing at Margate* (1798), *Salt Water* (1800), *A Back-side and Front View of a Modern Fine Lady, or the Swimming Venus of Ramsgate* (c. 1800), *Summer Amusement at Margate, or a Peep at the Mermaids*, in G. M. Woodward, *The Caricature Magazine, or Hudibrastic Mirror*, vol. 3, Folio 75.

22 On Thurlow's bathing habits, see *Morning Post*, August 21, 1795.

23 L.S., *The New Margate, Ramsgate, and Broadstairs Guide* (5th ed., Margate: G. Witherden, 1809), p. 51.

24 *Isle of Thanet*, p. 15, and see *Margate Guide*, p. 23.

25 *Letters of Momus, from Margate; Describing the Most Distinguished Characters There; and the Virtues, Vices and Follies, to Which They Gave Occasion, in What Was Called the Season of the Year 1777* (London: John Bell, 1778), p. 8. (This ed. reprints the letters of Momus from *St. James's Chronicle*).

26 *Momus*, pp. 51, 47; Lewis, *Excursion*, p. 23.

27 Leeson and McCarthy quarreled over a gambling debt. See M. Dorothy George, *Catalogue of Political and Personal Satires in the British Museum*, vol. 6, 1938, on *The Tipperary Duellists or Margate Heroes* (London: S. W Fores, September 19, 1790), and William Dent, *Honorable Situations the Tipperary Duellists or Margate Heroes Have Hitherto Stood In* (London: James Aitken, October 20, 1790), cited in British Museum Collections Online.

28 It is not always easy to distinguish between Catton's work and Rowlandson's, but Catton, who died in 1798, is unlikely to have worked on the image in his final years. His name does appear on the later engraving. See [Anon.], "Catton, Charles, the Elder (1728–1798)," Rev. Martin Myrone, in *Oxford Dictionary of National Biography* (Oxford University Press, 2004); online edn., January 2008, www.oxforddnb.com/view/article/4901, accessed March 2, 2015.

29 Philippe-Jacques de Loutherbourg's watercolor of the *Arrival of a Margate Hoy* and Joseph Smith's sketch of the hoy can be viewed in the online collection of the Yale Center for British Art at http://britishart.yale.edu/collections/search.

30 *Balnea*, pp. 7–8. On the Margate Theatre see Malcolm Morley, *Margate and Its Theatres* (London: Museum Press, 1966), chapters 1–4, and on assembly rooms and theatres see Brodie and Winter, *Seaside Resorts*, pp. 122–9.

31 See for example the Epilogue to Thomas Holcroft, *The German Hotel. A Comedy* (London: G.G.J and J. Robinson, 1790), p. 72, and Mary Ann Hanway, *Ellinor, or, The World as It Is. A Novel*, 4 vols. (London: Minerva Press, 1798), vol. II, pp. 14–7, and [Anon.], *The Female Gamester; or, the Pupil of Fashion. A Novel*, 2 vols. (London: Vernon and Hood, 1796), vol. I, pp. 180–215.

32 *Farther Excursions of the Observant Pedestrian, Exemplified in a Tour to Margate*, 4 vols. (London: R. Dutton, 1801), vol. III, p. 66.

33 Kenneth Garlick and Angus Macintyre, eds, *The Diary of Joseph Farington. Volume VI, April 1803-December 1804* (New Haven, CT: Yale University Press, 1979), August 14, 1804, p. 2393; August 15, 1804, p. 2394; August 21, 1804, p. 2395; August 22, 1804, p. 2396. The Dandelion was an open space within easy reach of Margate where picnics and public breakfasts were held. When Farington went there he wrote that the company "breakfasted in boxes, & at long tables on one side of a space of ground like a bowling green. A Stage for dancing was also laid & a small band of music in a circular Orchestra." August 22, 1804, p. 2395.

34 See Keate, *Sketches*, pp. 102–104. On Cozens's position at the Sea Bathing Hospital, see Strange, *History*, p. 37.

35 [Zechariah Cozens], *The Margate Guide, A Descriptive Poem*, with elucidatory notes. Also *A General Account of Ramsgate, Broadstairs, &c. By an inhabitant* (Margate:1797), n51a, 50, n53a. On the Duke of York see pp. 14–16, and n17a, and Harriet Guest, *Unbounded Attachment: Sentiment and Politics in the Age of the French Revolution* (Oxford: Oxford University Press, 2013), ch. 1.

36 Charlotte Smith, *Marchmont*, ed. Kate Davies and Harriet Guest, vol. 9 of *The Works of Charlotte Smith*, 14 vols., gen. ed. Stuart Curran (London: Pickering and Chatto, 2005–2007, vol. 9, 2006), pp. 267, 241–2. For further discussion of the representation of women's work in Smith's work, and in *Marchmont* in particular, see Jennie Batchelor, *Women's Work: Labour, Gender, Authorship, 1750–1830* (Manchester: Manchester University Press, 2010), ch. 2.

37 *Marchmont*, p. 268.

38 Ibid., pp. 268, 269, 273, 275. The Marchmont's reprieve is a thinly veiled allusion to the generosity of the Duchess of Devonshire, which Smith herself had experienced.

CHAPTER 10

Lower Deck Narratives and Sociability in the British Navy, 1750–1815

Nicholas Rogers

The public perception of the sailor was of Jack ashore. He is flush with money, roistering through the streets and taverns, looking for grog, women, and merriment. Robert Hay depicted the "jolly tar" in Plymouth, "with his white dimity trowsers fringed at the bottom, his fine scarlet waistcoat bound with black ribbon, his dark blue broadcloth jacket studded with pearl buttons, his black silk neckcloth thrown carelessly about his sunburnt neck." With his cocked hat and pigtail, his switch under one arm and "his doxy under the other" Jack set out "in good sailing trim" as he puts it, striding along "with all the importance of an Indian nabob."[1] Conspicuous consumption is his game, with an insouciant disregard for rank: frying gold watches, riding high on coaches. He is trim, dashing, and dangerously reckless.

The public perception of Jack Tar was made more dramatic because of the vast numbers of seamen who were demobilized with few safety nets. The navy was slow to consider ways of integrating men back into society and it did not seriously consider it their responsibility. Moreover, the Navy Board was bureaucratically slow in paying off men, so that young men had to hang around ports waiting for back pay and prize money, and this spelt trouble once they had spent their accessible pay and exhausted their credit. Demobilizations spawned crime waves and even moral panics. They saw young sailors dispensing various forms of rough justice: avenging wrongs committed afloat (particularly on officers), wrecking brothels where they felt cheated; robbing the rich and the mail. Highway robbery rose dramatically in the aftermath of war, sometimes with an alarming edginess, as if the humiliations of ship hierarchies were played out or displaced by a class hostility for the wealthy. In October 1749, for example, two seamen collared and robbed a Lombard street merchant of his watch, diamond ring, silver, and linen handkerchief, as he walked back home. Suspecting the merchant had not handed over all his valuables, the younger of them, Edward Dempsey, fingered his fob and threatened to blow his brains out.

Later Dempsey was arrested wearing the merchant's wig. As for his brother, Patrick, he defied the judge by refusing to remove his hat at his trial, and "could scarce be prevailed upon to stop his unruly Tongue."[2] Even at the gallows, he was resolved to die hard, knowing that his brother tars would rally with cudgels and cutlasses to ensure that his body would not be handed over to the surgeons. Demobilizations were often liminal moments of freedom between wars that carried with them the dangers of both youthful rebellion and collective strength. The public prints tried to defuse this predicament with the image of the "jolly tar," burlesquing the pastimes of the sailor, attributing them to feckless, drunken, youthful exuberance. The sailor was passionate, sensual, and guileless to the point of simplicity, childishly simple some thought. They tried to forget the fact that Britain's safety and commercial future rested with the set of men who sometimes hailed from the vagabond class, seaworthy men who had been coerced into the navy to serve the state for years at a time. Only the representations of the "Sailor's Return" hinted at the potential difficulties of Jack Tars re-entering society after years at sea.

Contemporaries were aware of the dualities of the sailor's life. Print-sellers published their naval pictures in pairs. They represented Jack doing his duty in war as well as disporting himself ashore, reminding the public that the wild cavorting of the tar was a price to be paid for his service to the nation. Henry Fielding remarked in 1740 that the "good qualities" of the seamen were left "behind them on shipboard: the sailor out of water, is, indeed as wretched an animal as the fish out of water."[3] He could survive like other amphibians, but if he was kept "any time" on land, "he never fails to become a nuisance."

Fielding assumed, like so many other contemporaries that sailors were essentially a breed apart. They wore distinctive clothing, blue jackets, skirts, bell-bottoms, and colorful scarves. They had a rolling gait, and a very distinctive way of speaking, laced with nautical referents. Fielding's half-brother, Sir John, who followed him as the magistrate of Bow Street, thought a man who walked through London's "sailor-town" at Wapping or Rotherhithe might think himself in "another country," for the tars' "manner of living, speaking, acting, dressing and behaving are so peculiar to themselves."[4] Yet it is worth reminding ourselves that this life-style was acquired rather than inherited, and it belied the very diverse origins from which seamen were recruited. Taking to the sea might mean a break with the land. This was undoubtedly the case with Edward Barlow who left one of the most detailed seafaring journals that has survived in the era of sail. His wanderlust caused him to abandon his agrarian roots in Lancashire, where his father was a very poor husbandman, for a life at sea took him to different ports in Europe, Africa, India, and the Far East over the course of almost fifty years. Although he married a poor servant girl at age thirty-six and had five children by her, he never really settled down and remained, throughout his life, something of a displaced outsider, living a life of continual spatial mobility that seems to have inhibited deep emotional relationships.[5]

Patricia Fumerton has cast Barlow's life as exemplary of the culture of mobile wage-earners in the early modern era, and while this seems to hold true for the seventeenth century, it carries rather less weight in the eighteenth century when there was noteworthy expansion of coastal trades and a consolidation of coastal communities. Many seamen of the eighteenth century lived by the sea as much as they were of it, and sometimes gravitated from coastal to oceanic trades, moving back to their communities in their thirties when they married, perhaps continuing short-haul trips, but also working along the wharfside using skills they had acquired at sea. Ashley Bowen of Marblehead falls into this category.[6] In his twenty-four years at sea he worked as a fisherman, whaler, boatman, coaster, deep-water mariner, and as a midshipman in the British navy. He never acquired much wealth, but at thirty-five, five years after he had married a servant from a local lodging-house, he settled down in Marblehead as a ship rigger, having failed to become a shipmaster. For all his travelling he remained rooted to his town, more so than to his country, as his response to the Anglo–American conflict revealed.

Induction into The Royal Navy

Bowen was the kind of man that the British navy was anxious to recruit in the long eighteenth century, when the demand for seaworthy people was insatiable and when the press gangs actively sought out men between the ages of 18 and 55 who "used the sea" and worked on rivers, a capacious definition that went well beyond the usual definition of mariner.[7] Indeed by the end of the eighteenth century, the navy found itself in a position where it was so desperate to man its fleets that it had to conscript landsmen under the Quota Acts to accomplish the task. By 1797 there were 36 captains and 58 lieutenants who were assigned the task of recruiting on land, with a further 31 lieutenants in charge of tenders to take those men to places like Plymouth where they would be assigned a berth. In that year about 119,000 men were borne, that is, entered on the books of the royal navy, and about 115,000 of these men were actually mustered. At least

20 percent were landsmen, many of them Quota men. The historian Michael Lewis calculated that 25 percent were probably non-seamen, including some who had been impressed.

It is difficult to determine just how many had been coerced into joining the navy, especially because impressed men were sometimes given the option to "volunteer" to ease their entry into the service. It is likely that the figure reached 40 percent. The vast majority were born in Britain and her colonies, probably 85 percent. The rest were foreigners, with the Americans making up a significant proportion.[8] Just how many were men of color is a contentious issue in the current literature; by my calculations probably 5 to 8 percent on average.[9] But to greenhorns like Robert Hay, who hailed from Paisley in Scotland, the diversity of the crew was noteworthy. Viewing the men on the Plymouth guardship in 1805, as they awaited their assignments, Hay remembered "complexions of every varied hue, and features of every cast" and "people of every profession . . . from the brawny ploughman to the delicate fop; the decayed author and bankrupt merchant who had eluded their creditors; the apprentices who had run from servitude; the improvident and impoverished father who had abandoned his family, and the smuggler who had escaped by flight the vengeance of the laws . . . To the ear came a hubbub little short of Babel: Irish, Welsh, Dutch, Portuguese, Spanish, French, Swedish, Italian, together with every provincial dialect prevailing from Land's End to John O'Groats."[10]

Even allowing for some plausible embellishment, Hay's description registered the fact the British navy became occupationally and ethnically more diverse during the long eighteenth-century, with a noteworthy increase of men from Ireland in particular, who often constituted a quarter of naval crews. The pattern of recruitment posed problems for the navy since it always required a critical core of experienced seamen to run any ship, and it inevitably meant that more new men had to be rapidly disciplined into a fighting machine. That meant tougher inductions into the service. Entry into the royal navy was already dramatic enough. For impressed men it meant imprisonment in filthy holds for days and sometimes weeks, breathing foul air, fending off potential attacks from drunken and irritable inmates. William Robinson recalled not only the wretchedness of traveling down the Thames to the Nore in one of the London tenders, but the marines who guarded the squad with fixed bayonets, "as though we had been culprits of the first degree, or capital convicts."[11] This only reinforced the impression that service in the royal navy was a form of servitude, as indeed did the fumigation aboard receiving ships. For landsmen it meant learning unfamiliar terms and duties, often to the pain of the boatswain's rope-end; in the words of Charles Pemberton, "to come at a whistle and run at a blow."[12]

Merchant seamen, too, had to adjust to the different rhythms and rigors of royal navy. They certainly had many of the skills that the royal navy wanted, but they had to operate in a very different social context. To begin with, most seamen roved the sea and coasts in relatively small crews in which the distance between master and men was not always very great. Small coasters had only three people, master, man, and boy. Most seagoing vessels and larger coasters such as colliers had crews raging from eight to forty men, with a master, mate, carpenter, four or so foremast-men, and sometimes a boatswain who acted as a foreman of the total crew and was responsible for the rigging. There were more complex crews than this, of course. East Indiamen often had a crew of over 100 with several mates, a midshipman, various quartermasters, stewards and a cooper, gunner, boatswain and their mates. This crew approximated the smaller frigates in the royal navy, although not large ships of the line, and like the navy, an East India crew was paid by the month. But even here there were significant differences. Offices such as boatswain, gunner, or second mate were within the range of any competent sailor, which was not necessarily the case in the royal navy. And voyages were shorter, at best two years in an East Indiaman, a year for a slaver, six months for a whaler or a transatlantic round trip, and a matter of months for ships bringing timber from the Baltic. A round trip for a collier from Newcastle to London took only six weeks.

The fact is that most merchant seamen had regular contact with their communities ashore and were never entirely proletarian, being paid by the share, by the voyage, by the monthly wage, or by a combination of the three.[13] Many had expectations of owning or commanding a small vessel; and most saw seafaring as part of a life-cycle of maritime work, returning to shore in middle-age. Impressment in the royal navy disrupted this pattern. Once in the navy, seamen were held for the duration of the war, which might mean five and sometimes even ten years in the service. Because of the possibility of desertion, officers transferred their crews to other vessels when their ships required repair, or kept them in the roads like Spithead, offshore of Portsmouth. Seldom did captains allow crews shore leave, and when they did they usually did so in small rotations, trusting that the camaraderie of crews would restrain men from deserting because it would deny others the opportunity to go ashore. Unless one was on some kind of coastal duty, royal naval vessels were in effect total institutions.

Dr. Johnson thought them floating prisons; places, moreover, where discipline was military, formal, and class based. To say this is not to suggest that harsh discipline was absent from merchantmen. Masters abused apprentices; mates or boatswains bullied seamen. Ashley Bowen never forgot the beatings he received at the hands of his master, Captain Peter Hall of Boston, who on one occasion tied him to the rail and gave him twelve lashings with a temporary cat of nine tails, rubbing the wounds with pickle, until, remembered Bowen, "the Mate interfered for me and said if I should die on the passage . . . he would be a witness against him."[14]

The incident is instructive. It is unusual in that the captain used the cat, which was not very common on merchant ships.[15] The mate interfered with what he saw as excessive punishment, something that would not happen in the navy where a hierarchy of command was strictly observed and where a mate would not question an officer over a matter of twelve lashes. Had Bowen not been bound by his indenture, he could have left the ship after the voyage and taken his labor elsewhere. This was not possible in the royal navy, where the cat was used routinely to punish drunkards, deserters, sailors who seemed insolent or were simply careless. On the Leeward Islands station in the late eighteenth and early nineteenth century, there were nearly 7500 occasions when the cat was used over a period of twenty-five years, an average of nearly 300 (297) floggings per year, or between three and four floggings per month on each ship. At least three of these monthly floggings would have been formal affairs, conducted at the gangway by the boatswain's mate. As George Cruickshank's print of this practice instructively reveals, officers and crew congregated to watch this spectacle of judicial violence, and marines were in attendance, just in case there was any trouble.

Ship logbooks track these punishments where the number of lashes was twelve or more, but logbooks say nothing about lesser punishments, especially "starting," the arbitrary use of a rope's end or cane by boatswains or other junior officers to chivvy seamen along. These were not trifling punishments. Pemberton remembered receiving a blow "which sent the blood whizzing and boiling back upon my heart, for the blow seemed to fall through my bones into my breast, so ponderous was the stroke."[16] Some "men's backs have often been so bad from the effects of the starting system," remarked William Robinson, "that they have not been able to bear their jackets on for several days."[17] Particularly galling were the summary punishments inflicted by young officers upon experienced, older mariners. Robinson recalled one midshipmen of twelve or thirteen years who would stand on "the carriage of a gun, call a man to him, and kick him about the thighs and body, and with his fist would beat him about the head; and these, though prime seamen, at the same time dared not murmur."[18] Samuel Leech echoed this judgment, even when he was a youngster of same age as many midshipmen. "These little minions of power ordered and drove me round like a dog," he remembered, "nor did I and the other boys dare interpose a word. They were *officers*; their word was law."[19]

In the seventeenth century, midshipmen were sometimes experienced men from the lower deck who aspired to become officers. But by the eighteenth century the great majority were sons of gentlemen, who through the patronage of the captain and their own family's interest, were able to aspire to join the officer class. Indeed, right down to 1794, and for some time thereafter, captains informally controlled the entry of recruits to the naval hierarchy, producing an increasingly in-bred oligarchy of naval leaders from the hitherto younger sons of aristocratic, gentry, and professional families, people who preferred the sea to the battlefield, pulpit and the bar. Many of these families stayed the course over the generations, so that by the end of the Napoleonic era nearly half of the new officers were themselves sons of former naval officers.[20] This oligarchy may not have been as closed as that of the army, but it was tight enough, and imparted a patrician air to the top naval ratings. In essence, naval careers were an important adjunct to a predominately landed society where inheritance was dominated by male primogeniture. A good windfall of prizes in wartime could put a naval officer firmly back in landed society. Although it has been suggested that merchant ships were deinstitutionalized sites, relatively free from the influence of church and state,[21] this was manifestly not the case with British naval ships. They echoed the structures of authority on land, especially on smaller ships like frigates where captains used local patron–client relationships to recruit landsmen to their crews.[22]

Space and Sociability on the Lower Deck

The spatial arrangements of the British men of war replicated this class structure. The sailors slept forward on the gun deck or in the case of smaller vessels, below the forecastle, where conditions were cramped, fetid, and without any privacy. On HMS *Bounty* thirty-three men shared an unventilated, windowless area 22 by 36 feet, with barely enough room to stand. On a 74-gun ship of the line, 500–600 men shared a space of about 165 feet by 45.[23] That meant that if the ship had a full complement, each man had theoretically 12 to 13 square feet in which to live, half of what the seamen of the *Bounty* enjoyed. Of course, half the men were on watch while the others slept; even so, men rubbed shoulders with one another a lot of the time, and in their small groupings of eight or nine in which they ate, slept, and sometimes relaxed, there must have been a lot of jostling about personal space and informal pecking orders, and undoubtedly the constant threat of interpersonal violence. One gets only a few hints of this in seamen's narratives. Lower-deck stand-offs were simply taken for granted; crews did not like seamen complaining about fights to the officers.[24] Samuel Leech encountered some hostility from a weather-beaten tar when he joined his mess on the *Macedonian*. "He treated me with so much abuse and unkindness that my messmates soon advised me to change my mess," he recalled, "a privilege which is wisely allowed, and which tends very much to the good fellowship of ship's crew."[25] The seamen preferred to regulate their own rough justice below decks, and took a dim view of men who grassed to the officers. Robert Wilson remarked on this with respect to drunkenness. "Sailors in general would rather screen than report a brother-sailor in his cups. Even should one do so, he would be ill looked upon."[26]

So seamen lived in cramped quarters where the threat of violence was very real. When they worked, they congregated on the forecastle or main deck, reefing or furling the sails, hauling in the rigging, washing the decks. The officers slept aft in the warmer and drier parts of the ship and inhabited the quarterdeck. The marines, the midshipmen and the warrant officers slept between them, although warrant officers with wives on board might sleep elsewhere. Every man had an assigned job afloat. "For every task, from getting up the anchor to unbending the sails, aloft and below, at the mess-tub or in the hammock," remarked Samuel Leech, "each task has its men, and each man his place. A ship contained a set of human machinery, in which every man is a wheel, a band, a crank, all moving with wonderful regularity and precision."[27] This near-Newtonian vision contained a hierarchy of skill and experience. Apart from the warrant officers, carpenters, caulkers, coopers, and sail-makers practiced essential skills. The forecastlemen were generally older seamen whose task was to manage the lower riggings, foreyard and bowsprit, and also to attend in the holds, stowing goods away and bringing up water. The topmen were the smart sailors, known for their agility and daring, because they were required to shorten or reduce sails in a sudden squall. As Robert Wilson remarked, "it not only requires alertness but courage to ascend in a manner sky-high when stormy winds do blow."[28] Then there was the afterguard, who attended the quarterdeck and trimmed sails, and the waisters, who did the drudgery work on the main deck amidships, pulling and hauling on falls and tackles, scrubbing decks. The organization of the ship was also undergirded by the structures of social class. The quarterdeck was off limits to seamen. Unless they were in the tops, they looked up at the officers on duty. Officers wore breeches; men "trowsers." Officers expected deference; men could get into trouble for not doffing the cap and pulling the forelock, although not every captain was super-punctilious about such proprieties. When Captain Patrick Campbell took command of HMS *Unité* in 1806, so Robert Wilson recalled, he "did away with the formality of touching our hats at quarters, except when spoken to."[29]

For the lower deck, the living and fighting quarters were one and the same; hammocks were stowed above guns, and tables were affixed to the beams. When sleeping and eating, seamen were literally on top of the guns and their tackle, which had to be ready for instant action.[30] Although some pen-pushing volunteers like Charles Pemberton could ruminate about the grandeur of the ship and the majesty of the sea, most seamen recognized they were part of a fighting machine that spelt death and danger. "The breadth of an inch-board is betwixt him [the sailor] and drowning," remarked Richard Braithwaite, "yet he swears and drinks as deeply as if he were a fathom from it."[31] Foul language and grog, he continued, were the means by which the tar armed himself "with a kind of dissolute security against any encounter." And plenty of both could be heard or found on the lower deck. When he went to sea as a cooper in 1776, John Nichol was glad he messed with the steward aboard his 20-gun ship, the *Proteus,* a transport bound for New York. The "swearing and loose talking of the men" troubled him. "I had all my life been used to the strictest conversation, prayers night and morning; now I was in a situation where family worship was unknown." For a while he said his prayers and read his bible, but over time, he became "more and more remiss, and before long" he recalled, "I was a sailor like the rest."[32]

Whether Nichol drank to the same degree as the rest of the crew is uncertain but even if he didn't, the daily ration was formidable: a gallon of beer on the home station, a pint of wine on the Mediterranean run, and a half pint of rum elsewhere, diluted with a quart of water and served at two sittings, one at noon and the other at five. By today's standards, historian Jonathan Neale has calculated that meant four double rums at lunch and another four at teatime. For men who averaged 5 foot five in height[33] and were likely no more than 160 lbs in weight, this was a formidable amount to drink, even if one allows for the recuperating powers of active twenty-year-olds, the age cohort into which most of the lower deck fell. Rum and other liquors were also smuggled aboard ship, so one is hardly be surprised by the frequent accounts of inebriation, the accidents of tipsy men drowning, and the regular punishments at the gratings for being drunken and disorderly. Samuel Leech thought the culture of drink was actively encouraged by officers who valued "your jolly, merry-making, don't care sort of seaman" because it dissipated discontent aboard ship. He thought liquor lubricated the "forced merriment of minds ill at ease," becoming a consolation for the subordination, privations, and danger seamen had to confront. Historians have sometimes agreed. "Liquor was the only bright spot in a seaman's life," writes Jack Laffin, "his consolation, compensation, anodyne, anesthetic and soporific."[34]

Drink was central to a sailor's life, the "acme of sensual bliss" one dubbed it. It was an important component of shipboard masculinity, but it did not produce a ship of fools, a boatload of dysfunctional alcoholics. Men who worked the tops knew that one slip could mean serious injury and possibly death. They could not afford to be hopelessly drunk; their work experience taught them that. To survive they had to moderate their drinking to the tasks assigned them. And the evidence of the logbooks suggests that by and large they did. So, too, does the journal of a naval surgeon who in the course of ten months had to deal with 145 cases of fever but only 21 involving accidents. Only one man was killed falling from aloft.[35] Over the course of the eighteenth century, the percentage of deaths by accident did increase, although some of this might be attributed to inexperienced crews rather than drink. In the Napoleonic period it constituted 20 percent of all fatalities in the navy, but still less than a third of those who died from disease.

The drunken revelry for which Jack Tar was famed by and large occurred in port, or in the roads leading to the port where the ship was moored, or at Christmastime, on the Fifth of November, on royal anniversaries. When sailors crossed the equator there was a lot of mirth and diversion watching greenhorns being ritually shaved and ducked by Neptune and his emissaries, the former dressed in "a scaly coat, old wig powdered, which is the ship's swab dusted with flour, and a Trident in his right hand."[36] As Peter Cullen observed:

> This figure, with his train of sea gods, advances to the quarter deck – salutes, with true marine politeness, the Captain of the ship, and all his officers. Enquires of each whether he has ever been before in this part of Neptune's dominions. If he has, no more is said of him; but if he had not, he is then desired to do homage to the briny deep – which is being dipped or plunged into a bathing tub of seawater, or pay a fine of a bottle of rum to

escape this sometimes very unmerciful ducking. The officers generally pay this fine, and their passage is free over the imaginary line of ocean, but there is no such escape to their mess-mates who have not traversed this line before, and they must be both shaved and dipped in Neptune's suds which are worse than soapy. The whole process affords a great deal of sea fun and innocent merriment – and makes a complete marine holiday.

It was this carousing that fixated contemporaries and found its way into Georgian caricature. It is quite probable that the mess cooks who distributed the rum held back part of the ration for these spectacular blowouts on board ship, and "blowout" was a term that sailors used to describe the cathartic excess of a celebration. In this respect a seaman's drinking habits were not dissimilar to those of other plebeian groups in the eighteenth century, where work rhythms were both intense and sporadic, where time was made for revelry, where miners and agricultural laborers were partially remunerated with drink to slake their thirst during and after days of hard physical work.[37] The only significant difference was that when ships were moored offshore, captains turned a blind eye to the boatloads of women brought on board to gratify the sexual libidos of the crew. Technically seamen were allowed to bring wives on board when they were in the roads and not permitted shore leave, but too frequently men-of-the-line became floating brothels. Upon arriving at Portsmouth in 1809 Henry Walsh "was astonished in beholding the crowd of those women of pleasure that daily surround those ships of war and there remains until a man goes down into these boats and there chooses one ... I have seen above four hundred of these ladies on board at one time, and they are not very particular about the convenience of sleeping in private, as that is impossible to find among so many men. Their expressions in conversation is [are] quite beyond the limits of prudence or modesty."[38]

Drink lubricated a sailor's conviviality. It was the essential accompaniment to the songs and yarns that were central to lower-deck sociability. It made private reading more difficult among the minority of sailors who were literate, and some of them were ribbed for not joining in the general conviviality. After work, between watches, sailors would congregate to chat about the day, joke with messmates, and break into song. Good singers were cherished. On HMS *Macedonian* with 300 men, the crew was relieved when "Bloody Dick" Suttonwood, so called for his habitual swearing, was picked up after trying to desert. "The crew were all delighted at his return," remarked Leech, "as he was quite popular among them for his lively disposition and his talents as a comic singer, which last gift is always highly prized in a man of war."[39] Precisely what songs Bloody Dick favored is unknown: one doubts it was a ballad about seamen and their lovers at the point of parting; those tended to be sentimental rather than humorous, unless the seamen protested he must go and do his duty to avoid encumbering ties.[40] Perhaps it was the account of a captain rousing his men to battle, as in the "Adventurous Sailor," where the horrors of battle are handled with comic flippancy and black humor.[41]

> Our captain came up from the cabin,
> And roar'd with his nose unto me,
> You dog, sir, make ready for action,
> Or else I will halve you in three:
> Then the ships they began for to rattle,
> And fired a ball of broadsides,
> Till some that were headless and legless,
> Were running for fear of their hides.
> But long ere the action commenced,
> I found to the greatest surprize,
> Before that I came to composure,
> A swivel had blown out my eyes.
> So when that I look'd to my eye-balls
> And saw they were blown out indeed,
> I caught up my legs in my oxter, [under my arm]
> And walk'd on the crown of my head.

Songs like this one were designed to prepare crews for the realities of battle, just as others delved into the dangers of the deep, the storms and shipwrecks that were intrinsic to a seafaring life and the staple fare of castaway narratives. The songs reminded their audience that Jack Tar is often placed in predicaments beyond his control, which are best handled with a stoical courage or with a jocular, devil-may-care intrepidity. The same was true of the sailor's yarns, which veered to the fantastical and superstitious. They also reminded seamen of the perils of the seas and helped foster a camraderie to address those dangers. In a hyper-masculine space where stoicism and courage were admired, where the "confusion of the moment was followed by laughing and pleasantries" to quote Leech, spinning yarns played out the anxieties of plying the deep.[42]

After work assignments had been completed, sailors might congregate at the forecastle for a jig, for there were usually plenty of fiddlers on board ship. Robert Hay recalled the evenings aboard the *Culloden* in 1804 when "the instrument of black Bob, the fiddler, was in constant repetition, giving spirit to the evolutions of those who were disposed to trip a little to the light fantastic toe."[43] Some captains had bands to regale the men at the end of the day and even allowed musical shows and amateur dramatics on board ship as an antidote to long weeks on blockade. On the *Diamond* frigate off Brest in 1806, "the crew danced or got up some kind of farce" it was reported. On the *Royal George*, an altogether larger ship, there were no less than three acting companies when she was cruising the Mediterranean in 1807: one organized by the wardroom officers; one by the midshipmen; and one by the men. The seamen played Samuel Foote's well-known farce, *The Mayor of Garratt*, which recalled the plebeian mock-election in Wandsworth, south of London, an event which some tars had doubtless attended.[44]

Organized dancing or plays always raised the issue of lower-deck space or autonomy. How much of a sailor's life aboard ship should be regulated? Should it not be possible to have some time away from the prying eyes and ears of officers? The issue came to a head on the *Bounty* when Captain William Bligh insisted that the men should dance between 5 and 8pm every day on their voyage out to Tahiti because it was "conducive to their health."[45] The men didn't like it and on the October 19, 1787, two of them refused to co-operate, only to have their grog taken from them. Bligh's obsessive and self-righteous concern for his men's health – he also inspected their hands and fingernails to ensure they were clean – undermined the customary reciprocities that smoothed working relations between officers and men. It led eventually, and perhaps inexorably, to the most famous mutiny of the century.[46]

The give-and-take aboard ship was central to its governance. Under the articles of war, a royal naval captain was armed with incredible powers on a ship where nearly half the crew had been coerced into service and where others had recklessly volunteered to escape the authority of masters, parents, or family obligations. Captains had to use tact in such situations; they had to combine strict command with discretion; authority with discretion. Often they didn't.

Lower-deck narratives offer some interesting evidence on the customary expectations of seamen concerning the exercise of authority aboard ship. No-one opposed the right of captains to punish men by flogging, save Leech, a Brit turned American, who thought it a punishment unbefitting free men. William Robinson, one of the most outspoken critics of the navy, was more concerned with the forms of physical punishment than the principle. Like other members of the lower deck, he conceded that "discipline and subordination" was necessary on men of war, and that opinion extended to the mutineers of 1797, who flogged men who were drunk and remiss in their duty.[47] Even the crew of the Pompée, the only ship at Spithead that actually mutinied, declared they did not wish to encroach on "the Punishments necessary for the preservation of good order and discipline."[48] So flogging was tolerated in those extraordinary circumstances where one might expect some challenge to naval discipline, tout court. And in wartime, some tars actually welcomed a firm disciplinarian at the helm if it meant that laggards and landsmen were whipped into shape. That improved everyone's chance of survival. What was universally condemned was the custom of flogging around the fleet, where a seaman might receive anything from 100 to 600 lashes in plain view of every boat, subject to the discretion of the surgeon, who would stop the punishment when it had clearly imposed an intolerable injury.[49] That was considered barbarous, although from a strictly hierarchical point of view, the horror of the occasion was probably what the Admiralty intended.

For many sailors, the key issue was the arbitrary nature of punishment on board ship and the degradation it inflicted or signified. Starting was acceptable, but the victimization of particular greenhorns was not; nor should a boatswain use the cane indiscriminately on seasoned seamen, especially those who worked on the tops, the elite of young seamen. Flogging at the grating was tolerable if the offence merited it, yet when a captain miscalculated the punishment, trouble could ensue. Whether it did or not depended on the collective action of the seamen, and that in turn depended on the general opinion of the lower deck. In the interlude between watches, when crews were eating and entertaining themselves, these matters were discussed. Sometimes, amid the jokes and jests of the forecastle, sailors simply blew off steam about "cruel usage." But it is clear that crews constantly debated their officers' style of authority, particularly the captain; whether he was bluff and benevolent, or an "old rip," that is an officer who ripped into seaman and allowed no concessions, a "complete rough knot," a "tarter," [tartar] a tyrant. Jacob Nagle remarked of Lieutenant Edward Riou aboard the *St Lucia*: "He made it his study to punish every man he could get holt of, and gloried in having the name of a villen and a terror to the seamen."[50] Officers were rated by crews as well as by the Admiralty. Sometimes seamen tried to negotiate with them. In 1778, aboard HMS *Glascow*, Thomas Pasley had Samuel Hall whipped for "Drunkenness and Mutiny. "Hall responded, Pasley noted, by saying

> that I had declared I would Flog every Man I saw drunk, and that he had seen me so once having Company on board in a harbour. I confessed that he had reason to say I was that day in Liquor, but there was a considerable difference – I had no duty to do, and always retained sufficient sense to walk quietly to my bed

Hall, on the other hand, was drunk on duty, for the second time in four days, and fully deserved the flogging, Pasley continued, and for good measure he awarded him another twelve lashes for his impertinence.[51]

Hall clearly tried to push the boundaries of paternalism, if not for himself, then for fellow tars. Others used more anonymous, collective methods. In 1793 the young inexperienced commander of HMS *Minerva*, Captain Whitby, decided to punish his crew for swearing and kept a list of those who should be flogged for the offence. The crew didn't like it, and signaled their discontent by refusing to dance in the evening, smashing the lanterns on deck, and thudding the door of the admiral with a gunner's wad, the cotton wool used to keep the powder in place in the barrel of the cannon. Admiral Cornwallis got the message, even if Captain Whitby didn't, and promptly ordered him not to use the lash on such "light occasions, and never to flog a man again without his permission."[52]

Mutiny

There were other occasions, however, when the early signals and protests of the crew proved in vain, where confrontations became bloody and violent. Between 1794 and 1795, there were a rash of munities in the fleet that fractured the traditional structures of command. Some of these conflicts involved perquisites and privileges that should have been negotiated quickly; the loss of a wine ration, the dilution of grog, rotten bread, quarrels between top-men and officers over menial jobs like swabbing decks, the removal of visiting rights between ships.[53] They escalated into full-scale mutinies because commanders were too intransigent to meet the challenge. Partly it was because the regional affiliations that had conventionally undergirded naval recruitment, with captains recruiting key seamen from their own localities, no longer held sway as naval complements expanded dramatically to encompass more Irishmen and more landsmen under the Quota system. Partly it was because the new crews were politically literate and more experienced in collective bargaining. From the 1760s there had been a growing willingness of the part of merchant seamen and allied groups such as the Newcastle keelmen to use the strike weapon, and by the beginning of the French revolutionary wars, Painite ideas and radical clubs were added to the toxic mix of strikes and anti-impressment riots, especially on the Tyne.[54]

The confidence and growing sense of entitlement among lower-deck seamen is most visible in the naval mutinies of 1797. Conventionally the mutinies have been attributed to outside influences, either to the politically conscious Quota men or to the rapid influx of Irish republicans in the fleet. Both of these interpretations play down the self-generating collective action of the seamen themselves. Certainly the actions at Spithead, which essentially amounted to a strike, a refusal to sail until certain collective demands had been agreed upon by the Admiralty and confirmed by parliament, took the naval hierarchy completely by surprise. One captain described it as "a revolution in the fleet," and symbolically so it seemed.[55] Not least because it revealed an organizational sophistication officers simply could not imagine: a red flagship, HMS *Charlotte,* which communicated with each vessel through elected delegates; democratic decision-making in the name of the British navy; and an appropriation of Admiralty control while the conflict lasted. Seaman assumed control of the ships, occupied the cabins of commanders, removed officers from the quarter deck, over fifty of them permanently on the grounds that they were detrimental to naval morale, and considered setting up their own court martial of Jack Tars to try officers responsible for the deaths of some of their colleagues on HMS *London.* One admiral was even dressed down for not removing his hat before the delegates.

It was indeed a topsy-turvy world, but it did not come from nowhere. Merchant seamen had been negotiating with employers for decades, usually through the conventional forms of collective violence and intimidation that characterized eighteenth-century labor conflicts. A series of mutinies over back pay and prize money at the end of the American war had also taught naval crews to be wary of single-ship mutinies where the Admiralty might renege on promises and execute ringleaders.[56] The significance of these struggles was not lost on the delegates, in particular, who were not new to the navy but experienced and skilled seamen in positions of authority: quartermasters, quarter gunners, yeoman of the sheets, able seamen. Five were actually midshipmen. Having worked in the Channel Fleet from two to four years, they had the heavy responsibility of following through on demands for better pay originally outlined in petitions to the Admiralty in ways that would not be construed as treasonable mutiny. This was one reason why they wanted to articulate their demands on the public stage and have them confirmed by parliament. And why, amid continuing Admiralty resentment at their insubordination and impertinence, they were anxious to learn from the newspaper press how their demands were received in parliament. In the end, the Spithead sailors successfully negotiated a new contract which not only involved higher pay, but shore leave, better provisions in port, better pensions for the injured, and a pardon for all participants. In the circumstances, in the face of repeated provocations by outraged officers such as Admirals Gardner and Colpoys, the discipline and solidarity of the Spithead crews was remarkable. It was the most successful strike action of the century, and it forced the navy to think twice about the collective actions that might flow from the sociability of the lower deck. It eventually led the Admiralty to demand greater accountability from their captains and to end their virtual sovereignty of the ship.

Old Jack Back on Shore

Working in the navy was a young man's game. Although the Admiralty's recruiting officers went after every seaworthy person between the ages of eighteen and fifty-five, they were really interested in twenty-year-olds. By my calculations, the average naval crew had twice as many twenty-year-olds as their age cohort in the general male population. The number of thirty-year-olds in the navy was roughly proportionate to that outside. And the number of seamen over forty shrank to a quarter of what it might be on land. Even in an older crew, such as HMS *Bellerophon* in the early nineteenth century, the proportion of adult males over forty was 17 percent. In Liverpool and Blackburn, in 1821, the proportion was twice as high.[57] Scrabbling to the tops and hauling in sails without winches was very tough work. Few forty-year-olds could handle it.

For the aging Georgian tar, particularly those that fought in the years 1793–1815, a twenty-two-year run with a one year interlude, re-entry into British society was fraught with difficulty. Seamen who were recruited early in these wars could expect eight or so years at sea without a break. During that time youthful courtships were disrupted, parents had died, and relatives had dispersed. William Richardson returned home after years in the merchant and then royal navy to discover North Shields was not "the merry place" he left behind; too many of his pals had been impressed, his parents were dead and his uncles, who ran an alehouse in the town, proved cool and distant.[58] Other tars felt the same estrangement. Even those who managed to marry during wartime found their peripatetic life a corroding influence on domesticity. Francis Bergh married after four years' duty in the Mediterranean: his mother-in-law disliked him and exposed him to the press gang, with the result he was hauled off to sea again, only to discover years later that his wife and baby had died in childbirth. Jacob Nagle, after a series of sexual exploits in London, Calcutta, Rio de Janeiro and Portsmouth, eventually settled down in 1795, marrying a Stepney girl whom he met through her maritime brothers. Within weeks he was taken up by the press gang on Tower Hill, and spent the next two and a half years in the navy. When he returned and was promoted to boatswain's mate, he tried to have his wife brought on board his frigate. But the Navy Board turned him down and so again he spent four years at sea without seeing his wife and child. When they were reconciled at the Peace of Amiens in 1802 and Nagle decided to return to his native Philadelphia for a new start, tragedy befell them. Both wife and child died of yellow fever in Lisbon on the voyage over.[59]

Nagle was thirty-five when he married, a late age for the 1790s when the mean age at first marriage was twenty-six, and in London somewhat younger. Clearly the homo-social world of the mariner, with its interludes of youthful gadding, had a strong attraction. Why marry when one could be footloose and fancy-free? Seamen continually encountered messmates who had negative things to say about marriage. Some married mariners delayed going home before the revelries of shore leave were played out. This was the case with a Bristolian whose wife knew he had landed at Gosport and wondered why he had not returned home. "I believe you have more love for your ship and ship mats (mates) than for me and your hous (e)," she told him, and unwisely sent him money to get back to Bristol and enlist in a privateer, signing off "I remaine, your unhappy wife tell death."[60]

This particular seaman, William Richards, aged twenty-seven, clearly seems to have wanted the best of both worlds. Others joined the navy to shirk all family responsibilities, as the toll of desertions reported in parish examinations explicitly reveal, particularly, it would seem at that point in the life cycle when the burden of small children was a heavy one. As one ballad stressed, marriage might mean trouble.[61]

> 'Twas at Stepney church I was splic'd to Doll,
> Pull away, pull away together;
> In wedlock you'll oft-time meet with a squall,
> But I found it all foul weather.

Of course sooner or later, Jack Tar had to recognize that a seafaring life was part of his life cycle, that re-entry ashore was necessary because of age or injury. Many seamen of the Napoleonic era tended to congregate in the larger ports where they hoped to pick up casual work on the wharfside and perhaps find a woman to provide some companionship in old age. Sometimes this proved to be a matter of serial monogamy in a subculture that took common law relationships for granted. William Kerwood was demobilized at the Peace of Amiens and within three days married a woman, one

Tryphena Hamlyn, who had been seeing one of his shipmates. He lived with her for about six months, working as a shoemaker, and then moved on. When he found himself a party to a bigamy suit, Tryphena was in fact already married, he responded with bemused attachment and wondered what the fuss was all about.[62]

Others took their marital responsibilities more seriously. John Nicol spent twenty-five years at sea traversing the globe and in 1789 struck up a relationship with Sarah Whitlam, a convict on the first female transport to Australia. He hoped to link up with her again after her servitude, but she married a first-fleet convict and left him high and dry; and so on coming ashore at the end of the war, he married his cousin in his native Edinburgh, his thoughts of Sarah now fading into a "distant pleasing dream." He hoped to make a go of it as a cooper, the maritime skill he had acquired, but the press gang had wind of his presence and he was forced to sell his stock in trade and quarry for a living. His marriage to Margaret lasted seven years, but he was unable to save enough and found himself a destitute widower at age fifty-eight.[63] Francis Bergh, who apprenticed in the Yorkshire coastal trade, had better luck handling old age, although his marital course was checkered. As we have seen, his mother-in-law betrayed him to the press gang, and for years he didn't know his wife had died in childbirth. He married a second time some twenty years later, to a widow in New Orleans who died within a year of a fever. Returning to England in 1833, he married a widow from Chatham. She "had a heavy family to bring up," he recalled, "and I thought I could do no better with my money to [than] assist the widow and fatherless." Unfortunately she died in less than a year as well, and his adopted family rejected him, absconding with everything he possessed. He then tried a fourth time, marrying a widow of a shipmate who also had a family to feed. After three more years of service in the navy, he was discharged with a pension of £21 per annum.[64]

What do these stories reveal? Three things: the difficulties of linking a peripatetic life to a domestic one, at a time, interestingly when domesticity was more highly prized, at least among the more respectable. The way in which state imperatives, particularly impressment and the prohibition of shore leave, disrupted courtship patterns and familial ties, and made the sorts of transitions back to coastal communities so difficult. Finally, these tales suggest that the seamen of the Napoleonic era were a lost generation, adrift in a world that offered few material returns outside of an overstocked merchant marine, unless one had enough savings to run a quayside pub or chandler's shop. Of the seadogs of Britain's great battles, Camperdown, the Nile, Trafalgar, recalled Thomas Haswell, the son of a sailor, "Scores were to be found on the quays, the wharves, the landing places and lower streets of old Shields, in every state of picturesque dismemberment ... grimly suggestive of the peculiar horror of 'tween deck fighting."[65] Paradoxically the bleak endings of many maritime lives heightened the romance of youthful adventure and naval heroism, for Jack Tars could not psychologically consider the personal cost of their endeavors over the long term without a hint of nostalgia for the dangerous days of sail.

Notes

1 Robert Hay, *Landsman Hay. The Memoirs of Robert Hay*, ed. Vincent McInerney (Barnsley: Seaforth Pub., 2010), pp.170–71.

2 Old Bailey Proceedings Online, December 1749, Edward and Patrick Dempsey (t17491209-21); Ordinary of Newgate's Account, February 1750 (OA17509207).

3 Henry Fielding, *The Journal of a Voyage to Lisbon* (London, 1755), p. 199.

4 John Fielding, *A Brief Description of the Cities of London and Westminster* (London, 1776), p. xv.

5 Patricia Fumerton, *Unsettled: The Culture of Mobility and the Working Poor in Early Modern England* (Chicago: University of Chicago Press, 2006), part 2.

6 *The Autobiography of Ashley Bowen 1728–1813*, ed. Daniel Vickers (Peterborough, Ontario: Broadview Editions, 2006), pp. 11–30.

7 Nicholas Rogers, *The Press Gang. Naval Impressment and its Opponents in Georgian Britain* (London: Continuum, 2007), p. 8.

8 Michael A. Lewis, *A Social History of the Navy, 1793–1815* (London: Allen & Unwin, 1960), pp. 129, 139; Rogers, *Press Gang*, pp. 4–5. Cf. J. Ross Dancy, *The Myth of the Press Gang* (Woodbridge: The Boydell Press, 2015), pp. 120–156.

9 Rogers, *Press Gang* pp. 93–49.

10 Hay, *Landsman Hay*, pp. 52–53.

11 Jack Nastyface [William Robinson], *Nautical Economy: or Forecastle Recollections of Events during the Last War* (London, 1836), p. 2.

12 Charles Reece Pemberton, *The History of Pel Verjuice, the Wanderer* (London: James Watson, 1853) pp. 96–7.

13 Peter Earle, *Sailors: English Merchant Seamen 1650–1775* (London: Methuen, 1998), ch. 3.

14 Bowen, *Ashley Bowen*, p. 45.

15 Peter Earle, *Sailors*, p. 153.

16 Pemberton, *Pel Verjuice*, p. 97.

17 Robinson, *Nautical Economy*, p. 117.

18 Ibid., p. 27.

19 Samuel Leech, *Thirty Years from Home, or A Voice from the Main Deck, Being the Experiences of Samuel Leech* (Boston, 1844), p. 37.

20 Lewis, *Social History of the Navy*, parts 1 & 2.
21 Marcus Rediker, *Between the Devil and the Deep Blue Sea. Merchant Seamen, Pirates and the Anglo-American Maritime World, 1700–1750* (New York: Cambridge University Press, 1987), chs. 3–5.
22 N.A.M. Rodger, *The Wooden World. An Anatomy of the Georgian Navy* (London: Collins, 1986), pp. 155–57, 344–46.
23 Caroline Alexander, *The Bounty: the True Story of the Mutiny on the Bounty* (New York: Viking, 2003), p. 69; Rodger, *Wooden World*, pp. 60–61.
24 Leech, *Thirty Years from Home*, pp. 95–96.
25 Ibid., p. 37.
26 *Five Naval Journals 1789–1817*, ed. Rear-Admiral H. G. Thursfield (London: Navy Records Society, vol. 91, 1951), p. 154.
27 Leech, *Thirty Years from Home*, pp. 39–40.
28 *Five Naval Journals*, p. 245.
29 Ibid., p. 145.
30 Lewis, *Social History of the Navy*, p. 270.
31 Cited in Lewis, *Social History of the Navy*, p. 278.
32 John Nicol, *The Life and Adventures of John Nicol, Mariner*, ed. Tim Flannery (New York: Atlantic Monthly Press, 1997), p. 28.
33 David Cordingly, *Billy Ruffian*, (London: Bloomsbury, 2003), p. 209.
34 John Laffin, *Jack Tar: The Story of the British Sailor* (London: Cassell, 1969), p. 88. See also Isaac Lamb, *War, Nationalism, and the British Sailor* (New York: Palgrave Macmillan, 2009), pp. 36–7.
35 N. A. M. Rodger, *The Command of the Ocean: a Naval History of Britain, 1649-1815* (New York: W.W. Norton, 2005), p. 214.
36 *Five Naval Journals*, 69–70; see also Thomas Pasley, *Private Sea Journals 1778-1782*, ed. Rodney M.S. Pasley (London: Dent, 1931), p. 74, where Captain Pasley gave his men "liberty ... to get drunk if done without noise and quarrelling." See also Simon J. Bronner, *Crossing the Line. Violence, Play, and Drama in Naval Equator Traditions* (Amsterdam: Amsterdam University Press, 2006).
37 E. P. Thompson, *Customs in Common* (London: Merlin Press, 1991), esp. ch. 6; and Hans Medick, "Plebeian Culture in the transition to capitalism," in *Culture, Ideology and Politics. Essays for Eric Hobsbawm*, ed. Raphael Samuel and Gareth Stedman Jones (London: Routledge & Kegan Paul, 1982), pp. 84–113.
38 Cited in Roy and Lesley Adkins, *Jack Tar: Life in Nelson's Navy* (London: Little, Brown, 2008), p. 155. See also Christopher Lloyd, *The British Seaman 1200-1860. A Social Survey* (London: Collins, 1968), pp. 245–7, and Lamb, *War, Nationalism and the British Sailor*, pp. 46–9.
39 Leech, *Thirty Years from Home*, p. 72.
40 Fumerton, *Unsettled*, p. 139.
41 "The Adventurous Sailor," in *A Garland of New Songs* (Newcastle, 1790?), p. 6.

42 Brian J. Rouleau, "Dead Men Do Tell Tales: Folklore, Fraternity and the Forecastle," *Early American Studies*, 5/1 (Spring 2007), 30–62; Leech, *Thirty Years from Home*, p. 82.

43 Robert Hay, *Landsman Hay*, ed. Vincent McInerney (Barnsley: Seaforth Publishing, 2010), p. 93.

44 Rodger, *Command of the Ocean*, p. 205; John Brewer, "Theatre and Counter-Theatre in Georgian Politics: The Mock Elections at Garratt," *Radical History Review* 22 (1979–1980), 7–40.

45 Alexander, *Bounty*, p. 102.

46 On the failure of those customary reciprocities, see Greg Dening, *Mr. Bligh's Bad Language: Passion, Power and Theatre on the Bounty* (Cambridge: Cambridge University Press), pp. 113–47.

47 William Richardson, *A Mariner of England* (London: John Murray, 1908), p. 106.

48 The National Archives, London [hereafter TNA], Adm 1/4172, cited in Kathrin Orth, "Voices from the Lower Deck: Petitions on the Conduct of Naval Officers during the 1797 Mutinies," in *The Naval Mutinies of 1797. Unity and Perseverance*, ed. Ann Veronica Coats and Philip MacDougall (Woodbridge: The Boydell Press, 2011), pp. 99–100.

49 Lloyd, *British Seaman*, pp. 240–2.

50 Richardson, *Mariner of England*, pp. 178, 187; Jacob Nagle, *The Nagle Journal: a Diary of the Life of Jacob Nagle, Sailor, from the Year 1775 to 1841*, ed. John C. Dann (New York: Weidenfeld & Nicolson, 1988), pp. 65, 73, 76.

51 Pasley, *Private Sea Journals*, p. 12.

52 Richardson, *Mariner of England*, p. 106.

53 Jonathan Neale, *The Cutlass and the Lash: Mutiny and Discipline in Nelson's Navy* (London: Pluto Press, 1985).

54 Rogers, *Press Gang*, pp. 106–107; Norman McCord and David E. Brewster, "Some Labour Troubles of the 1790s in North East England," *International Review of Social History* 13 (1968), 365–83. See also Joseph Price Moore III, "'The Greatest Enormity that Prevails': Direct Democracy and Workers' Self-Management in the British Naval Mutinies of 1797," in *Jack Tar in History: Essays in the History of Maritime Life and Labour*, ed. Colin Howell and Richard J. Twomey (Fredericton, NB: Acadiensis Press, 1991), pp. 82–83.

55 Ibid., p. 87.

56 Ann Veronica Coats, "The Delegates: A Radical Tradition," in *The Naval Mutinies of 1797* (Woodbridge: Boydell Press, 2011), ed. Ann Veronica Coats and Philip MacDougall, pp. 39–60.

57 Cordingly, *Billy Ruffian*, p. 210; the Liverpool and Blackburn figures are taken from the 1821 census. See *British Parliamentary Papers*, 1822, xv, 425.

58 Richardson, *Mariner of England*, pp. 121–22

59 Nagle, *Journal*, pp. 186–246.

60 TNA, Adm 1/2100 (Mostyn) enclosure with September 3, 1744; the letter is printed in *Manning the Royal Navy in Bristol: Liberty, Impressment and the*

      State, 1739-1815, ed. Nicholas Rogers (Bristol: Bristol Record Society, vol. 66,
      2014), no. 32.
61   *The Naval Songster, or Jack Tar's Chest of Conviviality for 1798* (London, 1798?),
      pp. 12–13.
62   Old Bailey Proceedings Online, April 1805, Tryphena Hamlyn (t18050424-34).
      On a sailor returning to find his wife living with someone else and for a
      time trying a ménage à trois, see Lamb, *War, Nationalism and the British Sailor*,
      p. 53.
63   Nicol, *Life and Adventures*, pp. 183–92.
64   Francis Bergh, "The Story of a Sailor's Life," *Household Words* 3 (1851), 216,
      227, 284, 308–10.
65   G. H. Haswell, *The Maister: A Century of Tyneside Life* (London: W. Scott,
      1895), p. 132.

Select Bibliography

Abinger Collection, Bodleian Library www.bodley.ox.ac.uk/dept/scwmss/wmss/online/1500-1900/abinger/abinger.html.

The Anti-Jacobin; or, Weekly Examiner, 2 vols. London, 1799.

Austen, Jane. *Emma*, ed. Richard Cronin and Dorothy McMillan. Cambridge: Cambridge University Press, 2005.

    Later Manuscripts, ed. Janet Todd and Linda Bree. Cambridge: Cambridge University Press, 2008.

Bage, Robert. *Man as He Is*, 4 vols. London, 1792.

Bee, John [John Badcock]. *Slang. A Dictionary of the Turf, the Ring, the Chase, Pit, of Bon-ton, and Varieties of Life*. London, 1823.

    Sportsman's Slang; A New Dictionary. London, 1825.

[Beloe, William]. *The Sexagenarian; or, The Recollections of a Literary Life*, second edition, 2 vols. London, 1818.

Bowen, Ashley. *The Autobiography of Ashley Bowen 1728–1813*, ed. Daniel Vickers. Peterborough: Broadview, 2006.

"Boxiana No. VIII." *Blackwood's* 8 (October 1820), 60–63.

Breslaw, Philip. *Breslaw's Last Legacy; or, The Magical Companion*. London, 1784.

Brightwell, C. L. *Memorials of the Life of Amelia Opie, Selected and Arranged from her Letters, Diaries, and Other Manuscripts*. Norwich, 1854.

Carey, George Saville. *The Balnea: Or, an Impartial Description of All the Popular Watering Places in England*. London, 1799.

Colston, Marianne. *Journal of a Tour in France, Switzerland, and Italy, During the Years 1819, 20, and 21*, 2 vols. London, 1823.

"Country Book-Clubs Fifty Years Ago." *Gentleman's Magazine* n.s. 37, pt. 1 (May–June 1852), 571–72.

Crabbe, George. *The Borough: A Poem. In Twenty-Four Letters*. London, 1810.

Dent, William. *Honorable Situations the Tipperary Duellists or Margate Heroes Have Hitherto Stood In*. London, 1790.

Dermody, Thomas. *Thomas Dermody: Selected Writings*, ed. Michael Griffin. Dublin: Field Day, 2012.

Egan, Pierce. *Boxiana, or Sketches of Ancient and Modern Pugilism*. London, 1829.

"Facts Relative to the State of Reading Societies and Literary Institutions in the United Kingdom." *Monthly Magazine* 51 (June 1821), 397–98.

Farington, Joseph. *The Diary of Joseph Farington. Volume VI, April 1803–December 1804*, ed. Kenneth Garlick and Angus Macintyre. New Haven: Yale University Press, 1979.

Farther Excursions of the Observant Pedestrian, Exemplified in a Tour to Margate, 4 vols. London, 1801.

The Female Gamester; or, the Pupil of Fashion. A Novel. London, 1796.

Fielding, Henry. *The Journal of a Voyage to Lisbon*. London, 1755.

Fielding, John. *A Brief Description of the Cities of London and Westminster*. London, 1776.

Fox, Charles James. *The Speech of the Right Hon. Charles James Fox: Containing the Declaration of his Principles, Respecting the Present Crisis of Public Affairs*. London, 1792.

"Fuss in A Book Club. As Related By a Copy Of Miss Martineau's 'Eastern Life,' Etc. Etc." *Fraser's Magazine* 38 (December 1848), 628–34.

[Geddes, Alexander]. *Bardomachia: Or, The Battle of the Bards, Translated from the Original Latin*. London, 1800.

Gifford, William. *An Epistle to Peter Pindar; Third Edition with Considerable Additions to the Postscript*. London, 1800.

Godwin, William. *Caleb Williams*, ed. David McCracken. Oxford: Oxford World's Classics, 1982.

    The Diary of William Godwin, ed. Victoria Myers, David O'Shaughnessy, and Mark Philp. Oxford: Oxford Digital Library, 2010. http://godwindiary.bodleian.ox.ac.uk.

    An Enquiry Concerning Political Justice, ed. Mark Philp, vol. 3 of *Political and Philosophical Writings of William Godwin*. London: William Pickering, 1993.

    The Letters of William Godwin, Volume I: 1778–1797, ed. Pamela Clemit. Oxford: Oxford University Press, 2011.

    The Letters of William Godwin, Volume II: 1798–1805, ed. Pamela Clemit. Oxford: Oxford University Press, 2014.

Gray, Thomas. *Correspondence of Thomas Gray*, ed. Paget Toynbee and Leonard Whibley, with corrections and additions by H. W. Starr, 3 vols. Oxford: Clarendon Press, 1971.

    The Poems of Mr. Gray, 4 vols. York and London, 1778.

Hanway, Mary Ann. *Ellinor, or, The World As It Is. A Novel*, 4 vols. London: Minerva Press, 1798.

Hay, Robert. *Landsman Hay. The Memoirs of Robert Hay*, ed. Vincent McInerney. Barnsley: Seaforth Publications, 2010.

Hays, Mary. *The Correspondence of Mary Hays, British Novelist*, ed. Marilyn L. Brooks. Lewiston, Lampeter: Edward Mellon Press, 2004.

Holcroft, Thomas. *The German Hotel. A Comedy*. London, 1790.

    The Noble Peasant. A Comic Opera in Three Acts. Dublin, 1784.

Hardy, Thomas. *Memoir of Thomas Hardy, Founder of and Secretary to, the London Corresponding Society, for Diffusing Useful Political Knowledge among the People of Great Britain and Ireland, and for Promoting Parliamentary Reform*. London, 1832.

Hutton, William. *An History of Birmingham to the End of the Year 1780.* Birmingham, 1781.

Iliff, Edward Henry. *A Summary of the Duties of Citizenship! Written Expressly for the Members of the London Corresponding Society; Including Observations on the Contemptuous Neglect of the Secretary of State, with Regard to Their Late Address to the King!* London: 1795.

Jameson, Anna Brownell. *Diary of an Ennuyée.* London, 1826.

Jones, John Gale. *Sketch of a Political Tour through Rochester, Chatham, Maidstone, Gravesend &c. Part the First.* London, 1796.

Lamb, Charles and Mary Lamb. *The Letters of Charles and Mary Lamb*, ed. Edwin W. Marrs, 3 vols. Ithaca, NY: Cornell University Press, 1975.

Lambeth Palace Archives. D675 and D 676, case number 3111; G 155/18; G 155/79; G 153/89; E45/100; G155/79; MS Film 104, 105.

"Letter to the Editor of the Monthly Magazine." *Monthly Magazine, and British Register* 4 (October 1797), 275–77.

Letters of Momus, from Margate; Describing the Most Distinguished Characters There; and The Virtues, Vices and Follies, to which They Gave Occasion, in What was Called the Season Of the Year 1777. London, 1778.

Lewis, Hardwicke. *An Excursion to Margate, In the Month of June, 1786: Interspersed with a Variety of Anecdotes of Well-known Characters.* London, 1787.

Lloyd, Sarah. "Amour in the Shrubbery: Reading the Detail of English Adultery Trial Publications of the 1780s." *Eighteenth-Century Studies* 39 (2006), 421–42.

London Corresponding Society. *Account of the proceedings of a meeting of the London Corresponding Society, held in a Field near Copenhagen House, Monday, October 26, 1795.* London, 1795.

Selections from the Papers of the London Corresponding Society 1792–1799, ed. Mary Thale. Cambridge: Cambridge University Press, 1983.

London Metropolitan Archive. DL/6/662/179/3; DL/C/0562/177–79.

London Unmask'd: Or the New Town Spy. Exhibiting a Striking Picture of the World as it Goes. London, 1785.

Mackenzie, Eneas. *An Historical, Topographical, and Descriptive View of the County of Northumberland*, second edition, 2 vols. Newcastle upon Tyne, 1825.

The Margate Guide. Containing a Particular Account of Margate, With Respect to Its New Buildings, Assemblies, Accommodations, Manner of Bathing, and Remarkable Places in Its Neighbourhood. London, 1775.

Marsh, John, *The John Marsh Journals: The Life and Times of a Gentleman Composer (1752–1828)*, ed. Brian Robins. Hillsdale NY: Pendragon Press, 1998.

Mathews, Henry. *The Diary of an Invalid: Being the Journal of a Tour in Pursuit of Health in Portugal, Italy, Switzerland and France in the Years 1817, 1818 and 1819.* London, 1820.

Mendoza, Daniel. *The Art of Boxing.* London, 1789.

Murray, John. *Handbook for Travellers in Central Italy, Including the Papal States, Rome, and the Cities of Etruria.* London, 1843.

National Archive. PROB 11/1591:129/110–12; Del 7/1; DEL 1/670; Del 5/35; and Del 6/52

The New Margate and Ramsgate Guide in Letters to a Friend. Describing the Accommodations and Amusements of those Delightful Watering Places in Prose and Verse. London, [1780?].

Nicol, John. *The Life and Adventures of John Nicol, Mariner*, ed. Tim Flannery. New York: Atlantic Monthly Press, 1997.

Pancratia, or a History of Pugilism. London, 1812.

Pasley, Thomas. *Private Sea Journals 1778–1782*, ed. Rodney M. S. Pasley. London: Dent, 1931.

Parsons, William. *Travelling Recreations*, 2 vols. London, 1807.

Pemberton, Charles Reece. *The History of Pel Verjuice, The Wanderer*. London: James Watson, 1853.

Pindar, Peter. *Lord Auckland's Triumph; or the Death of Crim. Con. A Pair of Prophetic Odes.* London, 1800.

Place, Francis. *The Autobiography of Francis Place (1771–1854)*, ed. Mary Thale. Cambridge: Cambridge University Press, 1972.

Pocock's Everlasting Songster, Containing a Selection of the Most Approved Songs. Gravesend, 1800.

Polwhele, Richard. *The Language, Literature, and Literary Characters of Cornwall: With Illustrations from Devonshire.* London, 1806.

Powell, James. *The Narcotic and Private Theatricals.* London, 1793.

Regulations Adopted at a General Meeting of the Members of the Edgbaston and Five Ways Book Society. March 27, 1816.

Richardson, William. *A Mariner of England.* London: John Murray, 1908.

Robinson, William. *A Trip to Margate: With a Description of Its Environs, Written in the Year 1805.* London, [1805].

Rules and Regulations of the Book Society at Sedgefield, With the Names of the Members, and a List of Books. Stockton, 1800.

[Shillito, Charles]. *The Country Book-Club. A Poem.* London, 1788.

Simond, L. *A Tour in Italy and Sicily.* London, 1828.

Smith, Charlotte. *Marchmont*, ed. Kate Davies and Harriet Guest. Vol. 9 of *The Works of Charlotte Smith*, 14 vols, ed. Stuart Curran. London: Pickering and Chatto, 2005–2007.

Starke, Mariana. *Travels on the Continent: Written for the Use and Particular Information of Travellers.* London, 1820.

Stephens, Alexander. "Stephensiana. No. VI." *Monthly Magazine* 53 (1822), 138–42.

"Stephensiana. No. XIV." *Monthly Magazine* 54 (1822), 425–28.

Thelwall, John. *Natural and Constitutional Right of Britons to Annual Parliaments, Universal Suffrage, and the Freedom of Popular Association.* London, 1795.

Ode to Science. Recited at the Anniversary Meeting of the Philomathian Society, June 20, 1791. London, 1791.

Tribune, 3 vols. London, 1796.

Trials for Treason and Sedition, 1792–1794, ed. John Barrell and Jon Mee, 8 vols. London: Pickering and Chatto, 2006–2007.

[Turner, David], *A Short History of the Westminster Forum: Containing Some Remarks upon the Laws; wherein the Nature of such Societies is Examined,* 2 vols. London, 1781.

[Walker, Eliza]. "Country Reading Societies." *New Monthly Magazine and Literary Journal* 22 (January 1828), 216–23.

Wordsworth, Dorothy. *The Grasmere and Alfoxden Journals,* ed. Pamela Woof. Oxford: Oxford University Press, 2008.

SECONDARY SOURCES

Adkins, Roy and Lesley Adkins. *Jack Tar.* London: Little, Brown, 2008.

Andrew, Donna. "Popular Culture and Public Debate: London 1780." *Historical Journal* 39 (1996), 405–23.

Appadurai, Arjun. "Putting Hierarchy in Its Place." In *Rereading Cultural Anthropology,* ed. George E. Marcus. Durham, NC: Duke University Press, 1992. 34–47.

Austin, Linda. *Nostalgia in Transition, 1780–1917.* Charlottesville, VA: University of Virginia Press, 2007.

Allan, David. *A Nation of Readers: The Lending Library in Georgian England.* London: The British Library, 2008.

Baer, Marc. *Theatre and Disorder in Late Georgian London.* Oxford: Clarendon Press, 1992.

Berry, Helen. "Creating Polite Space: The Organisation and Social Function of the Newcastle Assembly Rooms." In *Creating and Consuming Culture in North-East England 1660–1830,* ed. Helen Berry and Jeremy Gregory. Aldershot: Ashgate, 2004. 120–40.

Bailey, Joanne. *Unquiet Lives: Marriage and Marriage Breakdown in England, 1660–1800.* Cambridge: Cambridge University Press, 2003.

Barrell, John. *Imagining the King's Death: Figurative Treason, Fantasies of Regicide 1793–1796.* Oxford: Oxford University Press, 2000.

The Spirit of Despotism: Invasions of Privacy in the 1790s. Oxford: Oxford University Press, 2006.

Batchelor, Jennie. *Women's Work: Labour, Gender, Authorship, 1750–1830.* Manchester: Manchester University Press, 2010.

Beckwith, Frank. "The Eighteenth-Century Proprietary Library in England." *The Journal of Documentation* 3 (September 1957), 81–98.

Boddy, Ernest H. "The Dalton Book Club: A Brief History." *Library History* 9 (1992), 97–105.

Borsay, Peter. *The English Urban Renaissance: Culture and Society in the Provincial Town, c. 1680–1750.* Oxford: Oxford University Press, 1989.

Bourdieu, Pierre. *The Field of Cultural Production.* New York: Columbia University Press, 1993.

Brewer, John. "'The Most Polite Age and the Most Vicious': Attitudes Towards Culture as a Commodity, 1660–1800." In *The Consumption of Culture 1600–1800: Image, Object, Text*, ed. Ann Bermingham and John Brewer. London: Routledge, 1995.

The Pleasures of the Imagination: English Culture in the Eighteenth Century. London: Harper Collins, 1997.

"Theatre and Counter-Theatre in Georgian Politics: The Mock Elections at Garratt." *Radical History Review* 22 (1979), 7–40.

Brodie, Allan and Gary Winter. *England's Seaside Resorts*. Cambridge: English Heritage, 2007.

Bromwich, David. *Disowned by Memory: Wordsworth's Poetry of the 1790s*. Chicago: University of Chicago Press, 1998.

Bronner, Simon J. *Crossing the Line. Violence, Play, and Drama in Naval Equator Traditions*. Amsterdam: Amsterdam University Press, 2006.

Brown, Peter. *The History of the Market Drayton Book Society 1814–2008*. Market Drayton: Market Drayton Book Society, 2009.

Bugg, John. "Close Confinement: John Thelwall and the Romantic Prison." *European Romantic Review* 20 (2009), 37–56.

Butler, Judith. *Notes Toward a Performative Theory of Assembly*. Cambridge, MA: Harvard University Press, 2015.

Buzard, James. *The Beaten Track: European Tourism, Literature, and the Ways to Culture, 1800–1918*. Oxford: Oxford University Press, 1993.

"The Grand Tour and After (1660–1840)." In *The Cambridge Companion to Travel Writing*, ed. Peter Hulme and Tim Youngs. Cambridge: Cambridge University Press, 2002.

Carlson, Julie. "Hazlitt and the Sociability of the Theatre." In *Romantic Sociability: Social Networks and Literary Culture in Britain, 1770–1840*, ed. Gillian Russell and Clara Tuite. Cambridge: Cambridge University Press, 2002. 145–65.

Chard, Chloe. *Pleasure and Guilt on the Grand Tour: Travel Writing and Imaginative Geography, 1600–1830*. Manchester: Manchester University Press, 1999.

Clarke, Peter. *British Clubs and Societies 1580–1800: The Origins of an Associational World*. Oxford: Clarendon Press, 2000.

Coats, Ann Veronica and Philip MacDougall, eds. *The Naval Mutinies of 1797: Unity and Perseverance*. Woodbridge: The Boydell Press, 2011.

Conley, Tom. "Afterward: A Creative Swarm." In Michel de Certeau, *Culture in the Plural*, ed. Luce Giard. Minneapolis, MI: University of Minnesota Press, 1997.

Culler, Jonathan. *Framing the Sign: Criticism and Its Institutions*. Norman, OK: University of Oklahoma Press, 1986.

Curwen, Henry. *A History of Booksellers, The Old and the New*. London, 1873.

Cotlar, Seth. *Tom Paine's America: The Rise and Fall of Transatlantic Radicalism in the Early Republic*. Charlottesville, VA: University of Virginia Press, 2011.

Davis, Michael T. "'The Mob Club?': The London Corresponding Society and the Politics of Civility in the 1790s." In *Unrespectable Radicals?: Popular*

Politics in the Age of Reform, ed. Michael T. Davis and Paul A. Pickering. Aldershot: Ashgate, 2008. 21–40.

Day, John. *Coffee Houses and Book Clubs in Eighteenth and Nineteenth-Century Northumberland*. Newcastle upon Tyne: University of Newcastle upon Tyne, 1995.

Dening, Greg. *Mr. Bligh's Bad Language: Passion, Power and Theatre on the Bounty*. Cambridge: Cambridge University Press, 1992.

Downie, J.A. "How Useful to Eighteenth-Century English Studies is the Paradigm of the 'Bourgeois Public Sphere'?" *Literature Compass* 1 (2003), 1–19.

"Public and Private: The Myth of the Public Sphere." In *A Concise Companion to the Restoration and the Eighteenth Century*, ed. Cynthia Wall. Oxford: Blackwell, 2005. 58–79.

Earle, Peter. *Sailors: English Merchant Seamen 1650–1775*. London: Methuen, 1988.

Epstein, James. "'Equality and No King': Sociability and Sedition: The Case of John Frost." In *Romantic Sociability: Social Networks and Literary Culture in Britain, 1770–1840*, ed. Gillian Russell and Clara Tuite. Cambridge: Cambridge University Press, 2006. 43–61.

"Spatial Practices/Democratic Vistas." *Social History* 4 (1999), 294–310.

Everest, Kelvin. *Coleridge's Secret Ministry: The Context of the Conversation Poems 1795–1798*. Hassocks, Sussex: Harvester Press, 1979.

Fallon, David. "Booksellers in the Godwin Diaries." *Bodleian Library Record* 24 (2011), 25–34.

Fulford, Tim. *Landscape, Liberty and Authority: Poetry, Criticism and Politics from Thomson to Wordsworth*. Cambridge: Cambridge University Press, 1996.

Furness, Horace Howard. *A New Variorum Edition of Shakespeare, vol. 7, Merchant of Venice*. Philadelphia: Lippincott, 1888.

Felsenstein, Frank. *Anti-Semitic Stereotypes: A Paradigm of Otherness in English Popular Culture, 1660 -1830*. Baltimore, MD: Johns Hopkins University Press, 1999.

George, M. Dorothy. *Catalogue of Prints and Drawings in the British Museum: Division I: Political and Personal Satires*. London: British Museum, 1938.

Gilmartin, Kevin. "Popular Radicalism and the Public Sphere." *Studies in Romanticism* 33 (1994), 549–57.

Writing Against Revolution: Literary Conservatism in Britain, 1790–1832. Cambridge: Cambridge University Press, 2007.

Golinski, Jan. *Science as Public Culture: Chemistry and Enlightenment in Britain, 1760–1820*. Cambridge: Cambridge University Press, 1992.

"Humphrey Davy's Sexual Chemistry." *Configurations* 7 (1999), 15–41.

Goodman, Dena. *The Republic of Letters: A Cultural History of Enlightenment*. Ithaca, NY: Cornell University Press, 1993.

Goodwin, Albert. *The Friends of Liberty: The English Democratic Movement in the Age of the French Revolution*. Cambridge, MA: Harvard University Press, 1979.

Guest, Harriet. *Unbounded Attachment: Sentiment and Politics in the Age of the French Revolution*. Oxford: Oxford University Press, 2013.

Gutteridge, John. "Scenery and Ecstasy: Three of Coleridge's Blank Verse Poems." In *New Approaches to Coleridge: Biographical and Critical Essays*, ed. Donald Sultana. London: Vision Press, 1981.

Habermas, Jürgen. *The Structural Transformation of the Public Sphere: An Inquiry into a Category of Bourgeois Society*, trans. Thomas Burger and Frederick Lawrence. Cambridge, MA: MIT Press, 1989.

Hawkins, Edward. "Authors of the Poetry of the Anti-Jacobin." *Notes & Queries*, 1st ser., 3 (May 3, 1851), 349.

Helsinger, Elizabeth. *Rural Scenes and National Representation: Britain, 1815–1850*. Princeton: Princeton University Press, 1997.

Hill, Constance. *Jane Austen: Her Homes & Her Friends*. London: John Lane, 1902.

Hoare, Peter. "Nottingham Subscription Library: Its Organisation, Its Collection and Its Management Over 175 Years." In *Bromley House 1752–1991: Four Essays Celebrating the 175th Anniversary of the Foundation of The Nottingham Subscription Library, More Generally Known as Bromley House Library*, ed. Rosalys T. Coope and Jane Y. Corbett. Nottingham: Nottingham Subscription Library, 1991. 3–47.

Holmes, Richard. *Coleridge: Early Visions, 1772–1804*. New York: Pantheon Books, 1989.

Horden, John. *John Freeth, 1731–1808: Political Ballad-Writer and Innkeeper*. Oxford: Leopard's Head Press, 1993.

Humphreys, Arthur L. *Piccadilly Bookmen: Memorials of the House of Hatchard*. London: Hatchards, 1893.

Jackson, Heather. *Romantic Readers: The Evidence of the Marginalia*. New Haven, CT: Yale University Press, 2005.

James, Felicity. *Charles Lamb, Coleridge and Wordsworth: Reading Friendship in the 1790s*. Basingstoke: Palgrave, 2008.

Jordan, Nicolle. "The Promise and Frustration of Plebeian Public Opinion in *Caleb Williams*." *Eighteenth-Century Fiction* 19 (2007), 243–66.

Kaufman, Paul. *Libraries and Their Users: Collected Papers in Library History*. London: The Library Association, 1969.

Klancher, Jon. *Transfiguring the Arts and Sciences: Knowledge and Cultural Institutions in the Romantic Age*. Cambridge: Cambridge University Press, 2013.

Klein, Lawrence, *Shaftesbury and the Culture of Politeness: Moral Discourse and Cultural Politics in Early Eighteenth-Century England*. Cambridge: Cambridge University Press, 1994.

Laffin, John. *Jack Tar: The Story of the British Sailor*. London. Cassell, 1969.

Lamb, Isaac. *War, Nationalism and the British Sailor*. New York: Palgrave Macmillan, 2009.

Landry, Donna. *The Invention of the Countryside: Hunting, Walking and Ecology in English Literature, 1671–1831*. Basingstoke: Palgrave Macmillan, 2001.

Lewis, Michael A. *A Social History of the Navy, 1793–1815*. London: Allen & Unwin, 1960.

Lynch, Deidre Shauna. *The Economy of Character: Novels, Market Culture, and the Business of Inner Meaning*. Chicago: University of Chicago Press, 1998.

"Canons' Clockwork: Novels for Everyday Use." In *Bookish Histories: Books, Literature, and Commercial Modernity, 1700–1900*, ed. Ina Ferris and Paul Keen. Basingstoke: Palgrave Macmillan, 2009. 87–110.

MacCannell, Dean. *The Tourist: A New Theory of the Leisure Class*. Berkeley, CA: University of California Press, 1976.

Mackey, Brian. "The Market House and Assembly Rooms, Lisburn." *Lisburn Historical Society Journal* 6 (1986), 44–57.

Manogue, Ralph A. "The Plight of James Ridgway, London Bookseller and Publisher, and the Newgate Radicals, 1792–1797." *Wordsworth Circle* 27 (1996), 158–66.

Matlak, Richard E. *The Poetry of Relationship: The Wordsworths and Coleridge, 1797–1800*. New York: St Martin's Press, 1997.

McCalman, Iain. "Newgate in Revolution: Radical Enthusiasm and Romantic Counterculture." *Eighteenth Century Life* 22 (1998), 95–110.

McCann, Andrew. *Cultural Politics in the 1790s: Literature, Radicalism, and the Public Sphere*. New York: St Martin's Press, 1999.

Medick, Hans. "Plebeian Culture in the Transition to Capitalism." In *Culture, Ideology and Politics. Essays for Eric Hobsbawm*, ed. Raphael Samuel and Gareth Stedman Jones. London: Routledge & Kegan Paul, 1982.

Mee, Jon. "The Strange Career of Richard 'Citizen' Lee." In *British Literary Radicalism, 1650–1830: From Revolution to Revolution*, ed. Timothy Morton and Nigel Smith. Cambridge: Cambridge University Press, 2002. 151–66.

Conversable Worlds: Literature, Contention, and Community, 1762–1830. Oxford: Oxford University Press, 2011.

Mellor, Anne K. "Coleridge's 'This Lime-Tree Bower My Prison' and the Categories of English Landscape." *Studies in Romanticism* 18 (1979), 253–70.

Miller, Christopher R. "Coleridge and the Scene of Lyric Description." *The Journal of English and German Philology* 101 (2002), 520–39.

Modiano, Raimonda. *Coleridge and the Concept of Nature*. Tallahassee, FL: Florida State University Press, 1985.

Mole, Tom. *Byron's Romantic Celebrity: Industrial Culture and the Hermeneutic of Intimacy*. New York: Palgrave Macmillan, 2007.

Newman, Ian. "Edmund Burke in the Tavern." *European Romantic Review* 24 (2013), 125–48.

Nicassio, Susan Vandiver. *Imperial City: Rome under Napoleon*. Chicago: University of Chicago Press, 2009.

O'Quinn, Daniel. *Entertaining Crisis in the Atlantic Imperium, 1770–1800*. Baltimore, MD: Johns Hopkins University Press, 2011.

Staging Governance: Theatrical Imperialism in London, 1770–1800. Baltimore, MD: Johns Hopkins University Press, 2011.

"In the Face of Difference: Molineaux, Crib, and the Violence of the Fancy." In *Race, Romanticism, and the Atlantic*, ed. Paul Youngquist. London: Ashgate, 2013. 213–35.

O'Shaughnessy, David. "Caleb Williams and the Philomaths: Recalibrating Political Justice for the Nineteenth Century." *Nineteenth-Century Literature* 66 (2012), 423–48.

Page, Judith W. "'Hath Not a Jew Eyes?': Edmund Kean and the Sympathetic Shylock." *Wordsworth Circle* 34 (2003), 216–19.

Philp, Mark. "Preaching to the Unconverted." *Enlightenment and Dissent* 28 (2012), 73–88.

Pinch, Adela. *Thinking about Other People in Nineteenth-Century British Writing*. Cambridge: Cambridge University Press, 2010.

Piper, Andrew. *Dreaming in Books: The Making of the Bibliographic Imagination in the Romantic Age*. Chicago: University of Chicago Press, 2009.

Price, Leah. *How to Do Things with Books in Victorian Britain*. Princeton: Princeton University Press, 2012.

Probert, Rebecca, Julie Shaffer and Joanne Bailey. *A Noble Affair: The Remarkable True Story of the Runaway Wife, the Bigamous Earl and the Farmer's Daughter*. Brandram: Kenilworth, 2013.

Raiger, Michael. "The Poetics of Liberation in Imaginative Power: Coleridge's 'This Lime Tree Bower My Prison.'" *European Romantic Review* 3 (1992), 65–78.

Ragussis, Michael. *Theatrical Nation: Jews and Other Outlandish Englishmen in Georgian England*. Philadelphia: University of Pennsylvania Press, 2010.

Raven, James. *The Business of Books: Booksellers and the English Book Trade 1450–1850*. New Haven, CT: Yale University Press, 2007.

Bookscape: Geographies of Printing and Publishing in London before 1800. London: British Library, 2014.

Rediker, Marcus. *Between the Devil and the Deep Blue Sea: Merchant Seamen, Pirates and the Anglo-American Maritime World, 1700–1750*. New York: Cambridge University Press, 1987.

Ridley, Ronald T. *The Eagle and the Spade: Archaeology in Rome during the Napoleonic Era*. Cambridge: Cambridge University Press, 2009.

Robbins, Bruce. "Introduction: The Public as Phantom." In *The Phantom Public Sphere*, ed. Bruce Robbins. Minneapolis, MN: University of Minnesota Press, 1993. vii–xxvi.

Rodger, Nicholas A. M. *The Wooden World: An Anatomy of the Georgian Navy*. London: Collins, 1986.

The Command of the Ocean: A Naval History of Britain, 1649–1815. New York: W. W. Norton, 2005.

Rogers, Nicholas. *The Press Gang. Naval Impressment and Its Opponents in Georgian Britain*. London: Continuum, 2007.

Rogers, Nicholas, ed. *Manning the Royal Navy in Bristol: Liberty, Impressment and the State, 1739–1815*. Bristol: Bristol Record Society, 2014.

Russell, Gillian and Clara Tuite, eds. *Romantic Sociability: Social Networks and Literary Culture in Britain, 1770–1840*. Cambridge: Cambridge University Press, 2002.

Russell, Gillian. *Women, Sociability and Theatre in Georgian London*. Cambridge: Cambridge University Press, 2007.

Scrivener, Michael. "Habermas, Romanticism, and Literary Theory." *Literature Compass* 1 (2004), 1–18.

Shattuck, Charles H. "Introduction to Shakespeare's *Merchant of Venice*." In *John Philip Kemble Promptbooks*, 11 vols. Charlottesville, VA: University of Virginia Press, 1974.

Shaw-Taylor, Desmond. "Eighteenth-Century Performances of Shakespeare Recorded in the Theatrical Portraits of the Garrick Club." In *Shakespeare Survey 51, Shakespeare in the Eighteenth Century*, ed. Stanley Wells. Cambridge: Cambridge University Press, 1998. 107–24.

Stillinger, Jack. *Coleridge and Textual Instability: The Multiple Versions of the Major Poems*. Oxford: Oxford University Press, 1994.

Smith, Ruth. *Handel's Oratorio's and Eighteenth-Century Thought*. Cambridge: Cambridge University Press, 1995.

Snowdon, David. "Drama *Boxiana*: Spectacle and Theatricality in Pierce Egan's Pugilistic Writing." *Romanticism on the Net* 46 (May 2007).

Springer, Carolyn. *The Marble Wilderness: Ruins and Representation in Italian Romanticism, 1775–1850*. Cambridge: Cambridge University Press, 1987.

St. Clair, William. *The Reading Nation in the Romantic Period*. Cambridge: Cambridge University Press, 2004.

St. Clair Strange, F. G. *The History of the Royal Sea Bathing Hospital, Margate, 1791–1991*. Rainham, Kent: Meresborough Books, 1991.

Starobinski, Jean. *The Invention of Liberty, 1700–1789*, trans. Bernard C. Swift. Geneva: Skira, 1964.

Staves, Susan. *Married Women's Separate Property in England, 1660–1833*. Cambridge, MA: Harvard University Press, 1990.

Stockdale, Eric. *'Tis Treason, My Good Man! Four Revolutionary Presidents and a Piccadilly Bookshop*. Delaware and London: Oak Knoll Press and the British Library, 2005.

Swanton, M. J. "A Dividing Book Club of the 1840s: Wadebridge, Cornwall." *Library History* 9 (1992), 106–21.

Sweet, Rosemary. *Cities and the Grand Tour: The British in Italy*, c. 1690–1820. Cambridge: Cambridge University Press, 2012.

Taylor, Diana. *The Archive and the Repertoire: Performing Cultural Memory in the Americas*. Durham, NC: Duke University Press, 2003.

Thale, Mary. "Women in London Debating Societies in 1780." *Gender & History* 7 (1995), 5–24.

Thompson, E. P. *Customs in Common*. London. Merlin Press, 1991.

Thompson, Judith. "From Forum to Repository: A Case Study in Romantic Cultural Geography." *European Romantic Review* 15 (2004), 177–91.

Ulmer, William A. "The Rhetorical Occasion of 'This Lime-Tree Bower my Prison.'" *Romanticism* 13 (2007), 15–27.

Urry, John. *The Tourist Gaze: Leisure and Travel in Contemporary Societies.* London: Sage, 1990.

Wagner, Corinna. "Domestic Invasions: John Thelwall and the Exploitation of Privacy." In *John Thelwall: Radical Romantic and Acquitted Felon*, ed. Steve Poole. London: Pickering and Chatto, 2009. 95–106.

Walton, John K. *The English Seaside Resort: A Social History, 1750–1914.* Leicester: Leicester University Press, 1983.

Whale, John. "Daniel Mendoza's Contests of Identity: Masculinity, Ethnicity and Nation in Georgian Prize-Fighting." *Romanticism* 14 (2008), 259–71.

Wharman, Dror. *The Making of the Modern Self: Identity and Culture in Eighteenth-century England.* New Haven, CT: Yale University Press, 2004.

Williams, Raymond. *Marxism and Literature.* Oxford and New York: Oxford University Press, 1977.

Wolfson, Susan J. *Romantic Interactions: Social Being and the Turns of Literary Action.* Baltimore, MD: Johns Hopkins University Press, 2010.

Worrall, David. *Theatric Revolution: Drama, Censorship and Romantic Period Subcultures 1773–1832.* Oxford: Oxford University Press, 2009.

"'Imperfect Sympathies': The Early Nineteenth-Century Formation of Responses to Black Fighters in Britain." *Moving Worlds* 12 (2012), 5–18.

Index